Common Threads

Festivals of Folklore and Literature for Schools and Libraries

by
Alan Heath

The Scarecrow Press, Inc.
Lanham, Md., and London

SCARECROW PRESS, INC.

Published in the United States of America
by Scarecrow Press, Inc.
4720 Boston Way
Lanham, Maryland 20706

4 Pleydell Gardens, Folkestone
Kent CT20 2DN, England

British Cataloguing-in-Publication Information Available

Library of Congress Cataloging-in-Publication Data

Heath, Alan, 1946–   .
Common threads : festivals of folklore and literature for schools and
libraries / by Alan Heath.
p.   cm.
Includes bibliographical references and index.
1. Festivals—Study and teaching (Elementary) 2. Multiculturalism—Study
and teaching (Elementary) 3. Festivals—Planning. 4. Festivals—Management.
5. Libraries—Cultural programs.   I. Title
GT3930.H42   1996   372.83—dc20   95-15439   CIP

ISBN 0-8108-3036-1 (cloth : alk. paper)

⊖™ The paper used in this publication meets the minimum requirements of
American National Standard for Information Sciences—Permanence of
Paper for Printed Library Materials, ANSI Z39.48–1984.
Manufactured in the United States of America.

For Marguerite Law ("Miz Law")
the best high school English teacher ever
and my inspiration

Acknowledgments

The recipes for Rose Water Cookies and Mother Ann's Birthday Cake, pages 117–119, are reprinted with the kind permission of Amy Bess Miller and Persis Fuller, the authors of *The Best of Shaker Cooking* (New York: Macmillan, © 1985).

The recipes for Miss Wattie's Brownies and Lemon Cornmeal Cookies, pages 80–82, are reprinted from *A Taste of Homecoming* (© 1985, 1989), edited by Daisy King, with the kind permission of The Rutledge Hill Press, Nashville, Tennessee.

The Shaker fence logo on page 105 is reprinted with the kind permission of Paul M. Van Kolken and Diane L. Van Kolken, editors of *The Shaker Messenger,* published by The World of Shaker, P.O.B. 1645, Holland, Michigan 49422-1645.

Contents

Illustrations

Introduction

Common to cultures around the world is a longing to celebrate special occasions. People gather for games, storytelling, dancing, religious and civic rituals, and good food. It is rare to find a community anywhere that doesn't have an annual celebration. They may not call it by a grand name, but there will be a time when folks get together. In some rural areas of the United States this will be Decoration Day at the cemetery with dinner on the ground, an afternoon of music in the country church, and time to catch up on news of people that have moved away. Children's cheeks will be pinched by distant relatives as they intone, "My, how you've grown!" In some places, there will be a festival based on a special crop, such as cotton, corn, strawberries, apples or oranges. Bands will parade down Main Street, a queen will be crowned, and farmers will exhibit their produce in hopes of winning first prize. Cities celebrate, too. Some festivals are annual ethnic feasts when immigrant Americans and their friends and descendants remember their roots. Other celebrations occur around anniversaries, sports events and national holidays.

Across America there are many other celebrations, known, perhaps, to only a few: celebrations based on local heroes, legends and folklore, festivals that may enliven an autumn weekend with all the classic celebratory elements—fellowship; good food; books, arts and crafts to buy; lectures, speeches, and seminars; games and music; and maybe a play. People wait excitedly for the annual festival to roll around, a highlight of the year. *Schools and libraries, too, can enrich the academic year by choosing something special to celebrate so that students and teachers are lifted up from the ordinary run of things into a concentrated atmosphere of enjoyable learning.* This book, a companion volume to *Windows on the World: Multi-cultural Festivals for Schools and Libraries,* suggests nine celebrations based on folklore, literature, or a cross-pollination of both. The festivals can be used as they are, or elements from several festivals can be combined to create yet other themes for celebration. The ideas here can also be used as frameworks to create still other festivals, related in organization, but different in content.

School librarians may want to organize festivals that occur totally within the media center environment. Teachers may want to use a festival as a culminating event for a class project or unit of study. On the other hand, librarians and teachers may want to work together to facilitate a school-wide festival in which every child is involved—in arts and crafts projects, reading, writing creatively, storytelling, rehearsing a play, and listening to experts in the chosen field. Every bulletin board in school can be devoted to the festive theme, just as every academic discipline, from mathematics to physical education, can use *some* elements of the theme to tie into the festival. *Common Threads* offers ideas for intracurricular cooperation so that teachers and students can, during festival time, work toward common goals along various academic paths. There are festival activities that will be suitable for all school-age levels. Creative teachers and librarians will, of course, adapt some of the suggested activities for ages other than those for which they were originally intended.

Each festival chapter includes a bookmark to be photocopied and used in your school. There is space for the addition of your school's name, and the dates of the festival. The bookmark can be given away to advertise the festival, and it can be used as a cover design for bibliographies or printed festival programs. "Creating a Festival Ambience" is a special page in each chapter devoted to decorative things that can be done to enhance the atmosphere, with ideas for making flags, paper friezes, artificial flowers, and more. Each festival has its share of thematic art and craft activities (including displays), a special edible treat to make, and a list of books which can inspire the celebrations. In addition, there are reading-related activities and four play scripts to perform.

"Horsefeathers and Hen's Teeth" (Chapter 1) is a festival of storytelling and folklore that uses the inventive arts to get everybody involved. Through folklore anthologies, students explore tall tales, legends, and myths. Through drama, they experience the fun of sharing them with others. "History in My Own Backyard" (Chapter 2) uses local folklore, literature and traditions, as exemplified by those in a small Tennessee town, to encourage rural schools to celebrate regional peculiarities which, in our techno-crazed age, are threatened by "progress" with oblivion.

Two festivals will appeal directly to elementary schools: "A Festival of the Imagination: Puppets and Literature" (Chapter 7) encourages creativity with glove puppets and books, while "Grin and Bear It" (Chapter 6) capitalizes upon the growing popularity of Teddy Bears by offering several "excuses" for bringing them to school. Both festivals, however, offer activities for older students, so that the fun can be enjoyed by the entire school.

One festival in particular celebrates the history of a uniquely American utopian movement: the United Society of Believers in Christ's Second Appearing, or the Shakers. "Simple Gifts" (Chapter 3) can, of course, be celebrated by schools in the "Shaker Belt" from Kentucky northwards into New England. But geography need not limit the festival, for as the Shakers are gradually dying out, so American awareness of the great contributions they made to society is growing.

Since holidays are obvious times for celebrations, we send each other a Valentine (Chapter 5) of poetry and literature, holiday games, and folklore. Schools could plan similar festivals around other holidays, such as Groundhog's Day or a President's birthday, using the theme as a basis for a lively exploration of related topics.

The art of children's picture books is the springboard for "Out of the Frame" (Chapter 8), in which we write, illustrate and bind our own books while looking at art in many forms. We "Reach for a Star" (Chapter 4) in a look at the zodiac. While asking if it is sensible to base our actions on galactic alignments or stellar patterns, we have fun with star cookies and crafts. Finally, we "Roll on the River" (Chapter 9) to celebrate the things great waterways have given us, from steamboats to music to leisure opportunities.

Planning a thematic festival and seeing it through, from brainstorming ideas and events to cleaning up afterwards, can involve a not inconsiderable amount of work. But the learning and fun shared by teachers and students make it worthwhile—and inevitable that another festival is just around the corner.

Scale Down!

Some, if not many, teachers and librarians may feel too rushed already. The *idea* of taking on a major festival, in addition to correcting essays, recording grades, filling in forms, circulating books, planning lessons, and teaching, may bring on paroxysms. There is an answer: Scale Down! A festival can be small!

Put up a bulletin board, even if it's just a poster. Tell a story to a class and help them make a pop-up card. Serve cookies. And call it a festival!

Brainstorm with the kids. Ask them to decide on things *they'd* like to do to celebrate. Divide them into cooperative teams so that small groups are responsible for different elements of the festival, from books, music, and games to food, crafts, and displays. Set aside some class time for planning and research, and let the students create their own special celebrations.

Use one or two ideas from the choices which follow. Try to do something visual (display), something aural (a story or a booktalk), something tactile (a craft), and something active (browsing among books, baking cookies, improvising a play). If nothing else, put up balloons, turn on the CD player, and call it a festival of fun! Once you've experienced one special festival, I know you'll want to have some more. Celebrating is contagious!

Down to Basics

In outlining the nine festivals which follow, there are some assumptions, or givens, underlying the use of recycled/recyclable craft materials, cooking and cooking space, and certain theatrical possibilities. If these assumptions apply only in part, or not at all, in your library, classroom, or school, then adapt or discard, going on to activities which you deem most feasible. As I have said before, *if a particular project seems too daunting, either spend some time studying and practicing it, adapt it to suit your specific abilities and talents, or move on to another. Conversely, if a project seems too simple, enrich it with your own peculiar insights to give the impact you require.*

The Assumptions

1. That you have access to discarded cardboard boxes, newspapers, magazines, brown grocery bags and other papers.
2. That you have access to "artroom"-type materials:
   a. plain white paper
   b. butcher's paper
   c. colored construction papers

    d. Paints: tempera, watercolors, acrylic, discarded household latex paints

    e. Glues: stick, PVA (polyvinyl adhesive, or white glue)

    f. Tapes: clear, masking, Mystic®

    g. Staples, pins

    h. Measuring and cutting tools: rulers, scissors, craft knives, compasses

    i. a tabletop, floor, or other workspace, either under your control or available for your use (or the use of a colleague who is assisting you).

3. That you have certain cooking facilities in your room or school:

    a. work surface

    b. area for students to join in demonstrations and preparations

    c. water

    d. a kitchen stove (oven and burners)

    e. a refrigerator

    f. standard pots, pans, utensils.

4. That you have a "performance space" that may or may not be a theatre or auditorium:

    a. a nook or corner in the classroom or library

    b. a separate room

    c. a stage in an auditorium

    d. any kind of space that could be used for a reader's theatre, choral reading, improvisations and games, or a scripted performance by students or students and puppets.

5. That you have a lively book and materials collection upon which to base these (and other) festivals.

6. That you are professionally involved in an educational atmosphere of cooperation, scholastic adventure, cultural exploration, and the pursuit of the wholeness of and wide potential of the human being.

7. That you will make time to let celebrations happen on a grand scale at least once a year, and more often on a small scale, dipping into these festival examples for one or two displays and activities with which to punctuate the school year in a frisson of gaiety.

Chapter 1
Horsefeathers and Hen's Teeth: A Festival of Storytelling and Folklore

When the rush of modern life closes in, and the noise of traffic, clustering human voices, and the ever-present hum of personal stereos compete with car radios and television screens, it is good to escape to one's own laughing place, that secret spot where thoughts provide the furniture and daydreams feed the soul. Time was when America reverberated with the sounds of silent nature—wind in the leaves, the tumble of water over boulder-strewn stream beds, the calling of birds, and the gentility of non-industrial sounds: the strain of harness as horses pulled iron-shod wagon wheels, the thwack of axes clearing timber, the laughter of children playing in the frontier forests. Time was when folks would gather on the porch after supper to watch the sun go down, to talk about times past, to swap stories about lands that never were except in the imagination. No television to disturb the night. No music unless you made it. Within the lifetimes of many people alive today, this idyll is a "once upon a time" memory, available only in secret laughing places.

A festival of folklore and storytelling can recapture some of that early American peace. It can also create a lot of noise: laughter, screams of fright, and even a few tears. Folklore and storytelling are inseparably linked with music, too, for a good storyteller in full swing is more like a one-man band than anything else. A festival of folklore and storytelling will restate the joy of myths. It can recreate, in part, the feeling of days not so long gone when electricity hadn't quite reached into "our neck of the woods." It can connect us with days when heroes walked the trails, when horrible specters dwelt in the surrounding forest, and when horses had feathers and chickens had teeth. A festival of folklore will reopen doors on human history while neatly fitting into several areas of a school's curriculum, from language arts to social studies, drama, music, and, yes, even math and science.

A festival like this one offers opportunity for many people to tell stories, from books, from memory, and from the imagination. It provides ample scope for drama—for the improvisation of children's stories, folk tales and myths, and for the performance of more highly structured theater pieces. Music, too, is integral to folk culture. This is the time to look for exotic recordings from local and world cultures to play at special times during the festival; time, also, to encourage students to perform on their instruments during folk music concerts in the library or classroom. Art work can flourish in the climate of storytelling. And storytellers have to eat—there can be a festival feast of magic foods.

The telling of folklore helps children develop thinking skills. Youngsters (and adults!) enjoy the repetitive cycles of events and objects, and once they have heard them will join in with successive occurrences in the tale. The telling and the hearing of folk tales helps in language development, and in reading and writing. When the teacher or librarian tells or reads a story from a book, most of the children want to take the book home to their own laughing places. It has a laudable effect on logical, lateral, and sequential thinking processes. A story like the "Three Little Pigs" helps children think about what comes next. It encourages good listening and memory skills. A skillful storyteller will have the audience in the palm of his or her hand. No one would hear the proverbial pin drop, for all eyes and ears are riveted on the tale and the teller. Folktelling is good for the soul: it helps in emotional understanding and in psychological development. The plaintive "Barbry Allan" moves hearts to ponder loneliness and unrequited love, just as the wanton abandonment of Hansel and Gretel raises a lump in many throats.

Stage a Festival of Storytelling and Folklore when autumn days draw people in to firesides. Combine folklore and the Halloween season with a Festival of Frightful Tales. Turn the pre-Christmas holidays into a Festival of Northern Tales, with snow and ice from Scandinavia and the Eskimo regions of North America. Set the stage for a local or national storytelling festival by holding one in your school first, whetting students' appetites for more. Let spring blossom with Tall Tale Times when outdoor games and dramatics could re-enact some river rafting or land-taming. Hold this festival anytime, for there is always room for a storyteller, always time for a story. No matter when the Festival happens, its stories will cast their spells.

Displays

1. Look through an assortment of folktale books, collections of fairy stories, or books about folk art and folkways. Often the dust jacket or inside illustrations will provide the right idea for a major bulletin board display. If the festival is eclectic, the task is easier, for any character from legend and lore can represent the celebrations. For a narrower focus, locate books on the specific subject, such as Danish folklore, or African folklore, for ideas.

2. Since folklore goes hand in glove with music, set a line drawing of a banjo, fiddle or other instrument across the display, with the title of the festival in large lettering beside it. Within the display, camouflage a small compact disc or cassette player with paper cut-outs to give added impact through recorded folk music.

3. If a well-known storyteller will visit the festival, ask for a publicity photograph, or use one from a magazine, as the focal point

Create a Festival Ambience

PLAY RECORDED FOLK MUSIC softly at selected times throughout the day, as the audience assembles for story-telling, during quiet reading, or at lunch.

WHITE ⇒ DISGUISE the machine and portable speakers with cutout cardboard designs, painted with tempera: wooden buckets, animals, shrubs, musical instruments, or books.

And they lived Happily Ever After.

HANG A PATCHWORK QUILT on a wall. Dress a department store manikin in old-fashioned clothes. Pin hats to the wall.

BURN INCENSE to capture campfire memories. Burn (out-of-reach) in metal or ceramic containers. Order special aromatic incense sticks from: Mesquite Piñon Incienso de Santa Fe Cimarron, New Mexico 87714 or Campfire Products Cedar Box 86 Kalispell, Montana 59901

BORROW A POTTED TREE from the nursery and bring in a garden bench. Reserve this spot for sole use of FOLKLORE readers. Put folktale books and magazines on tables nearby. Add wooden barrels, farm tools, musical instruments...

Figure 2

of a display. Some storytellers, such as the North Carolina-based Folktellers, have recordings on the market. These make eyecatching displays, especially when they are interspersed with books and appropriate objects (old tools, ceramic jars, antique kitchen equipment, outmoded costumes).

4. Capture the down home atmosphere of the chimney corner, fireside, or front porch with a silhouette of a storytelling session. Feature the storyteller higher and taller than the rest, hands animated in gesture, and all heads raised to listen. To make silhouettes, pose students or colleagues between a bright light and a paper-covered wall. Trace around the shadows.

Guest Speakers, Artists and Performers

Despite our noisy lives in the dying years of the twentieth century, the magic of tale spinning is a potent force. When we take time to be quiet, and to *listen* to a story, adults reenter the world of childhood, the realm of What If. There are many ways of telling stories, and all of them weave spells to take us from the here and now into the timeless. Make storytelling *the* focus of the festival.

1. Search for someone who can tell stories well. This may be a local Sunday school teacher or the president of a folklore organization, or it might be one of the teachers at the school. Ask them well in advance so they can prepare a really special entertainment for the festival.

2. Blow your own trumpet! Don't overlook your own talents. Plan to tell stories to as many classes as possible during the festival. Organize special storytellings for large gatherings during which you do the performance of your life. Select your favorite stories, provide bibliographic handouts, and set the world spinning with tales from your childhood or from your home state.

3. Organize a rota of teachers who don't ordinarily read or tell stories to children to do just that during the festival. In advance, put notices in teachers' mailboxes, or talk it up during the lunch hour. Invite science teachers and high school physical education instructors to read a short tale to a group of third graders. Ask

Figure 3. Members of a storytelling audience don't have to sit still! Arthur Luce Klein, president of Spoken Arts recording company in New Rochelle, New York, fascinates his listeners as they join in the adventure and movement in the middle of the school library. From time to time, Klein directs the action back to the props table from which he selects baskets, glasses and jugs, and other objects which students use to enliven the tale.

lower school teachers to read a favorite tale to a group of high school English students.

4. Is there a program in your school whereby middle and high school students provide tutorial assistance to lower schoolers? Or is there a course in children's literature in the English department? If there is, this will pave the way; but if there isn't, you will blaze trails and organize a group of older students to read from picture books to younger children. Some students will have a natural affinity for this, and will become expert storytellers and readers with just a little practice. Prior to the festival, organize a student aide club, the members of which can share folklore and stories with lower school students not only during the festival, but throughout the year.

5. Bring in folk musicians. Some areas will have old-fashioned Southern gospel quartets who would be prepared to give a half-

hour concert. Other areas will have fiddlers, guitarists, and balladeers. There may be dulcimer players, harpists, or tin whistlers, none of them professional musicians, but enthusiasts keeping folk music alive. Organize an Irish tale-telling with a story of the little people, and a short program of Celtic music on the accordion, piano, harp, or other instruments. Follow up a series of African tales with some percussion music on drums, or a concert by kora players. Tell some tales about Beale Street, New Orleans and the blues, surrounded by demonstrations of jazz performed by the school stage band. Be inventive: find out which teachers and students play instruments, and invite them to be part of the festival.

6. Invite some dancers to talk about the origins of folk dancing. Demonstrate with a square dance, a clog dance, or country dancing from the British Isles. Listen to recordings of Native American dance music, and where possible (as in New Mexico and Arizona), visit a public tribal dance. In areas of international university students, there may be people who would talk about and demonstrate the dances of their native countries, culminating with a workshop for interested teachers and students.

Old Wives' Tales: Projects in Folklore

1. *Organize Folklore Seminars.* In cooperation with teachers of language arts or social studies who have planned units of folklore to coincide with the festival, organize public seminars on relevant topics, such as:

> "Creation Stories in World Cultures"
> "The Truth Behind Tall Tales"
> "Appalachian Folk Legends"
> "How to Tell a Story from Memory"
> "Vampires and Werewolves—Do They Exist?"
> "Old Wives' Tales and Superstitions"

Prior to the festival, plan with the teachers to provide bibliographic backup for research projects in folklore which would result in papers and essays, which in turn could be focal points for seminars.

These topics can become springboards for student journalism, too, either for the school paper or for special festival brochures and handouts. An interested student or teacher could write a short essay on "Vampires and Werewolves" to accompany a library bibliography of books about the supernatural. Use creative writing wisely to perk up booklists and to spark interest in reading.

2. *Dig into Family Histories.* Teachers can ask students to interview elderly members of their families, or older neighbors and friends, looking for tales from times past. Students may formulate their own questions, or the teacher and librarian can offer samples to get them started, such as:

> "What toys did you play with as a child?"
> "Did your parents tell you stories?"
> "Was there a certain time of day that stories might be told, and a certain place?"
> "What stories did you like to read as a child?"
> "Did you ever see a ghost?"
> "What was the funniest thing that ever happened to you?"
> "Can you remember the first car you ever rode in?"
> "What was the best present you ever received?"
> "Can you remember the days before television? What did you do for entertainment?"

Questions need not relate to folk *stories,* since new tales can be told based on family events, tales unknown outside the close-knit circle.

Instead of requiring a written report, ask students to prepare an oral report of their findings. Suggest that they *tell* the most interesting answer to one of their questions as if it were a story, tall tale, or fable.

3. *Uncover local history.* Why are villages and towns named as they are? Do country roads follow ancient trails? Was there *really* a ghost in the Willow Shade Cemetery? An exciting, term-long project can be to discover origins of names, stories about local characters, histories of ghosts, witches, or supernatural legends, information about native inhabitants (Indians, for instance), or documents and maps about urban expansion over rural land. Reports may be *told* or written, and made into stories of "once upon a time."

4. *Learn about a different culture.* Students may choose the folklore of their ethnic or national heritage, the folklore of their immi-

grant ancestors, or the lore of a culture that interests them. They may learn well *one* story that springs from the culture they have chosen, and tell it during the festival. They may learn a song or a tune, or discover something of native art, costume and food, or learn a folk dance, using these elements to present a flavor of the culture.

5. *Focus on a particular genre*. A folklore enthusiast may want to study giant myths from several cultures, or ghost stories, animal fables, ballads or proverbs from many lands. It would be interesting to compare similar stories and themes from various cultures, countries, religions, and ethnic groups. A classroom teacher could decide on the genre, and with the librarian's help find materials to support student research into the ways different countries' tales have evolved on that theme, culminating in the shared telling of the tales. Follow-up activities could include discussions of differences and similarities, common threads that run through all cultures' tales.

6. *Keep a Folklore or Storytelling Journal*. This is a long-term project, and is excellent for real devotees. Journals are a good idea for anyone who enjoys a topic enough to want to remember information about it. A journal may be written, or dictated into a tape recorder. A folklore or storytelling journal could contain local idioms of speech or grammatical oddities, beginnings and endings of story ideas, bibliographic notes, outlines of stories that other people tell, metaphors and colorful phrases—in short, anything that can help the user retain images to use later in formulating stories and histories. These oddments can be used to flesh out the bare bones of a story, or to revitalize an old story—to make a story one's own.

The journal could be expanded into or combined with a scrapbook in which to keep newspaper articles, photos and drawings, posters and handbills, and other collections related to folklore. This, in turn, could prove valuable to a succeeding generation of folklore enthusiasts.

Trips to Take

Organize a school trip to a folklore festival or a storytelling convention. If one of these events is too far away to contemplate,

write to the National Association for the Preservation and Perpetuation of Storytelling, Jonesborough, Tennessee, for information
about festivals near you.

The Corn Island Storytelling Festival
  *Annually in September
  *Storytelling cruises on the Ohio River
  *Ghost tales in a cemetery
  *Contact: Joy Pennington, Coordinator
            Corn Island
            11905 Lilac Way
            Middletown, Kentucky 40243

Maryland Storytelling Festival
  *Annually (Write for varying dates)
  *Contact:
            Carroll County Public Information Office
            225 North Center Street
            Westminster, Maryland 21157

National Storytelling Festival
  Jonesborough, Tennessee
    *Annually in October
    *Up to 10,000 people in attendance
    *Championships in Lying and other forms of Story Telling
    *Folk Music
  Contact:
            National Association for the Preservation and Per-
            petuation of Storytelling (NAPPS)
            Jonesborough, Tennessee 37659

West Virginia State Folk Festival
  *Annually in late June
  *Crafts and Music
  *Old-fashioned country store
  *Mule swapping
  *Country dancing and food
  *Contact: Folk Festival
            Glenville, West Virginia 26351

Sundancing
  *Native American ritual music and dance
  *Annually in several locations
  *Contact: Thomas E. Mails
          The Center for Western Studies
          Augustana College
          29 S. Summit Road
          Sioux Falls, South Dakota 57102

The Folktellers
  *Professional storytellers travel to your school
  *Dynamic retelling of tales, children's stories, legends from
   America and the world
  *Contact: The Folktellers
          P.O.B. 2898
          Asheville, North Carolina 28802

International Story Telling Festival
  *Emphasis on cross-cultural stories
  *Annually (Write for varying dates)
  *Contact: ISTF
          40 High Street
          Brentford, Middlesex
          London TW8 DDS, England

Tale Swapping: Activities in Folklore

Storytelling doesn't come easy to some people, perhaps not to most people. Modern life in western culture precludes the gentler, slower pace that left time for the natural occurrence of storytelling in former times. To regain the power to entertain with folklore, people can be encouraged with some festival activities.

1. *Swap an anecdote with a partner*. This activity works well with people from lower school to adults, and since no public performance is required, there is no anxiety to succeed or to entertain.
   Divide the group into partnerships of two, and ask them to become Partner A or Partner B. Silently, each person thinks of an event to tell about: a Christmas party, an accident on a basketball court, the

arrival of a new puppy, what they ate for supper last night—anything at all that is based on experience. After a period for thinking and visualization (arranging the story mentally into a logical sequence of beginning, middle, and end), partner A tells partner B his anecdote. After three to five minutes, ask the partners to switch roles so that Partner B may tell his story while Partner A listens.

The group leader can watch the body language of the partners to see if the telling is going well. Storytellers will inevitably use large hand gestures, animated facial expression, and more movement of the torso, while the listener will sit more quietly, gaze intently into the teller's face, and try to listen.

Even when there are several partners telling their stories in one room at once, there is usually no hearing problem when conversational tones are kept low.

2. *Swap a story.* Using the method outlined above, have partners tell short stories to each other, beginning with ones that may be familiar to both, such as "The Three Little Pigs." Ideas for the partners may be based on written stories, a story told by the group leader or guest storyteller, recordings or films of stories.

3. *Tell an anecdote or story to the whole group.* Divide the group in half. Perhaps have all the A's become one group, and all the B's another. One by one, over a sequential period of time, each person should prepare a short tale or anecdote to tell to the small group, working on dramatic delivery. The leader or group may offer constructive criticism if this is appropriate.

4. *Tell a whopper.* Encourage outright (good-natured) lying (or if you prefer, *tall-tale-telling*) by asking group members to make up outlandish answers to the group leader's questions, such as:

> "What did you have for breakfast this morning?"
> "When did you start laying eggs?"
> "How many trees did you chop down before coming to school this morning?"
> "Where did you go before you got to school today?"
> "Why can't you turn in your homework today?"

Imaginative children enjoy the scope this kind of game provides, and it lets the teacher know more about an individual's creativity.

This kind of game may be used as a roll-call device first thing in the morning, or as a creative writing stimulus.

The Whopper or Tall-Tale-Telling can become the most popular event of the festival, especially if there is a big culminating session in which the Best Liars (or Tallest-Tale-Tellers) compete. In school, each classroom can see who can tell the biggest, most interesting whopper, with a championship event on Liars' Day (or Whoppers Day, or Tall-Tale Day).

5. *Dress up as a folk character.* Plan a dress-up day when lower and middle schoolers can wear costumes to represent a character from legend, myth, fable, tall tale or any other form of folklore. Encourage eccentricity. Arrange with the powers that be for the students to wear the costumes all day, to all classes and other activities, changing, of course, for physical education or courses in which costumes might prove hazardous or cumbersome. Plan a party so that as many people as possible can see the costumes.

Play a simple guessing game, such as Twenty Questions, in small groups. The leader can choose a costumed character to stand in front of players, who must ask questions that may only be answered by "yes" or "no." If questioners receive a "yes," they may continue the interrogation to find out the identity of the character. If "no," the questioning passes to someone else. No-one may guess unless they are in possession of a "yes" answer.

A variation on this theme is to ask the costumed characters to perform a mime to illustrate there nature or one of their feats, while observers hold up hands if they wish to guess.

Another variation does not require costumes. Divide the small group or class into mime teams who will decide among themselves on a segment of a legend to act out before the others, using either speech and movement, or movement only. The leader may make their choices easier by writing synopses of episodes on pieces of paper which teams may pick at random, as in charades.

Art Projects

Use these student art projects to highlight the library folktale collection by displaying books on tables beneath the drawings.

1. Draw or paint a mythological, fantasmagorical creature. This may be focussed on a student's special interest, such as Irish legends or Caribbean folktales, or it could be a group assignment to follow the teacher's reading of a tale about dragons, sorcerers, or Native American animal spirits.

2. Illustrate a short folktale, anecdote, legend, fable, or ballad with at least one pen-and-ink or watercolor sketch for each sequence or event.

3. Write out a short folk poem, proverb or saying, ballad, or tale in calligraphy on fine paper, marbled paper, or brown grocery bags.

4. Branch out with a Reading Tree. From construction paper, cut out the bare trunk and branches of a tree and staple or pin it to a wall. When lower and middle school students have read a folktale, they can add a *leaf* to the tree. Students can make leaves by tracing around their hands on colored paper or by cutting out realistic leaf shapes. On the leaves, they write their own names, and the name and source of the tale they read.

Students who tell folktales to classmates or to students in other grades could add special leaves to the tree. These leaves can be made from a special color paper, from gift wrap, or from specially textured paper.

Variations. For seasonal folktale celebrations, try these ideas:

Halloween: Place leaves on a giant pumpkin vine. Students who share folktales aloud to others can place small pumpkins. Or make a creepy haunted house from construction paper for the wall. Instead of leaves, readers and storytellers can put a paper ghost or goblin on the house.

Spring: Put a green construction paper meadow on the wall to which students add cut-out tulips, daffodils, or irises. Storytellers could add rabbits.

Summer School, or July 4th: On a black paper sky, students put paper firecrackers for each folktale they read.

Winter: On a blue or grey sky, students put snowflakes. People who share folktales aloud with others could place cut-out evergreen trees along the bottom of the display.

Thanksgiving: A tried and true seasonal theme is the ever-indulgent turkey. Cut out a tailless turkey for the wall to which students can add a "tale-feather" for every folktale they read.

For a *Harvest Festival,* add apples to the bare tree, instead of leaves. Or instead of a tree, cut out a large cornucopia basket from which the Folktale Apples can spill down the wall.

February: For the month of Presidential Birthdays and Valentines, students can pin white paper hearts onto a red wall (or vice versa). Students who tell tales aloud to others can put a paper doily around their hearts. Or put a photograph of George Washington or Abraham Lincoln on the wall. Students can mark their achievements with medals (Figure 4) pinned to the wall around the portrait.

Lead up to *Groundhog's Day* on February 2 with a construction paper likeness of the meteorological rodent peeping out of the snow, or hibernating in his burrow beneath the ground. In keeping with the myth, students can pin tiny suns to the sky around him to keep six more weeks of winter, or tiny clouds to ensure that he does not see his shadow.

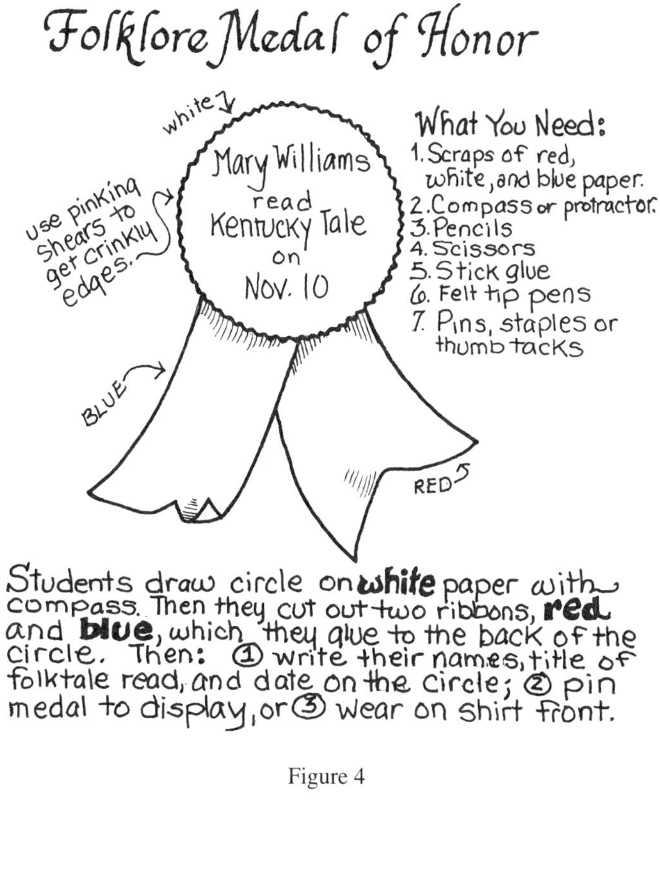

Figure 4

African-American History: In the center of the wall, place a portrait of an African-American leader, such as Martin Luther King. Student readers pin stars around the portrait for every African or African-inspired folktale they read. This can encompass African-Caribbean stories, too.

Sing a Folk Song

Lamentably, American children are getting farther and farther away from the joys of folk songs. Modern culture seems to have little time for traditional, home-made music. A festival of folklore offers time for listening to and learning some old melodies. Hopefully, youngsters will have learned "Yankee Doodle," "The Streets of Laredo," one of the many versions of "The Old Grey Goose," and "Go Tell Aunt Rhody." Since folk songs were originally spontaneous outpourings, and have gone through many changes and versions over the years, their tunes can be adapted to literary and library-oriented words today. When students have learned a traditional set of words, see how inventive they can be in creating their own lyrics on a reading theme. Get them started with "Go Tell Aunt Rhody" (Figure 5).

1. Go Tell Aunt Rhody,
   Go tell Aunt Rhody,
   Go tell Aunt Rhody,
   She left her book in bed.

2. The one that she'd been reading . . .
   At least that's what she said.

3. (softly) It was a scary story . . .
   I guess that's why she fled.

4. (more quietly) She left it on the pillow . . .
   Beside her new bedspread.

5. (loudly) Come back, Aunt Rhody . . .
   Please don't be afraid.

6. I've got another story . . .
   Why not read it instead?

Choose folksongs such as "Barbara Allan," "Robin Adair," "Greensleeves" and "Frog Went a-Courtin'." Reacquaint students with the songs by singing or playing them. Then discuss how the songs might have turned out differently had the protagonists had other concerns; instead of unfaithful love, no more books to read; instead of courting, learning to read; instead of a dying sweetheart, a new guitar or a trip to a folk concert.

Write a folksong for today's world. Having looked at folksongs of the past, students can get a picture of the world from which they

Figure 5

came: pre-automobile, pre-television, pre-airplane. Some folk-songs have nonsense refrains, such as "knick knack paddy-whack" or "diddle-dee diddle-dee dee." Folksongs speak of unrequited love, courtship, ocean voyages, and supernatural occurrences. What would a folksong for today be about? Famine, civil war, ter-rorism? Space travel, Caribbean cruises, new cars? Video-games, movies, the latest sports shoes? Students and teachers can work together to invent songs about daily life at school—the lunch-room, the principal, the famous basketball championship—to en-capusulate the flavor of time and surroundings. Feature the songs at a festival event, or publish them in the school paper.

A Celebration Dinner

On Dress-up Day, or to follow a guest story-teller's evening performance, serve a Fabled Feast, either as a finger buffet or as a sit-down "dinner on the ground" for which you could charge a fee, or organize as a pot-luck. Ask students to find references to food in folklore and tales, such as the fried chicken which the Rev. Dye Frye loved to eat in Richard Chase's *Grandfather Tales,* the coffee in Sooty Will's coffee mill in *The Pigtail of AhLee Ben Loo* by John Bennett, or the porridge in "Goldilocks and the Three Bears." While it might be difficult, unsavory, or downright unhealthy to duplicate the foods of some folktales, a dinner on the ground with down-home fried chicken, barbequed baked beans, and potato salad would be a grand way to round off the celebrations, and could, indeed, be the source of tales yet to come.

For special treats after a storytelling session or a student musi-cal program, offer some simple cookies or muffins. The first recipe comes from the folkways of England, where the elder-flower is used for making cookies, ice cream, tea, and wine. *Elders* are large shrubs native to many temperate climates, includ-ing the United States, so gathering the flowers in spring and turning them into muffins can be a true folkloric experience. The fragrant white flowers grow in compound sprays and produce berries in late summer. The berries are also used to make pre-serves, cake, and drinks. The second recipe has roots in various parts of the United States, and uses ingredients mentioned in many

Figure 6. Pick elderflowers in the spring when they have fully opened into large, creamy-white clusters. Plan a trip to the park or to a sunny woodland border to find the elder (*sambuccus canadensis*). The elder has been prominent in folklore on both sides of the Atlantic as an ingredient in both food and beverages. Elderflower Muffins, from Great Britain, capture the delicate scent and flavor of the blossoms.

folktales. Increase the enjoyment of these Molasses Cookies by cutting them into interesting shapes, either with commercially available cutters or by cutting around home-made cardboard patterns.

Folklore Taste Treats

Elderflower muffins

What You Need:
Recipe Makes 24-30 Muffins

1 cup flour, sifted
2 tsps baking powder

1/2 tsp salt
1/4 cup sugar
1-1/2 cups elder flowers, lightly rinsed in running water, and compressed lightly into measuring cup
2 tbsps butter or margarine, melted
1 whole egg, beaten
1/2 cup milk
1/2 cup apple juice

Muffin tray

What You Do:

Preheat oven to 400 degrees F, 200 degrees C. Grease and flour muffin cups.

Wash the elder blossoms in clear, cold water, and shake dry, or spin dry in a salad spinner.

Sift together the dry ingredients into a large bowl. Stir in the flowers. Add the liquid ingredients and stir until everything is moistened. Fill muffin cups 1/2 to 2/3 full. Bake for 20-25 minutes until golden brown on top.

Molasses Cookies

What You Need:

Group One

2 cups all-purpose flour, sifted
1/2 tsp salt
1/2 tsp baking soda
1 tsp double-acting baking soda
1 tsp ground ginger
1/2 tsp ground cloves
1-1/2 tsp cinnamon
1/2 tsp nutmeg
1/2 tsp allspice

Group Two

1/2 cup soft shortening
1/2 cup sugar
1/2 cup molasses
1 egg yolk

Extra flour
Rolling board or dry work surface
Cookie sheets
Cookie cutters
Cardboard templates and kitchen knife
Spatula
Oven gloves

What you do:

Preheat oven to 350 degrees F, 180 degrees C.

Sift all the Group One ingredients together into a mixing bowl.

Mix Group Two ingredients in another mixing bowl. When this is well blended, pour into Group One mixture, and stir until all ingredients are thoroughly combined.

Place dough on lightly floured surface, and roll until it is 1/8 inch to 1/4 inch thick (2 to 5 centimeters).

Dip cutters into flour. Cut out dough shapes and place on ungreased cookie sheets. Or cut around home-made templates. Lift cookies carefully with a spatula onto cookie sheets. Cookies should be at least 1/2 inch (7 cms) apart. Bake 8 to 10 minutes. Remove onto clean dry surface of plate to cool.

When cookies are thoroughly cool, decorate with this icing:

1-1/4 cups confectioner's sugar
1/8 tsp cream of tartar
1 egg white
1/4 tsp vanilla essence

Sift together first two ingredients into a bowl. Whisk in egg white with fork, wire whisk, or electric hand-mixer. Add vanilla, continuing to beat until mixture leaves stiff peaks, or until a clean knife drawn through it picks up no icing.

Put icing in a paper cone or cake decorator's tube, and paint the cookies, adding appropriate features, such as letters, faces, garments, or geometric patterns.

Drama in Folklore

Folktales lend themselves easily to the performing arena. Either as creative dramatics within storytelling or as rehearsed plays for presentation before audiences, folktales contain theatrical elements that young actors and actresses can bring to life with charm and humor. The festival organizer may wish to incorporate several folkloric dramas, concluding with a large production such as the Afro-Caribbean tale which follows.

Folktales may be performed with no sets, no costumes, and no props, or they may be outfitted as elaborately as time, talent, and energy can muster. Music before and during such performances will help establish setting and mood. This music may be performed by the actors themselves or played on a sound system.

Performers may travel from classroom to classroom to give several shows during the festival period, culminating with one major event in the library or school theatre. Each grade level, homeroom, or drama class could rehearse a different play to give the festival a true theatrical angle, with thematically related book displays and storytelling geared to accompany them.

Who's at the Door?
A Caribbean Folk Tale

CAST of CHARACTERS: Mapuri, a blacksmith
Abeyu, his wife
Rima, their beautiful daughter
Tiger, a trickster
Arawak, a young man
Orinoco, a young man
Trini, a young man

Pariah, a young man
Huracan, a young man

This story was told to the author in narrative form by a Jamaican friend who was a long resident in London. It was first performed at the American School in London during a Festival of Dramatic Folklore in December 1988 by "The Storytellers," a troupe of middle school actors and actresses who rehearsed after school for several weeks before the performances.

No set is required. Theatrical boxes or chairs may be used to create the smithy and the house in the jungle. The suitors may carry feathers, sea shells, or artificial fruit. The mother may carry a large basket into which she puts the suitor's gifts, and from which she takes the food.

The performance lasts about ten minutes.

To set the scene, a group of musicians may play "Yellow Bird" or another calypso song, fading away as Mapuri, Abeyu, and Rima step into the center of the stage.

Displays of books and other media about Afro-Caribbean culture, food, music, dress, and history should accompany this play.

MAPURI: Once upon a time, in the grasslands beyond the village

ABEYU: there lived a couple (*she hugs her husband*)

RIMA: with one daughter. That's me. (*giggle*)

MAPURI: As you can see, Rima our daughter is very beautiful.

(Suitors come on. Each should develop a special character with sunglasses, chewing gum, personal stereo, or hairstyle. Each kneels at Rima's feet as he speaks, then freezes into position, arms outstretched to her. Abeyu takes all the offerings for herself, and puts them with an appraising eye into her basket.)

ARAWAK: She is so beauteefull, mon.

ORINOCO: Rima, please sit beside me in the forest!

TRINI: Rima, *please* go with me to the beach!

PARIAH: Rima, *pleeee-ase* allow me to offer you these sea
                 shells.
HURACAN: Rima, *please, please, pleee-ase* walk with me to
                 see the sunset!

                 (All freeze. Mapuri walks to audience and says
                 his next line. Others become animated as Abeyu
                 speaks.)

MAPURI: Rima was so beautiful that every young man
                 within forty miles came courting her.
ABEYU: Offering her pretty coconuts and fancy seashells.
                 (*She pats her basket.*)
MAPURI: Pretty yellow birds from the jungle.
HURACAN: Buckets of clear, cold water from the mountain
                 springs.
RIMA: (*She raises both hands, palms out, in a grand ges-
                 ture of refusal as she says her line. Young men
                 fall backwards in defeat.*) But Rima refused to
                 marry, saying that she was the only child in the
                 family.
                 (*She puts her arms around her parents on either
                 side of her.*)
                 I do not wish to marry, father. I wish to stay here
                 to look after you and mama.
MAPURI: The father, impatient at the number of young men
                 who were continually asking for his daughter's
                 hand in marriage, said to his wife: Mama, these
                 people keep on pestering me! I am tired of them!
ARAWAK: Please may I marry with your daughter?
TRINI: Please allow me to marry Rima!
MAPURI: Go away! All of you! I must be left alone to think!

                 (Young men reluctantly leave. Mama pushes
                 them away. Rima waves to them.)

MAPURI: We must do something to keep our daughter out
                 of sight.
ABEYU: I agree, father. And I think I know just the thing!
RIMA: So my parents built for me a large house in the

woods. It was hidden deep in the forest by a large spring, and not easily seen.

MAPURI: You will live here, my child. No one will pester you here, Rima.

ABEYU: You stay here, Rima. I will bring you your breakfast every morning at ten o'clock, and dinner every night at four o'clock.

MAPURI: So we three went to the house at nightfall so no one might see.

(They tip-toe in a large circle on the stage, indicating their journey to the house. We see the tiger watching them from behind a tree.)

RIMA: My father gave me a beautiful necklace of coral. *(He puts it around her neck.)* And my mother gave me a valuable ring of pearls. *(Mama puts it on Rima's finger.)*

ABEYU: Now remember, Rima. Say your prayers every night. And when you hear me in the morning, coming with your breakfast, only open the door when you know that it is I.

RIMA: Yes, mama.

MAPURI: Open it to no one else!

RIMA: Yes, papa.

ABEYU: Open the door only when I say this:
Rima, dahlin', it is I,
Bringing you yo' piece of pie!

RIMA: Yes, mama. *(Rima moves into center of house, lies down, and goes to sleep.)*

TIGER: Now it happened that I, the Tiger, had seen all of this from my hiding place beneath the mango tree.
(Mother and Rima mime the following actions as Tiger describes them.)
At ten o'clock the next morning, the mother and father were at work. He in the blacksmith shop, and she bringing breakfast to Rima.

(Tiger hides downstage center by crouching low.)

ABEYU: Rima, dahlin', it is I,
            Bringing you yo' piece of pie!

TIGER: Rima let her mama in, and enjoyed breakfast of
            banana fritter and coconut milk. Then I have a
            plan! I go to see blacksmith! To ask him a favor!
            (Tiger moves to smithy.)

MAPURI: What do you want of me? I am a very busy man!

TIGER: There is a little rabbit in the jungle, a nice little fat
            bunny that I have been watching. I want you to
            forge my voice, file it and scrape it, so that I can
            sing sweetly, like a Jamaica bird. Then I will be
            able to speak like the rabbit's mother— and I can
            catch her!

MAPURI: This operation will hurt!

TIGER: I want to speak sweetly! I put up with the pain!

MAPURI: All right, Tiger! Open wide! I thrust the red hot
            iron down your throat!

TIGER: Arghhh! *(Loud screams, decrescendo to sigh.)*

MAPURI: Now try a little speech, Tiger.

TIGER: *(clears throat, then sings:)* Yellow bird, up high
            in banana tree. Yellow bird, can you sing as sweet
            as me?
            I spoke so sweetly, I could hardly believe it was
            me! Thank you very much, my friend. You have
            given me a new voice!

MAPURI: Now remember, Tiger, eat neither of the orange
            nor guava. If you do, your voice will get rough
            and deeper than before!

TIGER: So. I run away. Meaning to break into that house
            and eat Rima! But—as I ran along, *(tiger pants)*
            I get hungry, mon. Hey! Lookadat! Guavas! I love
            guavas! And oranges! My fav-o-reet! Mmmmmm.
            Ah, that stupid blacksmith! What does he know?
            I'm sure I can eat them! How could something as
            delicious as guavas and oranges make my voice
            go deeper? *(Tiger mimes plucking and eating
            fruit.)* So I tried out my voice!
            Yellow birrrd, up high in banana tree!
            Oh, no! I sounded like thunder! Never mind. I
            will run quickly. The roughness will wear off by

the time I get to Rima, and I will eat her for supper! *(Tiger runs, panting, to the house, and crouches beside it, looking left and right. Clears throat, and yells rhyme as loudly and roughly as he can.)*
Rima, dahlin', it is I,
Bringing you yo' piece of pie.

RIMA: That's not my mother! Go away! She doesn't have a voice like a hurricane! Go 'way!

TIGER: How embarrassing, mon! *(Creeps away to hide.)*

ABEYU: *(entering)* Soon, the mama, she come over the hill with the—mmmmmm—food!
Rima, dahlin', it is I.
Bringing you yo' piece of pie!

RIMA: Come in, mama. *(They hug and kiss.)* I'm so hungry!

ABEYU: Then Rima began to tell her mother about the strange thing that had happened, how a great rolling had shaken the ground, and how a voice like the pounding sea waves had rattled the grass roof of the house.

RIMA: Mama, please let me go home with you! I'm afraid to stay here!

ABEYU: No, your papa wouldn't like that! Remember those pestering boys! But I will tell him when I get home. *(Abeyu runs to smithy; Papa comes out to her; Rima lies down to sleep in her cottage.)*

MAPURI: Yes, of course she must come home if she is frightened of the spirits in the forest. Hurry back for her!

ABEYU: I will go back tomorrow morning. She will be safe until then.
(Abeyu exits; Tiger rouses, stretches, and approaches Mapuri.)

TIGER: I have been very stupid, brother Blacksmith!

MAPURI: What, did the rabbit escape you?

TIGER: I didn't catch the rabbit. I—I ate of the guava and of the orange.

MAPURI: What? Why you—

TIGER: I was very hungry mon. *(kneels)* PLEASE, put the hot iron down my throat again, please!

MAPURI:	I have a good mind to hit you with that hot iron, mon! But I will do this job for you once more. This time the iron will be VERY hot! You will listen to me, this time!
	The blacksmith heated the iron in the fire for five hours. Then pushed it down the Tiger's throat!
TIGER:	*(Groaning, screaming, then:)* Ahhhh.
MAPURI:	Smoke, steam, and vapor poured out of the Tiger's tonsils. Tiger leaped so high he bounced to the sun.
TIGER:	Eeeyowwwww!
MAPURI:	Sing, Tiger, so we can see if your voice is better.
TIGER:	So I shut my eyes. Cleared my throat. And sang. *(As he sings, both he and the blacksmith move in time to the calypso)*
	Yellow bird, up high in banana tree. Yellow bird, come dine in the woods with me.
MAPURI:	Excellent, mon. Very sweet.
TIGER:	Good. I am off.
MAPURI:	Remember, you stupid tiger! Eat nothing on the way. If you do, your voice will become rougher than ever!
TIGER:	Every time I see something sweet, I will shut my eyes! So the tiger hurried away. He passed beneath the banana tree, and he ran beside the orange grove, but he remembered the words of the blacksmith, and he did not stop to eat. Just before supper time, he crept up to the house in the jungle.
	Rima, dahlin', it is I
	Bringing you yo' piece of pie!
	(Rima plumps her hair and opens the door. Tiger growls. She screams. Tiger enters house and chases her offstage. Abeyu enters.)
ABEYU:	Rima, dahlin', it is I,
	Bringing you yo' piece of pie. *(pause.)*
	I said, Rima dahlin' it is I! *(another pause. Tap foot, look around sternly.)*
	I said, yo, Rima baby, let me in! Guess I'll just have to push the door open! *(She puts down food,*

rolls up sleeves, and starts to push.) Young people these days have no respect. Why, when I was a girl if I had disobeyed my mama . . . *(She heaves the door open.)* Unhhhhh! The mama, she look around but she find no Rima. She find nothing but the coral necklace and the fancy ring! She also find a few—gasp—Tiger hairs! I must tell my husband! Mapuri! Mapuri! (She runs to husband.)

MAPURI: Nonsense, woman. She must be there. You will have to find her.

ABEYU: At this, the mama, she fell speechless. And died —soon—thereafter.
(She collapses and dies.)

MAPURI: Taking to heart the loss of both his dear wife and beautiful daughter, I, Mapuri the Blacksmith, also died. *(He dies.)*
(Enter Arawak and other young men.)

ARAWAK: Seeing that they were left without the beautiful and charming Rima, the young men were desolate.

PARIAH: They, too, pined for their lost love.

HURACAN: And one by one, they all died.
(Young men collapse and die dramatically beside the parents center stage.)

ORINOCO: Goodbye, Rima.

TRINI: Goodbye, cruel world.
(Tiger emerges from forest, picking his teeth and looking very pleased with himself.)
And all because the Tiger was smart, mon. He learn to speak sweet, like the Jamaica bird to fool Rima. I think the moral of the tale be: Be sure you know who at the door before you open it.
(Tiger saunters off singing Yellow bird.)

SOURCES OF INSPIRATION:
Books about folklore and storytelling

Arbuthnot, May Hill. *Children and Books,* 3rd ed. Glenview, Ill.: Scott, Foresman, 1964.

This classic study runs the gamut of children's books, including folktales and storytelling in chapters 10 and 11.

———. *Time for Fairy Tales Old and New*. Glenview, Ill.: Scott, Foresman, 1952.
The introductions to each set of folk tales, fables, myths, legends, and modern fairy tales give background information about their origins.

Baker, Augusta, and Ellin Greene. *Storytelling: Art and Technique,* 2nd ed. New York: R. R. Bowker, 1987.
The authors advise on developing style and charisma as a storyteller.

Bettelheim, Bruno. *The Uses of Enchantment: The Meaning and Importance of Fairy Tales*. New York: Alfred Knopf, 1976.
Children's emotions can be liberated through the old classic tales of Cinderella, Beauty and the Beast, and other fairy stories.

———, and Karen Zelma. *On Learning to Read—The Child's Fascination With Meaning*. New York: Alfred Knopf, 1982.
Examines the way that reading stretches human imagination, emotion and knowledge.

Breneman, Lucille N. *Once Upon a Time—A Storytelling Handbook*. Nelson-Hall, 1983.
Breneman explains how to select, prepare, and tell a story, and discusses the importance of characterization, fluency, visualization, and body action. There is a vast and important annotated bibliography of stories to tell at the end of the book.

Cathon, Laura, and Marion Haushalter. *Stories to Tell Children, A Selected List*. Pittsburgh: University of Pittsburgh Press, 1974.
From this basis many an excellent storyteller can enlarge repertoire and entertainment value.

Clarke, Kenneth. *Introduction to Folklore*. New York: Holt, Rinehart, and Winston, 1963.
Clarke tells about the ancient roots of folk culture, and the place of storytelling then and now.

Cook, Elizabeth. *The Ordinary and Fabulous,* 2nd ed. Cambridge University Press, 1976.
This introduction to myths, legends, and fairy tales helps teachers and parents to select the most suitable versions of tales and stories.

DeWit, Dorothy. *Children's Faces Looking Up: Program Building for the Story Teller.* Chicago: American Library Association, 1979.
Sample story programs, based on folklore, center on specific themes to interest children.

Hale, Christina. *Dictionary of British Folk Customs.* New York: Granada, 1978.
This is a select calendar of annual events to see or to join, plus "all one needs to know about" folk traditions throughout the islands, from well dressing in Derbyshire to beating the bounds to pancake racing.

Huck, Charlotte S., and Doris Kuhn. *Children's Literature in the Elementary School.* New York: Holt, Rinehart, and Winston, 1968.
This well-known "kiddie lit" text is a comprehensive introduction to all forms of material suitable for storytelling.

Iarusso, Marilyn Berg. *Stories: A List of Stories to Tell and Read Aloud,* 7th ed. New York: New York Public Library, 1977.
The NYPL presents a useful compilation of stories.

Ohrman, Richard, ed. *The Making of Myth.* New York: Putnam, 1962.
Listen to a folklorist, a psychologist, and an anthropologist discuss the origins and values of myth, and how myths continue to originate.

Opie, Iona and Peter. *The Oxford Dictionary of Nursery Rhymes.* Oxford: Oxford University Press, 1969.
This is the most complete historical, annotated listing of English language nursery rhymes in existence, and is a handy reference tool for any storyteller.

Ramsey, Eloise. *Folklore for Children and Young People.* Philadelphia: American Folklore Society, 1952.
This bibliographic volume provides a huge source of material for storytelling.

Roche, Paul. *New Tales from Aesop (For Reading Aloud).* Notre Dame, Indiana: University of Notre Dame Press, 1982.
Retold in verse, the classic tales point out morals in animals' adventures.

Ross, Eulalie, ed. *The Lost Half-hour: A Collection of Stories.* New York: Harcourt, Brace, and World, 1963.
Here are many excellent stories arranged for telling by a master storyteller.

Sawyer, Ruth. *The Way of the Storyteller,* rev. ed. New York: Viking, 1962.
This great novelist presents storytelling as an art, with advice on selection and presentation.

Shedlock, Marie L. *The Art of the Storyteller.* New York: Dover, 1980.
The art of telling stories is not necessarily easy. This book sets the prospective teller on the way.

Smith, Lillian. *The Unreluctant Years.* Chicago: American Library Association, 1953.
Look in Chapter 4, "The Art of the Fairy Tale," for helpful hints on the presentation of folk tales.

Thompson, Stith. *The Folktale.* New York: Holt, Rinehart, and Winston, 1951.
Learn about the origins of themes, devices, and characters in folktales.

Tolkien, J.R.R. *Tree and Leaf.* London: Unwin Books, 1974.
Tolkien shows how to give to fantasy the inner consistency of reality as he rescues the fairy stories from academics, juvenilists, philologists, and anthropologists.

Tooze, Ruth. *Storytelling*. Englewood Cliffs, NJ: Prentice-Hall, 1959.
This is a comprehensive collation of helpful advice on storytelling, bibliography of tales to tell to three age groups, and a listing of holiday and seasonal stories.

Untermeyer, Louis, comp. *Story Poems: An Anthology of Narrative Verse,* rev. and enlarged. New York: Washington Square Press, 1968.
American and British verses and rhymes that tell tales.

Ziskind, Sylvia. *Telling Stories to Children*. New York: H.W. Wilson, 1976.
Suggestions and guidelines for developing skill in the art of storytelling include planning, poetry, and drama.

Collections of Songs, Tales and Stories

Aleichem, Sholom. *Some Laughter, Some Tears: Tales from the Old World and the New*. Trans. by Curt Leviant. New York: Paragon Books, 1979.
This great Jewish writer offers tales from the Jewish communities of Europe and America.

Barber, Richard, and Anne Riches. *A Dictionary of Fabulous Beasts*. London: MacMillan, 1971.
From A to Z, a look at mythic creatures reveals fantastic beings from folklore all over the world.

Baver, John. *Great Swedish Fairy Tales*. New York: Dell, 1966.
Gentle Sprites, malicious trolls, knights, princesses, elks and bears cavort through these pages from the northern European forests, fjords, and mountains of Sweden.

Bemister, Margaret. *Thirty Indian Legends of Canada*. Vancouver: J. J. Douglas, 1979.
First published in 1917, this book, full of awe at the marvels of nature, tells of mighty warriors and beautiful maidens in harmony with the plains, forests and mountains.

Blumberg, Rhoda. *The Truth About Dragons.* New York: Four
  Winds Press, 1980.
  At last, the mists clear and the unvarnished truth can be revealed—about what dragons eat, how they mate, what types of
treasure they truly prefer, and where they like to live. There is also
information on how to charm them away should they prove both-
ersome or frisky.

Boni, Margaret Bradford, ed. *The Fireside Book of Favorite
  American Songs.* New York: Simon and Schuster, 1952.
  Arranged chronologically by epochs in American history, this
"family" collection of songs includes many well-known folk
tunes as well as hymns, spirituals, and Victorian melodramatic
moral songs, all with interesting keyboard accompaniment.

Bowman, James C. *Pecos Bill, the Greatest Cowboy of All Time.*
  Chicago: Albert Whitman, 1937.
  Tall tales of a tall western cowboy who once believed he was a
coyote and who almost married Slue-Foot Sue will intrigue all
fans of sagebrush and wide-open spaces.

Briggs, Catherine. *An Encyclopedia of Fairies.* New York: Pantheon Books, 1976.
  A wonderful companion to the world of make-believe, this
guided tour spans ten centuries of mythological folk culture.

Buck, Pearl S. *Fairy Tales of the Orient.* New York: Simon and
  Schuster, 1965.
  From China, Iran, Arabia, India, and Japan comes an enchanted
procession of sultans and sultanas, peris and demons, ghost god-
desses, sorcerers, and fabled beasts.

Carroll, Lewis. *Alice's Adventures in Wonderland and Through
  the Looking Glass.* New York: Signet Books, 1973.
  Two of Charles Dodgson's classics that have passed into An-
glo-American folklore (here in one volume) entertain with their
tales of white rabbits in waistcoats, absurd tea parties, and potions
that urge passersby to drink them.

Chamberlain, Mary. *Old Wives' Tales, Their History, Remedies,
  and Spells.* London: Virago Press, 1981.
  From ancient healers in Greece and Assyria and witches in medieval Europe to the old wife and the sick poor of the nineteenth

century, these tales of medicine, cures, and healing offer fear, love, humor and superstition.

Chase, Richard. *Grandfather Tales*. Boston: Houghton Mifflin, 1948.
There are tales of witches and ghosts who turn up in the most unusual places, all told in a "country" dialect that evokes the charm of early America.

Cole, William, ed. *Story Poems, New and Old*. New York: World, 1957.
From before the days of the bards and troubadors, people have hungered for a good tale. This collection ranges from "Paul Revere's Ride" to "Abdullah Bulbul Amir."

Collodi, Carlo. *The Adventures of Pinocchio*. Soquel, Calif.: Four Winds Press, 1981.
A highly readable edition of this classic tale of a lonely old man and his puppet who has to learn how to live as a human being.

Colum, Padraic, ed. *Treasury of Irish Folklore,* rev. ed. New York: Crown, 1969.
This Irish poet presents a wealth of lore, from singing harps and fairies to leprechauns.

Courlander, Harold. *The Cow Tail Switch*. New York: Holt, Rinehart, and Winston, 1966.
West African folktales reveal customs, humor, and philosophy of this warm, tropical land.

———. *The King's Drum and Other African Stories*. New York: Harcourt, Brace and World, 1962.
Twenty-nine folk tales represent African storytellers from many tribes and traditions.

Curry, Jane. *Back in the Beforetime: Tales of the California Indians*. New York: McElderry Books, 1987.
Twenty-two creation stories, animal fables, and trickery tales are full of sly humor and wonder.

Dobie, J. Frank. *Puro Mexicano*. Austin: Texas Folklore Society, 1935.
"A pack load" of Mexican tales from La Cucaracha to Br'er Coyote, to the day that Juan Garcia went to heaven, make a great Tex-Mex event.

Dorson, Richard Mercer. *America in Legend: Folklore from the Colonial Period to the Present*. New York: Pantheon, 1973.
Dorson shows through tales how the values and ideas of a given epoch are reflected in ballad, lore, and legend.

Feuerlicht, Roberta Strauss. *The Legends of Paul Bunyan*. London: Collier-MacMillan, 1966.
Paul invented the Aurora Borealis so he could log by night. He invented the Rocky Mountains so the wind wouldn't blow away his soil. Twenty-five tales about this giant of a man.

Folklore, Myths, and Legends of Britain. London: Reader's Digest Association, 1973.
Typical of the Reader's Digest books, this collection is rich in illustration and attractive in format, presenting an exhaustive look at witches, trolls, stone circles, and walking stones, plus creatures and folklore and myth from all over the sceptered isles, such as the numinous Black Shuck, the giant hound that roams the north Norfolk coast bringing immediate death to any human being he meets.

Frimmer, Steven. *Neverland: Fabled Places and Fabulous Voyages of History and Legend*. New York: Viking Press, 1976.
Famous travelers (Odysseus, Jason, Sinbad, St. Brendan) go to exotic places (Atlantis, El Dorado). Then Frimmer tells us what is known about those places today.

Garner, Alan. *The Guizer: A Book of Fools*. London: Hamish Hamilton, 1975.
A collection of over 28 world stories about the Fool, advocate of uncertainty, creator and destroyer, helper and harmer, trickster and soother, suitable for readers from middle school and up.

Giants! Giants! Giants! From Many Lands and Many Times. New York: Franklin Watts, 1980.
Sixteen legends of giants from around the world who could make the earth shiver and split, the sea swell, and hearts quake from the core of this book.

Goaman, Muriel. *Touch Wood! A Book of Everyday Superstitions*. London: Chatto and Windus, 1973.

Superstitions cross cultures and boundaries, as revealed by this collection of European and British folk beliefs about amulets, salt, numerology, evil eyes, and other objects and rituals.

Grahame, Kenneth. *The Wind in the Willows*. Albertson, NY: Watermill Press, 1980.
The classic story of Toad, Mole, and the other riverbank residents has passed into the popular folk idiom as if it were a folk tale, and not the clever story of a Victorian English gentleman.

Great Children's Stories: The Classic Purnell Edition. Illus. by Frederick Richardson. Northbrook, Ill.: Hubbard Press, 1972.
People have their favorite children's story books; this one happens to be that of the author of this book because of its classic illustrations, large format, and large type.

Green, Margaret. *The Big Book of Animal Fables*. London: Dennis Dobson, 1965.
Read nearly a hundred legends, fables, and myths from folklore and from prominent writers such as James Thurber, Aesop, Leo Tolstoy, and Gotthold Ephraim.

Grimm Brothers. *Fairy Tales*. Illustrated by Arthur Rackham. London: Heineman, 1979.
Twenty tales include Rumpelstiltskin, Tom Thumb, and the Fisherman and His Wife, and are ideal for dramatic improvisation.

Grinnell, George Bird. *The Whistling Skeleton: American Indian Tales of the Supernatural*. Soquel, Calif.: Four Winds Press, 1982.
Tales of fright as ancient spirits walk the land may insure a few wakeful nights after reading these haunting stories from the lore of Native Americans.

Harris, Joel Chandler. *Uncle Remus and His Friends*. Boston: Houghton Mifflin, 1920.
A kindly old man tells a young boy tales of the animals in the surrounding countryside—Brer Fox and Brer Rabbit and Brer Bear are as fresh today as they were when they were collected after the Civil War.

Hausman, Gerald. *Sitting on the Blue-Eyed Bear: Navajo Myths and Legends*. Little Neck, NY: Laurence Hill and Co., 1975.
Stories from the southwest speak of precious turquoise, sun-baked earth, and of the humor of a great tribe.

Haviland, Virginia, ed. *The Faber Book of North American Legends*. London: Faber and Faber, 1979.
Black, Indian, European immigrant, and Tall Tales make an exciting melting pot of folk myth.

Holding, James. *The Skyeater and Other South Sea Tales*. New York: Abelard-Schuman, 1965.
Gather the sounds and climate of the southern seas in these nine Pacific tales of supernatural turtles, hermit crabs, clams, and other sea creatures, and of a boy who fished for the moon.

Hurston, Zora Neale. *Mules and Men*. Bloomington, Ind.: Indiana University Press, 1978.
This great black writer and collector of Southern folk tales traveled throughout her native Florida to write down these colorful fables and tall tales. They deserve a very wide audience.

Irving, Washington. *The Legend of Sleepy Hollow*. Albertson, NY: Watermill Press, 1980.
A classic tale of chills, love, jealousy, and colonial America that has passed into the folk culture.

Jagendorf, M. *New England Bean Pot*. Washington, DC: Vanguard, 1959.
Here are over forty regional tales from "the homeland of American chimney corner story-telling," including "The Devil in Red Flannel" and the "Haddam Witches."

Kaula, Edna. *African Village Folktales*. New York: World, 1968.
As the author traveled extensively in Africa, she gathered these twenty tribal tales which represent several tribes from south of the equator.

Knappert, Jan. *Myths and Legends of the Swahili*. Nairobi: Heineman, 1970.
Tales of warriors, fierce jungle spirits, and playful animals make compelling reading.

Lang, Andrew. *The Yellow Fairy Book*. New York: Dover, 1966.
Part of any school's basic folktale collection must be the series of Lang's fairy books, progressing from Yellow to Green, Red, and Blue Books.

Leach, Maria. *Noodles, Nitwits, and Numskulls*. New York: Dell Publishing Company, 1961.
Old jokes never die, they just keeping being funny in this world-wide gleaning of hilarity in myth and legend.

Lisker, Tom. *Tall Tales: American Myths*. Milwaukee: Raintree, 1977.
The Big Guys—Bunyan, Spink, and a host of others rip and roar their way through tree felling, seed planting, and river taming.

Littledale, Freya. *Snow White and the Seven Dwarfs*. Soquel, Calif.: Four Winds Press, 1982.
A readable version of this magic tale of poisoned apples, true love, and jealousy.

McHargue, Georgess. *The Impossible People: A History Natural and Unnatural of Beings Terrible and Wonderful*. New York: Holt, Rinehart, and Winston, 1972.
Trolls, witches, giants, pixies, demons, mermaids, minotaurs and other "impossible" people in European and American lore are the subjects of this book.

Mahlmann, Lewis. *Folktale Plays for Puppets: 13 Royalty-Free Plays for Hand Puppets or Marionettes*. Boston: Plays, Incorporated, 1980.
The Gingerbread Boy, Uncle Remus, Ali Baba, Baba Yaga, Anansi, Blue Willow and other folktales from around the world invite children to perform them with puppets.

Mayo, Gretchen Will. *Star Tales*. New York: Walker and Co., 1987.
North American Indian tales about the Milky Way and its many stars reveal "the race for the prize fish," "the spirit of the snow goose," and other adventures.

NicLeodhas, Sorche. *Heather and Broom: Tales of the Scottish Highlands*. New York: Holt, Rinehart, and Winston, 1960.
Eight tales reflect poetic Scots English, lordly tradition, and warrior spirit amongst the lochs and glens.

————. *Twelve Black Cats and Other Eerie Scottish Tales*. London: Hamlyn, 1976.
Ghosts in castles, black cats in the heather, and other supernatural frights in Scotland provide eerie reading.

Pyle, Howard. *The Wonder Clock*. New York: Harper and Row, 1943.
Favorites with children are "Bearskin," in which a young baby is saved from death, and "Peterkin and the Little Grey Hare," in which Peterkin outwits a giant; but this collection includes many others suitable for reading aloud.

Riordan, James. *Tales from Central Russia: Russian Tales, Volume One*. New York: Kestrel Viking, 1976.

————. *Tales from Tartary: Russian Tales, Volume Two*. New York: Kestrel Viking, 1976.
Wander the steppes with the babushkas and feel the biting eastern winds in these classic tales from Russia.

Rounds, Glen. *Ol' Paul, the Mighty Logger*. New York: Holiday House, 1976.
Paul Bunyan could outchop, outsplit, and outclimb any logging man anywhere. Nothing could stop big Paul and his mighty blue ox, Babe.

Schwartz, Alvin. *Chin Music: Tall Talk and Other Talk*. Philadelphia: Lippincott, 1979.
Chin wagging and tale telling make the lying and exaggerating into a fine art, as proven by these stories.

Shapiro, Irwin. *Heroes in American Folklore*. New York: Messner, 1962.
Tall stories reveal the truth about Casey Jones, Old Stormalong, John Henry, and Steamboat Bill.

Spink, Reginald. *Fairy Tales of Denmark*. London: Cassell, 1961.
Take a walk on the nether side of Hans Christian Andersen in this collection of Danish tales.

Stoutenberg, Adrien. *American Tall Tales*. New York: Viking, 1969.
Coyote Cowboy, Hammerman, Steelmaker, Sky-Bright Axe, and four other tall heroes stalk these pages.

Sutcliff, Rosemary. *The Chronicles of Robin Hood*. London: Oxford University Press, 1977.
Take a long trip to Sherwood Forest and right wrongs with Robin Hood and his band of merry men.

————. *The High Deeds of Finn MacCool*. London: Bodley Head, 1967.
Fifteen tales of this southern Irish hero, full of unexplained wisps of strangeness and of the soft air of Killarney, sing more of his heroic humanity than of supernatural power.

————. *The Sword and the Circle: King Arthur and the Knights of the Round Table*. New York: E. P. Dutton, 1981.
This master storyteller brings the legend of King Arthur to life, and destroys some of the Camelot image made popular by films and musicals.

Wentz, Evans. *The Fairy Tales in Celtic Countries*. Atlantic Highlands, NJ: Humanities Press, 1911.
First published in 1911, this classic study of "unlettered people furthest removed from the influence of modern civilization" discusses the nature of magic, religions and myth through the tales of Eire, Scotland, Cornwall, Brittany and the Isle of Man.

Wyndham, Lee. *Tales from the Arabian Nights*. Racine, Wis.: Whitman Publishing Company, 1965.
A magic carpet of tales from the spice-laden east introduces some old and familiar as well as a few new characters.

Zeitlin, Stephen J., ed. *A Celebration of American Family Folklore: Tales and Traditions from the Smithsonian Collection*. New York: Pantheon, 1982.
Contributed by ordinary American families during visits to the folklore tent in front of the Smithsonian Institution in Washing-

ton, D.C., these photographs and stories reflect a wide spectrum of tales from all over the U.S.A.

Folklore and Storytelling in Fiction

Barrie, J. M. *Peter Pan.* New York: Charles Scribner's Sons, 1980.
The enchanted story of the boy who wouldn't grow up and of his adventures in Never Never Land with Wendy and her young brothers never fails to weave a magic spell when it is read or told.

Brittain, Bill. *The Wish Giver.* New York: Harper and Row, 1983.
Thaddeus Blinn appears out of nowhere, and what stories he tells at the Coven Tree Church Social! Only young believers-in-magic are curious enough to listen.

Long, Claudia. *Albert's Story.* New York: Delacorte, 1978.
In this picture book, with help from his sister, Albert puts together an original tale about a junkyard and a dragon.

Marshall, Edward. *Three by Sea.* New York: Dial, 1981.
Lolly, Spider, and Sam, three children on a beach, share stories, including the scariest one by Spider about a child-eating monster.

Nixon, Joan Lowery. *The Gift.* New York: Macmillan, 1983.
A young boy determines to catch a leprechaun after visiting his Irish grandfather whose tales and lore beguile the lad.

Wilde, Oscar. *The Happy Prince and Other Fairy Tales.* New York: G.P. Putnam's Sons, 1962.
Oscar Wilde told these stories first to his own children, whose hearts were no doubt warmed by them, just as are hearts of readers and listeners today.

Wilder, Laura Ingalls. *Little House in the Big Woods.* New York: Penguin, 1982.
Pa tells tales and sings songs as he plays his fiddle on winter nights in the Wisconsin forest, entrancing young Laura and her siblings.

Folklore Societies

The following organizations can provide further information about various forms of folklore. All open their membership to interested individuals or organizations, and most of them publish newsletters and other periodicals.

1. *The American Folklore Society*
   Department of Behavioral Sciences
   College of Medicine
   Milton S. Hershey Medical Center
   Pennsylvania State University
   Hershey, Pennsylvania 17033
   The AFS holds an annual convention of individuals and institutes interested in the collection, discussion, and publication of folklore. They publish five periodicals, including bibliographies and memoirs.

2. *The Center for Southern Folklore*
   POB 40105
   Memphis, Tennessee 38104
   The CSF produces dozens of films, records, traveling exhibitions, books, and slide/tape shows on crafts, tales, music and lifestyles, serving educational institutions and museums in the U.S.A., Canada, and Europe. They have a library, media archives, and speakers bureau. The CSF publishes two periodicals.

3. *The International Society for Folk-Narrative Research*
   Nordic Institute of Folklore
   Henrikinkatu 3
   SF-20500 Turku 50, Finland
   This organization aims to develop scholarly work in the field of folk narrative research and to stimulate the exchange of this information through publications and annual meetings.

4. *The National Association for the Preservation and Perpetuation of Storytelling*
   Jonesborough, Tennessee 37659
   Not only do they publish a storytelling magazine, NAPPS is active in organizing what may be the largest gathering of storytellers

in the U.S.A. each autumn in this historic east Tennessee town, high in the mountains. This large storytelling festival also attracts folk artists and musicians.

5. *The National Council for the Traditional Arts*
   1346 Connecticut Avenue
   Washington, D.C. 20036
   The NCTA organizes the annual National Folk Festival in Washington, and assists the National Park Service in planning and directing presentations of traditional folk arts. They publish a valuable annual calendar of Folk Festivals.

6. Société Historique et Folklorique Française
   56-52 203rd Street
   Bayside, Long Island, New York 11364
   For anyone interested in French folklore and history, this organization promotes Franco-American cultural relations, publishes a bulletin of French folklore, and often prints newly-found songs, dances, and instrumental music.

7. *Ulster Folklore Society*
   c/o Ulster Folk and Transport Museum
   Cultra Manor
   Holywood
   County Down, Northern Ireland
   The UFS sponsors lectures, research, folkloric events, and visits to collect Irish lore.

(Many states have folklore societies dedicated to recording tales, music, and legends from their region. For details of these organizations, contact NAPPS or NCTA.)

Selected List of Folklore Magazines

American Folklore Society Newsletter. 1703 New Hampshire Avenue NW, Washington, DC 20009.
   A quarterly magazine, national in scope, that publishes news of research, bibliographies, and events.

Canada Folk Bulletin. 333 Carrall Street, Vancouver, British Columbia V6B 2J4.
   A bi-monthly magazine that reflects the growing interest in multi-racial, multi-ethnic Canadian folklore.

Center for Southern Folklore Magazine. 1216 Peabody Avenue, Box 4081, Memphis, Tennessee 38104.
A semi-annual magazine that covers the Southern states, with names of folklore gathering, festivals, and research.

Folklife Center News. Library of Congress, American Folklife Center, Washington, DC 20540.
A free quarterly that tells about activities of the Folklife Center and events around the nation.

Folklore. Indian Folklore Society, 3 British Indian Street, Calcutta 700069, India.
A magazine of the folk arts, literature, crafts, music, dance, tribal studies, and related social sciences.

Foxfire. Rabun Gap, Georgia 30568.
Since 1967 this magazine, researched and written by high school students, has been a popular showcase for the dying folkways of the north Georgia Appalachians, with book reviews, illustrations, and well-written articles.

Journal of American Folklore. 1703 New Hampshire Avenue NW, Washington, DC 20009.
Founded in 1888, this quarterly has a wide readership because of its research articles on lore and legend.

Western Folklore. California Folklore Society, c/o Folklore and Mythology Group, GSM 1037, University of Southern California, Los Angeles, California 90024.
Founded in 1942, this journal records lore of the old west, of native Americans, and developing folkways of western Americans.

World Cultures: Folk Music Recordings

Regrettably, not all producers print tape or compact disk numbers on the cover sheets or on the recordings themselves, but specialist shops should be able to offer these, or similar recordings, by title alone. Where possible, however, I have included the number of the recording.

Asian

The Buddhist Music, Best Hits. CD 280. Taipei, Taiwan, ROC:
Lee Tsai Chi, n.d.
Eastern Buddhist chanting, both *a capella* and with stringed in-
struments, evokes an atmosphere of calm.

Hill Tribe Music. Chiang Mai, Thailand: Hill Tribe Music, 1991.
This collection of instrumental and vocal music, including sung
folk tales in local dialect, was recorded in the northern Thai mountains among the Yao people.

Music and Dances of Tang Dynasty. Bejing: China Travel and
Tourism Press, 1987.
Recorded during a live performance, this cassette tape includes vo-
cals and traditional instruments to give an authentic flavor of China.

European

Bosna Moja, Divna Mila. Sumaji: Jugoton CAY 960, 1981.
Bosnian folk songs and dances were recorded before the out-
break of civil war in the former Yugoslavia. The photo on the
cover of the cassette shows the peaceful multicultural community
as it was, a village mosque and a village church side by side on the
square.

Budvarka Padesatiny. Prague, Czech Republic: Supraphon, 1991.
Czech and Slovenian folk music, played on brass instruments,
sets the stage for a feast or an afternoon picnic.

Carolan's Favorite. Derek Bell, Irish Harp. Baile Atha Cliath,
Eire: Claddagh Records, 1985.
Harpist with the Chieftains, Derek Bell plays 18th-century
Gaelic music by the last of the Celtic bards, O'Carolan.

Klenoty Renesancni Hudby (Gems of Renaissance Music), by the
Rozmberk Ensemble. Prague: Suprophon 11 034-4131, 1987.
Performed on original stringed instruments by a professional
Czech chamber group, this music provides good introductory or
background theme music for traditional European fairy tales.

The New Strung Harp, by Maire Ni Chathasaigh. Waterbury, Vt.: Temple Records CTP019, 1987.
Award-winning Maire Ni Chathasaigh plays Scottish and Irish folk music on the Celtic harp.

Secret Isles, by Patrick Ball. Tucson: Celestial Harmonies LC8878, 1985.
California storyteller and Celtic harper Patrick Ball plays music from Ireland and the Isle of Man on the ringing wire-strung harp.

Native American

Songs of the Indian Flute, played by John Rainer. Orem, Utah: Red Willow Songs, n.d.
Using five traditional Native American flutes of cane, pine, spruce and redwood, Rainer evokes the ancient past of his people with songs from the Plains, Taos, Sioux, and Crow.

Sundance Season, played and sung by R. Carlos Nakai. Tucson, Ariz.: Celestial Harmonies, 1988.
Nakai, a Navajo-Ute from Arizona, recorded this album of gentle music in the Lindisfarne Chapel, Crestone, Colorado, on flute, drums, and bells.

Taos Pueblo Round Dance Songs. IH 1006. Taos, New Mexico: Indian House, 1987.
Dance and chant from this ancient Native American community features drum and voice.

The Traditional and Contemporary Indian Flute of Fernando Cellicion. Moore, Okla.: Indian Sounds, 1990.
Gentle, mysterious, melodic, this recording of Native American music sets the stage for storytelling and dance.

American

Amazing Grace, by Aretha Franklin and the Southern California Community Choir. New York: Atlantic Recording Corporation CS 2-906, 1972.
Including "Mary, Don't You Weep" and "Precious Memories," this lively recording features the unmistakable sounds of a great African-American soloist and a gospel choir.

Lester Flatt and Earl Scruggs, The Mercury Sessions. New York: Polygram PSP 5003, 1985.

Traditional blue-grass music as it was played by one of the best-known Nashville bands of the 1950–'60s, this recording includes many well-known folk favorites, including "Foggy Mountain Breakdown" and "Boil That Cabbage Down."

Smoky Mountain Hymns, vols. 1–3. Brentwood, Tenn.: Brentwood Music C-5137, 1989.

Handmade instruments, including dulcimer, guitar, autoharp, mandolin, banjo, jaw harp and fiddle, play old-time Southern gospel.

White Horses and Whippoorwills, by The Folktellers. Asheville, NC: Mama-T Artists MT-1, 1981.

Contemporary folktellers Barbara Freeman and Connie Regan offer six tales on this lively album. No instruments here, just their lively voices as they tell a jazzy version of the Three Bears, the hilarious No News, and the sad Oliver Hyde's Dishcloth Concert. This is *the perfect* album to listen to with the lights down low, or to offer to listeners on the library headphones.

Chapter 2
History in My Own Backyard: A Small-Town Heritage Festival

It is often assumed that history happens somewhere else. Yet each community has its own story to tell, its own lineage, its folklore, its own sources of ancestral pride. Using the following festival as a guideline, any school or library—with research, and cooperation of local archivists, artists, historians, students and teachers—can focus on its roots. In an age of increased awareness of ancestors and family genealogies, a heritage festival will generate enthusiasm for reading (historical fiction, biographies, regional poetry and histories), arts and crafts, regional cuisine, and learning more about the region's geography. And like Eliot Wigginton and his "Foxfire" kids in Georgia, you may start something really big and very important in your community.

A general assumption is that

schools and libraries in large cities have more resources at their fingertips, so to illustrate how a small-town school can organize an interesting festival using local resources and those within driving distance, consider the town of Westmoreland, Tennessee, with a population of less than 2,000. Why this particular place when we could focus on countless others across America? The best reason is that I, the author, grew up there, and I know and love the area intimately. I lament that during my school days in the 1950s and '60s, the town showed little interest in the *local* story. In scrambling through old cemeteries, visiting Native American hunting grounds, exploring the ruins of a 19th-century health spa, and discovering the foundations of my great-grandfather's smithy (which helped supply the Confederate army with guns and ammunition), all within five miles of my boyhood home, I began to realize that even my small town had a story to uncover. There is still time to tell that story, and the stories of other small communities across the country.

Planning a Local Heritage Festival

When looking at the way this festival has been organized, brainstorm with colleagues at your school about a similar event where you are. While these suggestions are for a specific location, think as you read: *how could we turn this into a festival here?* Make notes about local sites to visit, speakers to invite, arts and crafts to make, and foods to eat—anything special that adds distinction and color to local life, anything that makes your town unique. This is a festival in which everybody can participate, from elementary schoolers to senior citizens of the community. Plan the festival to coincide with an already existing event: a town carnival, a homecoming football game, or other cultural event. While it is important to have one enthusiastic person responsible for organizing a heritage festival, it is even more important to gain the cooperation of friends and colleagues. Ask history and English teachers to coordinate curricular units to augment or give scholastic fiber to the festival, such as creative writing, research in local archives or libraries, interviews with older residents, and reading of books by or about local places and figures. Talk to art, music, and drama teachers to plan appropriate work that would fulfill the heritage

Create a Heritage Ambience

Display the flags that have flown over the area from times past to the present: British, Colonial, North Carolinian, and Confederate, along with flags and insignia of local clubs and organizations. Flags can be facsimiled in paper collage.

Musical instruments

Use local expressions and figures of speech on posters to invite participation in heritage festival events.

A display of Musical Instruments evokes the lighter side of regional culture, especially when home made ones, like this Tennessee box fiddle, are available on loan.

Kissin' COUSINS! Trace Your Ancestors! Find out how! Tuesday 11am James Anderson

COME AND SET A SPELL! Tennessee WITCH TALE Friday 2pm LIBRARY

Y'all come and see us! BASKETRY DEMONSTRATION Thursday 1pm Galightly Room

Recall times past with yesterday's gadgets and tools.

Horns of Plenty: Abundant baskets of produce in season showcase local farms and town gardens. Make a homey display in winter with pumpkins, apples, potatoes and home-canned fruits, preserves and pickles.

Strawberry Preserves Susie Sloan 93

Blackberry Jelly Carol Bentley Summer 94

Assemble a vintage collection of school yearbooks.

Figure 8

theme. See if a local phrase or by-word could become the title of the festival, such as the ubiquitous Southernism, "Y'all Come." Or look at "The Way We Were."

A *first* heritage festival could begin to uncover the hidden past through displays of early photographs which may lie hidden in the attics of elderly residents. Students can ask their relatives for photos of the area, and compare them with the way the town looks today. Another activity could ask students to predict the way the town will look in fifty or a hundred years, providing fodder for creative writing, sociology and demography studies, and artwork. Further celebrations of local heritage could focus on specific aspects of regional life. In Westmoreland, for instance:

Sounds of the South: Exploring Southern Music
The Civil War: Local Battles and Heroes
Quilts: A Pageant of History
Bubbling Waters: Tennessee Mineral Springs
Ivied Columns: College Day for High School Students
The Trail of Tears: Local Native American History
Vacation! Tennessee State Parks
Wrestling With Water: the Tennessee Valley Authority
Fine Fixin's: The Way We Eat in Tennessee
Dogwood Days: A Celebration of Wildlife

In a time when interstate highways, nationwide hamburger and pizza chains, and satellite communications tend to homogenize American life, making one place virtually like every other place, a school heritage festival makes students think about the things that make their community special.

A Heritage Display: Local Historic Architecture

Look at the oldest buildings in your region. Are they of stone, old mellowed brick, clapboard? Take photos of the house, church, or civic building that symbolizes the area's past. Have the picture enlarged to poster size, or use the photo to inspire artwork. With an overhead projector draw around the enlarged outline of the building, and cut out the silhouette. Experiment with colors—black on white, blue on grey, white on green. Here, to establish the festival mood in small-town Tennessee, place a pen and ink or felt-tip line drawing of a pioneer log house on a background of green trees cut from construction paper. The drawing is based upon historic Wynnewood (figure 9), near Westmoreland in Castalian Springs, built in the early 1800s as a coaching inn near the salt lick. As in all major displays, librarians and teachers should include relevant books, free bookmarks and program agendas, and other items to enhance the theme, such as locally made crafts.

Develop a festival logo by holding a competition for student artists. Use the logo on all printouts and publications, and feature it on bulletin boards.

Guest Speakers Bring History to Life

Authorities on local history can be found in most communities. They may be museum curators, docents at historic houses, crafts-

Figure 9. Begun in 1828, this largest of Tennessee's log structures is Wynnewood, and is today open to the public. There school students may see the bed in which Jesse James once slept, examine a pioneer doctor's office, look at relics from excavations in nearby Indian mounds, and imagine what life on the frontier was like. Use a photo or drawing of this historic structure as a display centerpiece.

Figure 10. A local heritage festival should highlight arts and crafts from the immediate area. Such an eye-catching display encourages regional pride and offers craftspeople a welcome showcase. These Tennessee baskets, carved decoy ducks and chicken silhouettes, and psaltery, are displayed with books about the state. Two patchwork quilts, made by Westmoreland resident Valera Heath, form a homey background.

people, teachers, or amateur genealogists with a burning interest in digging up the past. Invite an enthusiast to speak to classes about one aspect of local history, or schedule visits to their museums or places of work. A person who has researched his or her own family tree could help students learn about the processes involved in genealogy. A teacher could take groups on a tour of a cemetery, pointing out its uses in discovering the past. For this Tennessee festival, students visit historic sites and watch artisans making crafts with links to the past.

1. *The Curators of Wynnewood.* This log structure, under the care of the Tennessee Historical Commission and the Bledsoe's Lick Historical Association, was built as a coaching inn in 1828. Over the years, it was enlarged to accommodate more guests, and may have been the largest log building in the state. At 142 feet, it is certainly the largest to have survived to the present time.

Curators Lee and Doris Myers live in the house, care for its antique furniture and implements and its wooded grounds, and take visitors on guided tours. They are expert local historians, with detailed knowledge of the Indian earthworks nearby, of days when the house catered to visitors to the mineral springs, and of Civil War engagements when soldiers on both sides of the conflict treated the house with respect. They also lead visitors to the bed in which Jesse James slept while staying at the inn.

2. *Folk Artists and Craftspeople*. Increasingly, interest centers on early patchwork quilts, basketry, woodwork, and farm implements native to the area. Westmoreland artists Sam and Vicky Taylor perpetuate the skills that brought these things into being. He builds miniature Tennessee log houses and sells them in kit form. Vicky weaves split oak baskets and makes salt dough characters. Under their tutelage, students participate in workshops, trying their hands at making traditional egg baskets or finding out how a log house was built.

Figure 11. Students get an intimate picture of frontier Tennessee life when curator Doris Myers takes them through Wynnewood. The kitchen, shown here, was built separately from the main structure as a precaution against fire, but was later connected with a dog trot.

Patchwork quilting was often the only art form open to the hard-working women who settled the area. Most local families possess these heirloom 19th-century quilts, and would be familiar with their design and construction. Two recognized authorities on patchwork quilts are Annie Babb, of nearby Goodlettsville, and Lois Gardner, who teaches quilting at the Western Kentucky State University. Their discussion of patchwork quilting is accompanied by a show of local quilts.

Other areas of America, settled by people from various parts of Europe, Africa and Asia, should feature crafts peculiar to their area, either of the past or today's. In Pennsylvania, for instance, fraktur painting and scherrenschnitte; in the Southwest, pottery and weaving, bolo ties, adobe buildings; in the Plains states, sod houses and covered wagons. Local festival organizers will emphasize the lively arts and crafts which developed in their regions due to settlement patterns and agriculture or commercial development.

Festival Student Art Projects

A heritage festival focuses on the people whose lives led to the present. Art ties in well as students visit historic sites to examine the past. Visits should include specific time for sketching, for through close observation of detail one gains deeper impressions of texture, color, and age. Quiet observation leads to understanding of how things were made and helps people to take things less for granted.

1. *Drawing*. During the Festival, teachers and small groups of students take drawing materials on visits to parks and walks about the town, specifically to turn the commonplace into art. While looking at and drawing buildings of the past, students gain insights into the beauty of old structures and an appreciation for the people who built them. The sketches which result are displayed in classrooms and in the library.

2. *Photography*. Through social studies and creative writing units, students photograph the town, trying to document the contemporary houses, parks, industries, stores, churches, schools, and civic buildings. These photos, displayed in school, are especially effective when contrasted with old photographs from family collections to give historical perspective. Students' work, compiled into scrap-

books and albums, is not only a satisfactory tangible result of the project, but becomes a historical document for the future.

To increase the value of such a project, students must learn the history of the buildings and sites they photograph. Who built or developed them? When? For what purpose? Who lives in or uses these places today? Photographs should be accompanied with captions or essays that document the sites as they are today.

Photos, drawings, newspaper clippings, church bulletins, business posters—any printed documents can be collected into a school "year book" for future reference, to show *the way we are*. Forward-looking librarians might want to assemble a time capsule containing representative documents to be opened in fifty years. Heritage festivals, indeed, can look not just to the past, but also to the future.

3. *Building a Log House: A Major Craft Project.* Focusing on the predominant historic architecture of the region, students build log house replicas using cardboard boxes and rolled-up newspapers. Completion of this project can be achieved in one full-day workshop, or it may be stretched out over several shorter periods,

Figure 12. The finished paper log house makes a good home for antique toy animals. The removable roof is shingled with cardboard rectangles. The simulated stone chimney, the roof, and the rolled newspaper logs are painted with tempera. When several students build log houses like this the result is an attractive frontier village.

planned to coincide with the festival. This is a very interesting project, and the end results are inevitably a source of pride to the artists. Students may work in teams or alone.

For regions whose history does not include the log house, similar projects can be developed around other architectural styles, from clapboard to adobe, all using found materials as their base. (See *Windows on the World,* pp. 207–212 , for a project in making adobe structures.) Librarians or teachers may want to make the log house simply as a demonstration rather than a hands-on student project, in which case they should make up a finished house, a partly-finished box (steps 1-3, below), a few newspaper logs (steps 5-6), and a partly-finished roof (steps 3 and 8). Photocopy the building instructions and drawings to hand out to students after the demonstration.

What You Need:

Cardboard box (large grocery box, photocopy paper box) for each student or team
Cardboard, stiff card or small grocery box (cocoa, cereal)
Extra cardboard (for roof pieces)
Several stacks of used newspapers
PVA glue
Tempera or latex paints (browns, greens, yellows)
Construction paper
Craft knives and scissors
Paint brushes
Rulers
Masking tape
(Optional: newspaper strips, wallpaper paste, papier mâché, cardboard for porch roof and floor; twigs and dowels and panel pins for porch posts and supports)

What to Do

Refer to figures 13-15 while reading the instructions for making the log house.

1. On a cardboard box, sketch in doors and windows, measuring carefully to achieve proper proportion, dimension, and right-

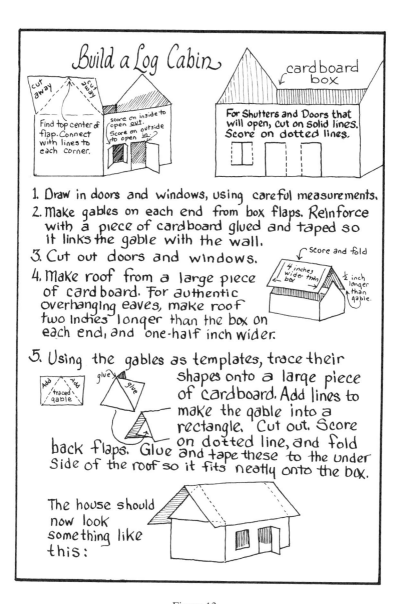

Build a Log Cabin

cut away — cut away

Find top center of flap. Connect with lines to each corner.

Score on inside to open out.
Score on outside to open in.

cardboard box

For Shutters and Doors that will open, cut on solid lines. Score on dotted lines.

1. Draw in doors and windows, using careful measurements.

2. Make gables on each end from box flaps. Reinforce with a piece of cardboard glued and taped so it links the gable with the wall.

3. Cut out doors and windows.

Score and fold

4 inches wider than box

½ inch longer than gable.

4. Make roof from a large piece of cardboard. For authentic overhanging eaves, make roof two inches longer than the box on each end, and one-half inch wider.

5. Using the gables as templates, trace their shapes onto a large piece of cardboard. Add lines to make the gable into a rectangle. Cut out. Score on dotted line, and fold back flaps. Glue and tape these to the under side of the roof so it fits neatly onto the box.

Add — Add
traced gable

glue — glue

The house should now look something like this:

Figure 13

6. Chimneys can be made from small cardboard boxes:

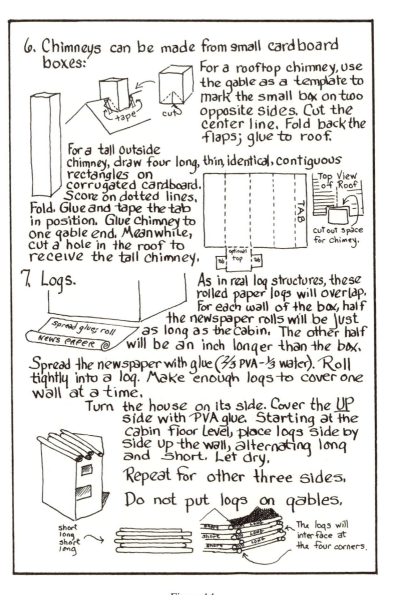

For a rooftop chimney, use the gable as a template to mark the small box on two opposite sides. Cut the center line. Fold back the flaps; glue to roof.

For a tall outside chimney, draw four long, thin, identical, contiguous rectangles on corrugated cardboard. Score on dotted lines. Fold. Glue and tape the tab in position. Glue chimney to one gable end. Meanwhile, cut a hole in the roof to receive the tall chimney.

TAB

optional top tab

Top View of Roof

cut out space for chimey.

7. Logs.

As in real log structures, these rolled paper logs will overlap. For each wall of the box, half the newspaper rolls will be just as long as the cabin. The other half will be an inch longer than the box.

spread glue; roll
NEWS PAPER

Spread the newspaper with glue (⅔ PVA–⅓ water). Roll tightly into a log. Make enough logs to cover one wall at a time.

Turn the house on its side. Cover the UP side with PVA glue. Starting at the cabin floor level, place logs side by side up the wall, alternating long and short. Let dry.

Repeat for other three sides.

Do not put logs on gables.

short
long
short
long

short
long
short
long

The logs will interface at the four corners.

Figure 14

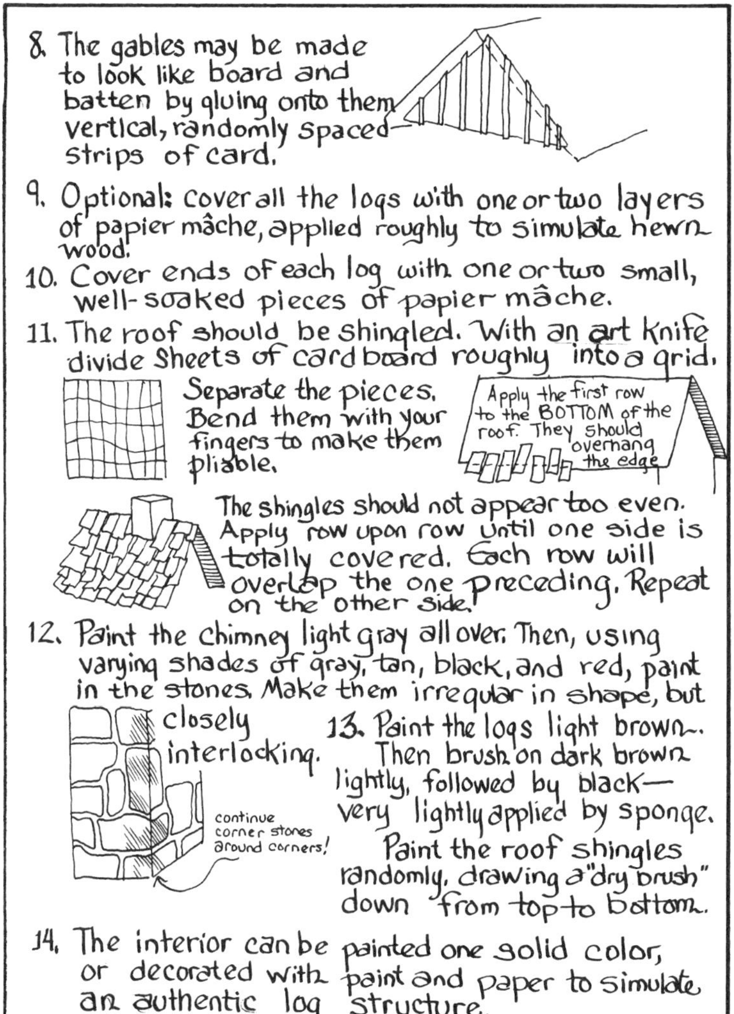

8. The gables may be made to look like board and batten by gluing onto them vertical, randomly spaced strips of card.

9. Optional: cover all the logs with one or two layers of papier mâché, applied roughly to simulate hewn wood.

10. Cover ends of each log with one or two small, well-soaked pieces of papier mâché.

11. The roof should be shingled. With an art knife divide sheets of card board roughly into a grid. Separate the pieces. Bend them with your fingers to make them pliable. Apply the first row to the BOTTOM of the roof. They should overhang the edge. The shingles should not appear too even. Apply row upon row until one side is totally covered. Each row will overlap the one preceding. Repeat on the other side.

12. Paint the chimney light gray all over. Then, using varying shades of gray, tan, black, and red, paint in the stones. Make them irregular in shape, but closely interlocking. continue corner stones around corners!

13. Paint the logs light brown. Then brush on dark brown lightly, followed by black— very lightly applied by sponge. Paint the roof shingles randomly, drawing a "dry brush" down from top to bottom.

14. The interior can be painted one solid color, or decorated with paint and paper to simulate an authentic log structure.

15. Coat with polyurethane varnish to seal.

Figure 15

angle squares. Early log houses had few openings, while modern ones have more. Students may decide which they want to build.

To help younger students or those with limited skill in accurate measuring, provide templates for doors and windows that can be traced around.

a. To *make a working door,* use a craft knife to cut out the top, one side, and the bottom of the door. Exercise caution to avoid accidents with the sharp knife! To make a door that opens inwards, score along the remaining outside door edge, and gently push the door in. If the door opens awkwardly, use the craft knife to cut away a millimeter or so from all three cut edges to reduce friction. To make a door that opens outwards, score along the remaining inside door edge, and push out.

Place masking tape along the non-scored edge of the working door to keep it from wearing out through usage.

b. To *make a window with working shutters,* cut along the top and bottom of the window. Draw a vertical line joining the halfway points of the top and bottom, and cut along it. To make the shutters open inwards, score along the remaining outside edges. To make them open inwards, score along the inside edges. Protect the non-scored working edge of the shutters with masking tape. (The outward opening shutters will not open all the way once the logs are in place.) To make a window without shutters, cut around all four edges. Save the cut-out cardboard to make outside shutters on the log facade later.

2. To *make gable ends* which will support the roof, find the halfway point at the top of the end-flaps on the box. Connect that point with pencil lines to the bottom corners of the flap. Score along the line, and fold the tabs inwards. Be sure to check each box before the students cut, to make certain that both gables are the same size.

Having cut the end flaps into triangular gables, fold the two *side flaps* up to support gables and tape them all in place securely, inside and out.

3. To *make a removable roof* each student or team will need cardboard large enough to cover the entire roof space. The easy way to do this is to take a piece of cardboard about an inch longer than the base box itself (to provide overhanging eaves) and score a straight line accurately down the middle. Bend the roof into

position over the gables. Adjust the width of the eaves and the overhang at the front and back of the house with the craft knife.

This roof will not hang realistically without adding two small gables at either end as structural supports. To do this, trace the log cabin gables on the base box onto some more cardboard. Label the bottom of the gable "a," and the sides of the gable "b" and "c." Draw tabs onto sides "b" and "c." Cut out the gable and tabs. Score along the lines dividing "b" and "c" from the tabs. Glue and tape them into place just inside the roof panel.

You can make the gables identical in size to those on the house, or you can make them much smaller, so that they are just big enough to keep the roof in shape. Please read instruction 7 below (*Cover the gables*) before making your decision. If you decide to make these gables full size, set them just inside the edges of the roof so that they form a "lock" to keep it in place. The small versions may be taped in place to fit either inside or outside the gables on the base box.

4. *Make a chimney.* Traditionally, log cabins had a stone chimney in one of the gables. To make one of these, cut a template from paper, and trace it onto stiff card or cardboard. You will need four sides. The chimney may have sides equal in size, or you may wish to copy other styles, such as those in the illustration.

Having decided upon the design, make certain that the chimney is at least three inches taller than the highest point on the gable. Cut out the chimney pieces and tape them together to make a solid form. Glue the chimney to one side of the house. Cut out an opening in the roof to allow the chimney to fit snugly inside it.

For further realism, cut a fireplace opening on the inside bottom of the chimney and in the corresponding wall of the base box. Later, a hearth may be added to the interior.

A chimney can also be placed on top of the roof itself. Use a small packaging box (cocoa, crackers, candy, or shampoo). Trace the shape of the gable onto opposite sides of the box. Draw a line from the top of the gable triangle to the bottom of the triangle. Cut through this line. Fold back the two sides of the dissected triangle to form tabs. These tabs can be glued and taped to the roof to secure this chimney in place.

5. *Make the logs* from individual sheets of newspaper, cut to fit the sides and the front of the box. For the front and back of the

house, the newspaper needs to be about two inches longer than the length of the box. The same holds true for the sides of the house. Each cabin will need four sets of logs: two long sets to cover the front and back, and two shorter sets to cover the sides and gables. All the logs should be rolled before any are glued in place.

It is difficult to determine how many logs will be required per house. Each one, in fact, will be different, and the total number needed will depend upon the size of the box and how tightly rolled the newspaper is. After the newspapers are measured and cut, they should be glued along the outside edges, one at a time, and rolled into tubes. Finally, apply glue to the outside overlapping edge.

6. *Position the logs on the house.* Begin on the front of the house. Place the box so that the back side lies flat against the work surface. Spread some PVA glue onto the bottom of the front wall, and press the first long newspaper log against it. Make certain that it is exactly level with the bottom of the box. Hold it in place for a moment to allow the glue to work. You will notice that the log covers the door opening, and that a choice must now be made.

Early log houses were built with whole logs, dovetailed to make strong corner bonds. They were then chinked to make them air-tight. Only then were windows and doors cut! Choices for builders of paper log cabins are these:

(a) measure the logs against the side of the house and with a pencil or pen, mark where they should be cut to allow doors and windows to function. Cut the logs then with scissors and glue them in place. This is the easier, neater, speedier method. Or:

(b) glue the logs into position. When they are dry, use a craft knife to cut away the portions that cover door and window openings. This may be historically accurate, but it is more imprecise and messier when working with paper models.

Study pictures of log houses, or drawings made on site, to see how the logs fit into each other when they form corners. Some settlers simply cut notches into the ends of each log. Another successful method was dovetailing. Paper logs are rather more flexible than the real thing, so notches will not need to be cut. Logs should be overlapped, however, so it is important to lay the paper logs from the ground up all around the house. Some students will be tempted to finish one wall, then go on to another. This is to be avoided!

Assuming that you have decided to use method (a) in placing the logs on the box, and that you have placed your first log in place (having first measured, and cut away the door opening), then proceed to cut a log to fit neatly the exact length of one *side* of the house. Glue it in place. Then place a log on the bottom of the back of the house. Then another on the other side. Continue in this manner, circling the house with intersecting logs until you reach the top of the wall, front and back. To finish off the open ends of the logs, students need to cut small circles of construction paper, and glue them in place. (Optionally, dip small strips of newspaper in wallpaper paste and apply them over the openings.)

Another option is to cover the completed logs with two layers of papier mâché to create a rough, bark-like surface texture. This also enables students to give a more realistic finish to the open ends of the logs. An added advantage to this optional finish is the extra strength the papier mâché gives to the overall construction.

7. *Cover the gables.* Most early Tennessee pioneers covered the gables of their log houses with board and batten, i.e., rough-sawn planks nailed vertically to horizontal support struts, and sealed with narrow strips of wood to cover the joints. This was effective in keeping out precipitation.

To approximate board and batten on this log house, return to the roof piece (instruction number 3). The gables will need to be identical in size to those on the actual base box, and should be glued onto the bottom of the roofpiece to leave about 3/4 of an inch (2 cm) airspace between them and the house. When the logs are added, therefore, the roof gables will sit neatly and realistically on top of the top logs.

Simulate board and batten by gluing long, narrow strips of stiff card or cardboard at fairly regular intervals, vertically down the side of the gable, from roof to log level.

8. *Shingle the roof.* From construction paper and brown grocery bags, students should cut a large tray full of irregular rectangular shapes. Use shades of green, gold, brown, and grey to simulate weathered wooden shingles, or shakes. Shingles can also be cut from cardboard. Press the cardboard shingles between thumb and forefinger to soften them before applying.

To hang shingles, spread a thin layer of glue onto one side of

Figure 16. Having painted the logs and shingles, these sixth graders are nearing completion of their project. Here are two styles of chimney, the small one made from a cocoa box, the tall one from cardboard. Both were painted to resemble stone construction. The house in the middle simulates clapboard construction with overlapping strips of card glued to the side of a cardboard box. Roofs are shingled with small rectangles of paper and cardboard, then painted to resemble weathered "shakes."

the roof. Then, starting at the bottom, attach a row of paper shingles, varying the color choices. Then place another row, overlapping the first one, and so on until the entire side is covered. Repeat on the other side of the roof. A cover may be laid across the ridge by folding shingles in half, and gluing them across the angle of the roof.

9. *Stone the chimney.* Begin by cutting random stone shapes from black, blue, brown, or tan paper. The shapes may be rectangular, square, or random field stones. Paint the chimney piece grey, to simulate mortar. When the paint has dried, glue the stones in place, beginning at the bottom and working up. Alternatively, cover the chimney with from two to five layers of papier mâché. Apply an overall base coat of light grey to simulate mortar. Then paint on stone shapes, allowing the base coat to show through between.

10. *Add finishing touches*. Paint the logs with tempera, latex or acrylics. Spread the paint on rather thickly. When it is dry, sponge on another layer lightly and randomly. To achieve realism, follow one of these color schemes:

Weathered

a) base coat dark grey
b) first sponge coat black
c) second sponge coat very light grey

Newly built

a) base coat dark brown
b) first sponge coat black
c) second sponge coat very light brown

Paint the gables, doors, and shutters with the same color scheme. Use a fine-tip brush or felt-tip pens to add woodgrain to shutters, doors, roof shingles, and some of the logs.

11. To *finish the interior,* glue a sheet of brown grocery paper onto the floor, and use a felt-tip pen to draw on planks. Paint the interior walls of the box white or light brown.

Build a fireplace from a cocoa box. Cut out an opening and paint it to simulate stone construction, or glue paper stones in place. Glue the box to the wall. Glue small broken twigs together and place on the hearth. Add tiny scraps of flame-colored tissue paper.

Recreate a frontier cabin by making furniture from cardboard, wood, or other found materials.

12. To *make a lean-to porch* you will need to glue a floor piece to the bottom of the cabin. Place the base box on a large piece of cardboard. Trace around the base, extending one side to make the porch. Cut out and glue to the base. Then cut a cardboard porch roof slightly larger than the area of the porch floor. Support the roof either by (a) rolling newspaper logs and gluing them in place, or (b) cutting posts from twigs or dowel rods. Attach the posts to the floor and the porch roof by inserting them in a base and capital of cardboard which is then glued to the floor and roof. Make

bases and capitals from a square of cardboard just larger than the diameter of the posts. Pierce a hole in the center just large enough to contain the post. Glue in position and insert the posts.

Cover the porch with shingles. Paint the porch floor to simulate rough planks. With a felt-tip pen, create wood grain.

13. Optionally, students may want to *join two or more cabins together* with a dog-trot, the traditional Tennessee breezeway that catches wind and cools the house in summer. The large log house, Wynnewood, not only has several porches, but also three dog-trots joining various parts of the structure.

When the log houses are completed, they make a terrific heritage display: "Did early Westmoreland look like this?" Students can turn their structures into stores, smithies, schools, churches, and other buildings by adding signs and miniature utensils and equipment made from paper. The houses may be displayed with roofs on or off. Place small potted shrubs from the garden center among the houses to simulate the original wooded landscape.

Dramatizing Our Heritage

Librarians, whose work gives them more literary expertise than they may realize, can offer to classroom teachers or drama specialists suggestions of regional books that can be adapted for dramatic presentation. Search biographies for episodes that lend themselves to choral reading. Look through history texts for paragraphs, captions, or charts that suggest dramatic possibilities. Fiction and poetry are obvious choices for dialogue and descriptive narrative.

Using books from the Southern writers collection, the librarian, English and drama teachers, and participating students will find that compiling a readers' theatre brings local history to life. The focus can be general, including dramatizations of wood-felling, laying the railroad, quilt-making or floating produce down the river, or as specific as "The Civil War in Westmoreland," "The Day Our Town Changed Its Name" (which it did, in honor of the man who brought the Louisville and Nashville spur line through the town), or "Grandpa Cried Glory—When Electricity Came to

Town." Local legends include that of the notorious Bell Witch. She is an obvious choice for dramatization. Andrew Jackson also passed through the town when it was only a crossroads settlement, and various legends have grown up around this. "Andrew Jackson Slept Here" could be the dramatized result of a creative writing workshop.

During the heritage festival, dramatizations need not be for public consumption. Drama class improvisations which are based on growing knowledge of area history can be enriching for the participants without their having an audience for a polished, rehearsed performance.

Stroll Down Memory Lane:
Create Working Displays

1. *Photographs, maps, and pamphlets from historic sights,* pinned to walls and arranged on tables for reading, encourage students to take advantage of the region's offerings. While some class groups will visit them as a field studies opportunity, other students may wish to take brochures home so that the family can visit together later. The librarian or festival facilitator, in addition to displaying pamphlets, should organize at least one community tour during the festival, featuring a guided visit to places of historic importance.

School libraries should be clearing houses for local information. Sometimes, lacking professionally published materials, the librarian may have to gather regional information and put it together into a printed handout. This is a great class project, since it involves map work, geography, and historic research.

Begin by enlarging a map of the surrounding area on the overhead projector. Trace the outline on paper on the wall, but make this a map with a difference. Put Westmoreland in the precise center of the map. With a compass draw circles around Westmoreland at intervals: five miles, ten miles, fifteen miles, and so on. Then have students locate historic sites accurately on this map.

Some of the sites will never have been written about nor published before, so this project is truly about recording local history. In addition to mills, railways, and important buildings, include old cemeteries, especially if they have fallen into disrepair over time.

Organize teams of students and adults to visit these places to record names and dates on tombstones, or to cut away overgrown trees and bushes. Though the railway has been discontinued, and the tracks removed, some of the life of the L and N can still be seen. Westmoreland, in fact, boasts the shortest railroad tunnel in the world; it lies beneath a hill on the southern part of town. Should more people know about this? Is this part of local heritage? The importance of such unique sites is amplified by the transitional nature of the epochs which built them. The train no longer passes through with its loads of timber, cotton, and tobacco, but the tunnel still exists, a hole through a wooded limestone hill, and it appears today much as residents would have found it 100 years ago.

Within easy driving distance of Westmoreland are numerous opportunities to examine relics of the past. While a heritage festi-

Figure 17. Old photographs bring local history to life. Though the railroad has been dismantled, the tiny tunnel still exists, and today's students can compare the changes that have occurred, both in the topography and in modes of dress, over the past 100 years.

Figure 18. Though Dr. Bell's Pine-Tar-Honey no longer features among the remedies offered in Westmoreand, the drug store still exists, though much changed from this century-old photograph.

val can offer chances to visit a few during school hours, there will be many others to see later. Publishing a brochure of sites to be found within the rings around the town puts the school in the forefront of learning and adventure. Festival organizers may want to use the map projects to plan monthly excursions to historic sights, so that the festival itself extends throughout the academic year, making local, small-town history come to life.

2. *Photographs and family genealogies* prepared by students illustrate settlement patterns, social movement, and European immigration into the area. Old photographs also show how life has changed over the years in clothing, architecture, and transport.

3. *Native American artifacts and Civil War bullets* are still found during spring crop planting on surrounding farms and in town gardens. Collections of flint arrowheads displayed in a case show

Figure 19. Early tintype photographs take students even further back in their community history. This gentleman, a gunsmith and Confederate soldier, was Andrew I. Heath, great-grandfather of the author of *Common Threads*. Heath's smithshop no longer exists, but his tools and examples of his work are in the local county museum.

evidence of the first people who lived in this area, while Civil War bullets are reminders that matters of national importance are also felt at home.

4. *Yearbooks* from earliest days of the Westmoreland schools provide stimulus for discussion of changing and recurring styles in hair and clothing. Where possible, take photographs of older residents to show along with their yearbook photos. Schedule short seminars with small groups of students and one or two alumni to talk about the way things used to be on the sports field, in popular music, in travel.

5. *Patchwork quilts* from Westmoreland families, displayed securely in the library, classrooms, and school foyer, are focal points of tangible heritage. Student workshops in quilting can involve paper projects (see page 116, "Simple Gifts: A Shaker Festival") or sewing.

Classes can make a Westmoreland quilt. Give each student a square of paper. Determine the patchwork pattern to be used, such as a star, or combinations of geometric shapes to make circles or rectangles, or pictorial images. Provide colored paper (from a scrap box, left over from other projects), pencils, scissors and glue. Each student decides upon a theme from his or her own local heritage, and makes a collage picture on the square of paper. Glue all the squares together on a large piece of colored paper for display.

6. *Shape books* based on drawings of local houses and other buildings provide the space for creative writing inside. Shape books can be made accordion style, or with separate binding and pages (Figure 20).

Creative Writing

To encourage creative writing, publish a heritage festival booklet containing interviews with long-time residents of the town, poetry from students, and essays about life in the area. Give prizes for the best writing in categories such as these:

   a. Interview with long-time resident in which changes in local life can be traced.

   b. Poetry about the area (haiku, free-verse, rhyming couplets). Poetry can be about contemporary life or about some aspect of the past.

   c. Research paper about one segment of Tennessee history, written in conjunction with an on-going history class. Find out from social studies teachers what projects are under way. Set up an annual prize for the best local heritage research paper.

   d. Short story based upon one segment of local history, remembering that "history" doesn't necessarily have to be the sort that appears in books. The day the local timber mill burned is just as historic as any other event.

Writing stems naturally and easily from small-group seminars and discussions. Here students gain inspiration for expressing their thoughts on paper. A heritage festival should encourage discussion groups, based upon reading lists and library holdings, so that students and teachers can talk together about Southern writers. Do they mirror local life? Do they differ from writers from other regions?

Seminars can discuss how life in Westmoreland differs from

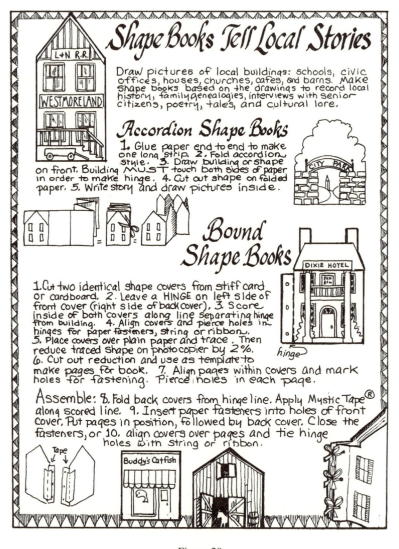

Shape Books Tell Local Stories

Draw pictures of local buildings: schools, civic offices, houses, churches, cafes, and barns. Make shape books based on the drawings to record local history, family genealogies, interviews with senior citizens, poetry, tales, and cultural lore.

Accordion Shape Books

1. Glue paper end to end to make one long strip. 2. Fold accordion style. 3. Draw building or shape on front. Building MUST touch both sides of paper in order to make hinge. 4. Cut out shape on folded paper. 5. Write story and draw pictures inside.

Bound Shape Books

1. Cut two identical shape covers from stiff card or cardboard. 2. Leave a HINGE on left side of front cover (right side of back cover). 3. Score inside of both covers along line separating hinge from building. 4. Align covers and pierce holes in hinges for paper fasteners, string or ribbon. 5. Place covers over plain paper and trace. Then reduce traced shape on photocopier by 2%. 6. Cut out reduction and use as template to make pages for book. 7. Align pages within covers and mark holes for fastening. Pierce holes in each page.

Assemble: 8. Fold back covers from hinge line. Apply Mystic Tape® along scored line. 9. Insert paper fasteners into holes of front cover. Put pages in position, followed by back cover. Close the fasteners, or 10. align covers over pages and tie hinge holes with string or ribbon.

Figure 20

that elsewhere. Has history affected the way we live today? Are we like people in the next county? Do we differ from people in different parts of the United States? Is Westmoreland like other towns portrayed on television and in the movies? During a heritage festival, students and teachers should ask and discuss many questions about what makes the local experience vital, or even unique. Does national television break down regionalisms? Is this good or bad? What has the interstate highway system done to make our part of the world look like other parts of America? Has this destroyed any local customs? How can Westmoreland maintain its identity in the face of modern technology, or should it? Does local history matter?

While some seminars will be private and informal, others should be festival events, with the public invited to hear a panel of students and teachers discuss a Tennessee author or their findings in researching an overgrown cemetery or the ruins of a nearby mineral springs spa. Here, the librarian can be a catalyst, publishing bibliographies, inviting bookstores and publishers to set up exhibitions, serving as an anchor for book discussion groups; in short, making the community aware of resources.

Blood-thinning: Festival Tales

The region abounds in legends: of headless ghosts seen wandering the now-abandoned railway tracks; of strangely eerie voices on the hillside below Mt. Olive Cemetery on dark nights; of the old mineral spa of Epperson Springs, which could have turned Westmoreland into a fashionable resort had not a fire raged through the large wooden hotels one hundred years ago; and of Civil War raids on local farms. Some older farmers rely on the *Farmers' Almanac* for planting and harvesting. There are still some people who drink sassafras tea every spring to "thin their blood." Others prefer to make their blood run cold with tales of the Bell Witch, probably the most famous apparition in Tennessee history, who haunted nearby Robertson County, with forays into the hills near Westmoreland. So called because she haunted the Bell family in the 1800s, pulling mischievous pranks and playing tricks on the crowds who turned up at the Bell's garden gate to hear her wild cackling, legends say that she still appears at infrequent, though regular, intervals.

A Heritage Festival has to include folklore. Librarians must offer booktalks to enthuse readers to take home volumes of folktales, folk remedies, and folk customs. The librarian and others should provide time to tell tales aloud to small groups. Creative storytelling keeps the old ways alive, and offers springboards of imagination to youngsters who may have never heard them, or who like to hear them again and again.

Use folktales to inspire creative writing and artwork. Visit abandoned sites, such as the railroad and the blackberry-infested remains of the Epperson Springs resort to make a video about the dreams that failed. Write the biographies of deceased residents, filming still photographs and interviewing surviving family members and friends. Investigate local folk practices, such as the drinking of sassafras tea, or the planting of crops by the signs of the moon. Imagine stories about people who fail to follow the signs. Use old hymns, such as "Poor Wayfaring Stranger," as a basis for atmospheric storytelling and writing.

Explore the Musical Heritage

About twenty years ago, long before Gorbachev and certainly before anyone thought the Soviet system would crumble, I was traveling on a train from Moscow to what was then Leningrad. Just to stretch my legs, I went into the dining car, a long, none-too-tidy place heated by a pot-bellied stove on which sat a pan of cabbage soup. I sat down at a table with a Russian. I could not speak his language, nor he mine, but by pointing at sentences in my tourist's Russian-English phrase book, he found out that I was a teacher, and I found out that he was a clothing merchant, going home to visit his family. He found it hard to believe that I, a foreign teacher, could travel in his country, since Russian teachers, along with everybody else in the USSR at that time, were not only forbidden to leave its borders, but were also restricted in internal travel.

He asked where I was from. I pointed to the tiny U.S. map in my phrase book, and said, "Tennessee." Immediately upon pronouncing the name of my native state himself, he burst into a big smile, and mimed the playing of a Tennessee fiddle! He had never been there, but he knew about Tennessee music! Before leaving

Moscow, I had spent an hour or two in the state department store, GUM. There wasn't really much on offer, but one stall on the ground floor had a huge crowd around it, so big, in fact, that I couldn't get near. But I could hear why they were there. It turned out to be a record stall, and they were playing country music on the sound system. The Russians were silent as they listened to the song. When it stopped, the crowd dispersed. There, in the middle of Soviet Moscow, was Tennessee!

Music has made Tennessee famous. And not just the plaintive twang of country, either. The Memphis sound and Elvis Presley, gospel quartets (largely unknown outside the South), bluegrass, and Appalachian folk melodies have all contributed to the fame of Tennessee music. A heritage festival that excludes music will not tell the full story. What activities can a Westmoreland, Tennessee Heritage Festival include? Here are a few short ideas:

1. Explore second-hand bookstores to find sheet music with the word Tennessee in the title. There are many songs from the first part of this century that do, and not just the famous "Tennessee Waltz."

2. Play recorded music daily at specified times in the library, including a wide variety of styles and artists. Include recordings by the Nashville Symphony Orchestra or ensembles from the Vanderbilt Blair School of Music. Feature Patsy Cline, who, though not a native of Tennessee, made her name there. Certainly include Elvis Presley and Pat Boone for glimpses into the fairly recent past, and showcase the country sound.

3. Encourage students to research the establishment and history of "The Grand Ole Opry" on Nashville's WSM radio.

4. Find out which Westmoreland residents have appeared on "The Grand Ole Opry" or play and sing in country groups.

5. Schedule performances of school music groups during the heritage festival. Bring a piano into the library for student recitals. Make Tuesday Guitar Day, and encourage everyone who can play the guitar to come to the library at 1 o'clock to play Tennessee folk songs.

6. Research Southern Civil War songs. Play them with small groups. Read the words. Do these songs have meaning for today, or have their sentiments become outmoded?

7. Organize a school field trip to a country church "singing" that features gospel quartets. Invite a quartet to perform at school.

Festival Fixin's: Southern Food

Southern cooking is a thriving heritage, famous throughout the world—fried chicken, cornbread, sweet potato pie; spicy sausage, grits, biscuits and red-eye gravy; Jack Daniel's, Wild Turkey, Rebel Yell; Lane Cake, triple-decker butterscotch pie, spoon bread, iced tea, and mint juleps—ideal for a potluck heritage supper, or, as Westmorelanders might expect, a dinner on the ground.

Westmorelanders hold church suppers in their fellowship halls, catfish-fries in the town park, and pancake breakfasts in the high school cafeteria—to raise money for band uniforms, to send the senior class on a trip to the nation's capital, to raise funds for charity, or just because it's fun to eat a meal together. To celebrate local cuisine, a heritage festival must feature cooking demonstrations. Teachers, students, and members of the community can show how they prepare their favorite regional specialties.

The festival organizer will find that a Southern cooking contest will bring out friendly rivalries as students compete to bake the best biscuits or make the tastiest grits casserole. Texans pride themselves on chili; Georgians on peanuts; Louisianans on seafood and their French heritage. What do Westmorelanders prepare that sums up local pride? As a theme, the festival cooking contest could search for the dish that is synonymous with the town. "As chili is to Texas, so _____ is to Westmoreland!" On the other hand, festival organizers could establish a theme that seeks to find the "best" variation on a local speciality, such as picnic potato salad or church dinner meatloaf, something simple enough that young cooks can enter without difficulty. For this Tennessee heritage festival, hold a Biscuit Bake-off or a Cornbread Cookoff, or concentrate on a seasonal crop, such as strawberries, blackberries, or pumpkins.

The contest can be held in conjunction with a Dinner on the Grounds in true Southern style, so that entries can be eaten after they are judged. Meal tickets can be sold to raise funds for Tennessee heritage books for the library, or items of food can be auctioned to the highest bidder. Or a team of volunteers can simply arrange the food on tables for a free festival buffet.

Cooking Contest: What to Do

1. Determine foods to be prepared for competition, either variations on one single item, or several categories, such as cornbreads, biscuits, cakes, or cookies.

2. Print and circulate entry forms, stating requirements, such as:
    a. Each entry must be accompanied by a list of ingredients and method of preparation.
    b. Each entry must be available for distribution in a specified quantity (enough to feed ten?).
    c. All utensils must be clearly marked on the bottom with owner's name and phone number.
    d. Entry must be delivered to required place at a specified time.
    e. Entry must be prepared by a student (teacher, or resident of the town).

3. Invite local cooks, the school catering manager, restaurant owners, teachers, and students to judge the foods. Prepare checklists for judges to use as they taste (appearance, texture, recipe, actual taste).

4. Award prizes, which may be ribbons, books, or a free meal or honored place at the Dinner on the Grounds.

Festival Dinner on the Grounds: What to Do

No matter what form it takes, a Tennessee meal will be the highlight of the festival. It can be a special school lunch prepared by the cooking staff to reflect regional specialties. It can be a Southern breakfast, prepared early in the day and enjoyed by the entire school instead of first period classes, or it could be a parent-and-child evening social function in conjunction with the cooking contest, and rounded off with a guest speaker. For an evening meal, organize a committee to schedule the place (outdoors in the park, school cafeteria, a church hall) and to arrange for seating and tables. They can organize musical entertainment by the school band, a local gospel quartet or bluegrass band, or a solo instrumentalist. Finally, the committee must arrange student/parent/teacher clean-up crews, and provide garbage bags, mops, towels, and other cleaning materials so that the area is left spotless after the meal.

Turn the meal into an occasion by giving awards to: (a) students whose creative writing, research, or artwork has been outstanding; (b) winners of the cooking contest; (c) long-time residents of the community; (d) residents with the longest local family tree; (e) the most recent newcomers to the community or school; (f) the crew of students and teachers who have restored a dilapidated site or an overgrown monument or cemetery; (g) the curator and staff of local historic sites whose help has given students new insights into their heritage.

Two Edible Festival Treats

Have plenty of paper napkins handy when you serve these special Tennessee treats after storytelling, at a reception for a lecturer or artist/demonstrator, or to launch the cooking competition. Chocolate brownies are a classic American delicacy, but this Tennessee version oustrips all others in flavor and texture. Thanks are due to the Rutledge Hill Press in Nashville for permission to share with readers of *Common Threads* the recipes for "Miss Wattie's Brownies" and "Lemon Cornmeal Cookies," which appeared in the *Tennessee Homecoming Cookbook* in 1986. The brownie recipe was submitted by Ms. Freda Wilson, a resident of Puryear, during a statewide search for regional recipes. Ms. Corinne Wells, of Columbia, gave the recipe for the cookies, utilizing a favorite Tennessee ingredient: cornmeal.

Both recipes are easy enough to be demonstrated during the festival by a group of students, and both are so tasty that one batch won't be enough. Pass the recipes around, and ask several cooks to help supply festival-goers with these treats.

Miss Wattie's Brownies

What You Need

1 cup margarine
8 tbsp cocoa
1/2 cup oil

1 cup water
2 cups sugar
2 cups all-purpose flour
2 eggs
1/2 cup buttermilk
2 tsp vanilla
1 tsp cinnamon
1 tsp soda
6 tbsp sweet milk*
1 package confectioner's sugar
1 cup nuts

1 long baking tray, greased and floured

Preheat oven to 350 degrees F./180 degrees C.

Bring to a boil 1/2 cup margarine, 4 tbsp cocoa, 1/2 cup oil and 1 cup water. Pour over a mixture of 2 cups sugar and 2 cups sifted flour. Mix well. Add 2 eggs, 1/2 cup buttermilk, 1 tsp vanilla, 1 tsp cinnamon, 1 tsp soda. Beat well. Pour into long greased and floured pan and bake for 45 minutes.

For Icing: Boil 4 tbsp cocoa, 1/2 cup margarine and 6 tbsp sweet milk. Pour over 1 package confectioner's sugar, 1 cup chopped nuts and 1 tsp vanilla. Beat well and ice the cake while it is hot.

When the brownies are cool, cut them into small squares and serve them on a plate. The above recipe will make around thirty one-inch brownies.

Lemon Cornmeal Cookies

1/2 pound butter or margarine at room temperature
1 cup sugar
2 egg yolks
1 tsp grated lemon peel
1 1/2 cups all-purpose flour
1 cup yellow cornmeal

---

*Sweet milk is a Southernism for milk, and does not imply that sugar has been added. Since Southerners use large amounts of buttermilk in baking, they always prefix the word "milk" with "sweet" for precision, not only in recipes, but in ordinary speech.

Beat butter and sugar with electric mixer until lighter in color and well blended. Add egg yolks and mix well. Stir in lemon peel, flour, and meal to mix well. Wrap dough in plastic bag and chill three to four hours. Heat oven to 350 degrees F, or 180 degrees C. Roll out dough on lightly floured surface or between sheets of waxed paper. Cut into heart shapes. Place on an ungreased baking sheet and sprinkle with additional sugar. Bake in center of oven 8 to 10 minutes until edges are browned. Or dough may be rolled into a 2-inch cylinder before chilling and cut into rounds 1/4 inch thick before baking. Yield: 3 dozen.

These cookies may be baked into other shapes successfully, and the inventive festival organizer or cook may wish to prepare a template in the shape of a log cabin or in the shape of the Tennessee state map to tie the treats even more closely into the theme.

In Print: Heritage Festival Publications

1. About a week before the festival, issue a brochure of events to each student and teacher, listing every speaker, booktalk, story-telling, drama performance, exhibition, dinner, and trip. Whether produced through desktop publishing or on a mimeograph machine, the festival brochure provides a handy reference for people who want to attend events, and also makes it easy for local radio or tv stations and newspapers to give the festival timely publicity. Place brochures in local public places, too, including churches, town library, doctor's office, and town hall.

2. After the festival, produce a cookbook of items brought to the dinner on the grounds, or of foods entered in the contest. Call it "High on the Hog: Westmoreland Eats," or "Festival Fixin's: A Mess of Something Good," to use local colloquialisms.

3. Use the student-designed festival logo on free bookmarks.

4. Produce "Exciting Things to See and Do Within a Fifty-Mile Radius of Westmoreland," a pamphlet that lists trips for classes, families, and tourists. Illustrate it with student drawings. Make certain that the school's name appears prominently on the brochure, with an invitation to drop by for books about Tennessee.

Place the brochure in service stations and tourist offices, cafes, and stores for distribution to travelers and local residents.

5. Publish a bibliograpy of Tennessee writers. Enlarge it to include a wide spectrum of Southern authors. Enlarge it further by including titles of newspapers and magazines that feature the South. Illustrate the booklist with student drawings.

6. Collect student interviews with older residents of the town, interviews with craftspeople, book reviews, poetry, short stories, photographs, and line drawings. Publish them as a festival magazine.

7. Combine any or all of the above into one large, professionally printed booklet. Market it through local shops to raise money for a worthwhile project, such as restoration of a historic sight.

8. Preserve videotaped interviews and program events in the library for future reference and research.

It may be that enough work has been generated to keep many hands busy. The festival facilitator must, of course, delegate jobs to colleagues when the work load exceeds time or skill limitations.

Sources of Inspiration:
Books About Tennessee and the South

Tennessee Fiction

Agee, James. *A Death in the Family*. New York: Bantam, 1971.
   A largely autobiographical story of a closely-knit family in Knoxville and of their intense sorrow after a sudden bereavement, this posthumously published book established Agee as a major American writer.

Cox, Elizabeth. *Family Ground*. New York: Atheneum, 1986.
   In this novel, a man returns to Sweetwater, Tennessee, after thirty years' absence to find that instead of having narrow, unrewarding lives, the people here are warm, friendly, and fulfilled, making his homecoming unexpectedly pleasant.

Crabb, Alfred Leland. *Journey to Nashville*. Indianapolis: Bobbs-Merrill, 1957.
   Dr. Crabb's epic story of the founding of Nashville takes readers from the Appalachian settlement of Watauga in 1779 to the bluffs of the Cumberland where, against hardship, warfare with

the native inhabitants, and deprivation, James Robertson and his colleagues establish a new fort on the frontier.

(Dr. Crabb's other historical novels are worth searching out, but since they are all out of print, few are available except through Elder's Bookshop, Elliston Place, Nashville. Titles to look for include *Dinner at Belmont, Supper at the Maxwell House, Breakfast at the Hermitage, Home to the Hermitage,* and *Home to Tennessee,* all of which are romantic evocations of great moments in Tennessee history.)

Ewing, James. *A Treasury of Tennessee Tales.* Nashville: Rutledge Press, 1985.
    Meet Casey Jones, W. C. Handy, Sequoyah, Jesse James, Davy Crockett and other Tennesseans in these thirty-five tales and legends.

Marshall, Catherine. *Christy.* New York: Avon, 1967.
    Christy Huddleston leaves home at 19 to teach school in the Smoky Mountains where she meets pride, superstition, poverty, beauty, and love.

Paschall, Douglas, and Alice Swanson. *Homewords: A Book of Tennessee Writers.* Knoxville: University of Tennessee Press, 1986.
    This is a compilation of the work of famous and less well-known writers for whom Tennessee is a motivating force.

Taylor, Peter. *A Summons to Memphis.* New York: Alfred A. Knopf, 1986.
    A tale of well-born Nashvillians leaving their privileged society and adapting (or not) to crass Memphis life, this novel won the Hemingway Prize for Fiction in 1987.

Southern Fiction

Arnow, Harriet. *The Doll Maker.* New York: Avon Books, 1972.
    Gertie Nevels suffers a terrible change when she is uprooted from her beloved backwoods home in the Kentucky Cumberlands and thrust into the chaos and confusion of wartime Detroit. She uses her native talent of woodcarving to hold on to beauty in the face of despair.

Beidler, Philip D. *The Art of Fiction in the Heart of Dixie: An Anthology of Alabama Writers*. University, Ala.: University of Alabama Press, 1987.
Twenty-one authors from the 1840s to the 1980s prove a credit to their time and place.

Brown, Mary Ward. *Tongues of Flame*. New York: Dutton, 1987.
These short stories by a contemporary Alabama author have been favorably compared to those of Welty and Porter.

Brown, Rita Mae. *Southern Discomfort*. New York: Bantam, 1983.
Peopled with the funniest, meanest, and kindest characters around, this is a raunchy, moving story of social conventions made to be broken.

Burns, Olive Ann. *Cold Sassy Tree*. New York: Ticknor and Fields, 1984.
Young Will Tweedy becomes chaperone, co-conspirator, and confidant to his renegade granddad, E. Rucker Blakeslee, and the old man's new young wife, Miss Love. This story is one of the best Southern novels in years.

Capote, Truman. *A Capote Reader*. New York: Random House, 1987.
This is a handy compilation of this Southern writer's stories, short novels, and essays.

————. *A Christmas Memory*. Mankato, Minn.: Creative Education, 1983.
One of Capote's most heart-warming stories, *A Christmas Memory* tells of tradition, love, and human relationships in a land of change.

Corrington, John William. *All My Trials*. Fayetteville: University of Arkansas Press, 1988.
Here are two novellas, one about growing up in a small Louisiana town, the other about divorce, both revealing the meaning of friendship.

Coulter, Hope Norman. *The Errand of the Eye*. Little Rock: August House, 1988.
Allie must deal with long-standing racial attitudes as well as her father's cancer in this observant novel of Southern transition.

Crabb, Alfred Leland. *Peace at Bowling Green*. Indianapolis: Bobbs-Merrill, 1955.
From 1803 to just after the Civil War, this chronicle tells of family division in this Southern town as it grew from frontier outpost to university city.

Edgerton, Clyde. *Walking Across Egypt*. Chapel Hill: Algonquin Books, 1988.
This is the heartwarming story of 78-year-old Mattie Rigsbee, matron of a small Southern town, who raises local eyebrows by befriending the downtrodden.

Ellison, Emily. *First Light*. New York: Morrow, 1986.
Mercy Betters returns from her job in Baltimore to help nurse her ailing mother in Georgia. Here she learns that her father's suicide on the day she was born shaped her mother's behavior.

Faulkner, William. *Selected Short Stories*. New York: Random House, 1961.
Included here are thirteen of Faulkner's locally-colored stories, including "Rose for Emily."

Fox, John R., Jr. *The Little Shepherd of Kingdom Come*. Lexington: University Press of Kentucky, 1987.
First published in 1903, when thousands of Civil War veterans still lived in the border states of the upper south, this is a bittersweet tale of people divided, and of Chad Buford, a literary hero as American as Tom Sawyer.

Godwin, Gail. *A Southern Family*. New York: Morrow, 1988.
The Quick family presents sibling rivalries, generation gaps, and struggles for achievements in a way that is Southern as well as universal.

Haley, Alex. *A Different Kind of Christmas*. New York: Doubleday, 1988.

North Carolinian Fletcher Randall finds himself at Princeton in the 1850s, caught between Rebel-hating Yankees and soft-spoken, Abolitionist Quakers. Haley reveals the two sides of the slavery issue while never letting up on its immorality.

Hankla, Cathryn. *A Blue Moon in Poorwater*. New York: Ticknor and Fields, 1988.
Set in the coal-mining towns of the Southern Appalachians, this story is told through ten-year-old Dorie Parks, whose dad works for miners' rights, and whose brother runs away to join a traveling tent revivalist.

Harris, Joel Chandler. *Uncle Remus: His Songs and Sayings*. New York: Grosset and Dunlap, 1921.
With the famous A. B. Frost illustrations, this collection contains the original Tar Baby as well as twenty-three other stories, nine poems/songs, and twenty-one proverbs.

Hurston, Zora Neale. *Jonah's Gourd Vine*. New York: Harper and Row, 1987.
Hurston's first novel, originally published in 1932, is fast-moving and vibrant, capturing the spirit and dialect of southern black experience. John Pearson discovers a taste for preaching, but his powers aren't limited to the pulpit.

————. *Their Eyes Were Watching God*. New York: Harper and Row, 1987.
First published in 1937 by this leader of the Harlem Renaissance, this is the story of a Southern black woman's quest for fulfillment.

Jones, Loyal, and Billy Ed Wheeler. *Laughter in Appalachia*. Little Rock: August House, 1987.
Tap the Southern mountain funnybone by reading these stories, collected at the Berea College Festival of Appalachian Humor.

Keneally, Thomas. *Confederates*. London: William Collins, 1979.
General Stonewall Jackson leads his troops north into the big battle they thought would win the War. Keneally, an Australian, gets to the heart of the Southern soldier and family man in this powerfully-written novel.

Koon, George W. *A Collection of Classic Southern Humor*. Atlanta: Peachtree Publishers, 1986.
A volume of short stories by notable writers who lift everyday experience to an art form: Welty, Caldwell, Capote, Twain, Jesse Hill Ford, Wolfe, and others.

Lee, Harper. *To Kill a Mockingbird*. New York: Harper and Row, 1961.
Pulitzer Prize-winning novel of a violent, intolerant, prejudiced, humorous South seen through the eyes of children.

Mitchell, Margaret. *Gone With the Wind*. New York: Macmillan, 1975.
The classic Old-South romance of Scarlett O'Hara and Rhett Butler is set amidst the destruction of the old way of life, the coming of the new.

O'Connor, Flannery. *The Complete Stories*. New York: Farrar, Straus, and Giroux, 1971.
Thirty-one stories by this great Southern writer are full of amusing, grotesque, and sometimes frightening characters.

Percy, Walker. *The Last Gentleman*. New York: Farrar, Straus, and Giroux, 1971.
Will Barrett's unusual capacity for forgetting and imagining involves him in the affairs of a Southern family.

Peyton, Jim. *Zions Cause: 1930–1950*. Chapel Hill: Algonquin Books, 1988.
Zions Cause is a "happening" place, though on the surface much like any other Kentucky town. A bumper crop of larger-than-life characters validates Peyton's premise that a town is nothing if not its people.

Poe, Edgar Allen. *Tales of Mystery and Imagination*. New York: Dutton, 1971.
This collection contains "The Fall of the House of Usher," "The Premature Burial," and forty-four other spine-tingling tales.

Roberts, Nancy. *Appalachian Ghosts*. Garden City, NY: Doubleday, 1978.

The ghosts of Appalachia reflect closely the unique character of the people of the region. In these stories ghostly fiddlers play in deserted cabins, long-dead coal miners moan beneath the earth, and phantom trains groan their way across cuts and tunnels.

Siddons, Anne Rivers. *Homeplace*. New York: Harper and Row, 1987.
This is a story of the civil rights movement in the 1960s, and of an enlightened white high school girl who receives the hatred of her family and peers. She discovers how hard it is to go home again after twelve years away.

Steadman, Mark. *Angel Child*. Atlanta: Peachtree Publishers, 1988.
A story of racial and physical prejudice, this is a novel about ugliness, beauty, and unwanted children.

Stuart, Jesse. *A Jesse Stuart Reader*. New York: McGraw-Hill, 1963.
Eighteen short stories, twenty-six poems, and passages from his biographies let readers enter the eastern Kentucky mountain world of this well-respected teacher and writer.

————. *Trees of Heaven*. Lexington: University Press of Kentucky, 1980.
Stuart's first novel uses spare, sinewy prose to create Ragweed Hollow and the rival families and philosophies of Anse Bushman and Boliver Tussie.

Walker, Alice. *The Color Purple*. New York: Harcourt Brace Jovanovich, 1982.
Walker depicts the struggles of Southern blacks in the 1920s and 1930s, and a triumphal ending, as Celie gains respect, rights, a thriving business, and the return of her children.

Wallin, Luke. *The Redneck Poacher's Son*. Scarsdale, NY: Bradbury Press, 1981.
Sixteen-year-old Jesse Watersmith lies in wait to shoot his redneck father whose dangerous deeds have kept the family prisoner in an Alabama swamp.

Warren, Robert Penn. *Wilderness.* New York: Random House, 1961.
This is a novel of the Civil War and of a Bavarian's adventures in the Union army.

Welty, Eudora. *Selected Stories.* New York: Modern Library, 1971.
Here are twenty-five stories, observations of human experience in Eudora Welty's south.

Weyr, Garrett. *Pretty Girls.* New York: Crown, 1988.
In this novel, three young girls grow into adulthood at the University of North Carolina, and band together for self-protection.

Wolfe, Thomas. *Look Homeward, Angel: A Story of the Buried Life.* New York: Charles Scribner's Sons, 1957.
This is the story of the coming of age of Eugene Gant in North Carolina, and of his growing passion to experience life outside a mountain resort town.

Young, Thomas Daniel, et al. *The Literature of the South,* rev. ed. Glenview, Ill.: Scott, Foresman, 1968.
This is a thorough anthology in four sections: The Early South to 1815; The Rise of the Confederacy, 1815–1865; The New South, 1865–1918; and Modern Renaissance, 1918–1965.

Tennessee in Non-Fiction

Bell, Charles Bailey. *A Mysterious Spirit: The Bell Witch of Tennessee.* Nashville: Charles Elder Books, 1972.
The Bell Witch appeared frequently to residents of northern middle Tennessee in the 1800s, playing pranks and performing benevolent deeds, as recorded in this history by a descendant of the early Bell family.

Black, Patti Carr. *The Natchez Trace.* Jackson: University of Mississippi Press, 1988.
This 300-year-old trail from central Tennessee down to the Mississippi River provides ample scope for exploration today. This collection of photographs and anecdotes takes the reader to

country stores, cemeteries, antebellum ruins, barns, mansions, cabins, and Indian relics.

Brachey, Doug and Dawn. *Rugby, Tennessee's Victorian Village.* Brentwood, Tenn.: J. M. Productions, 1987.
Photographs, maps, and drawings of this preserved Victorian village in the Cumberland Mountains, founded by British "colonists" in 1880, reveal the hopes and failures of idealism.

Brewer, Carson. *Just Over the Next Ridge: A Traveller's Guide to Little-Known and Out-of-the-Way Places in Southern Appalachia.* Knoxville: The Knoxville News-Sentinel, 1987.
Explore hiking trails, covered wooden bridges, white water, wildlife areas, log inns and catawba vineyards in this backpacker's companion that also lists state parks, national parks and forests, giving accommodation information.

Brumbaugh, Thomas B., ed. *Architecture of Middle Tennessee: The Historic American Buildings Survey.* Nashville: Vanderbilt University Press, 1974.
Take a look at early Nashville through descriptions, photos, architectural line drawings of thirty-five interesting structures, from houses, churches, and schools to factories and commercial buildings from the late 18th century to 1900.

Carpenter, Allan. *Tennessee.* (New Enchantment of America Series.) Chicago: Children's Press, 1978.
This fact-packed book highlights the art, music, history, and geography of the Volunteer State.

Crutchfield, James A. *The Tennessee Almanac and Book of Facts.* Nashville: Rutledge Hill Press, 1986.
The Tennessee Almanac contains information about nearly every town in the state, with details of annual festivals, fairs, elections, zip codes, and historical figures.

Cumberland General Store Wish and Want Book. Crossville, Tenn.: Cumberland General Store, 1982.
The Cumberland General Store tries to maintain an old-fashioned ambience through selling old-fashioned things that are un-

available elsewhere. Their mail-order catalogue looks like late 19th-century ones.

Dalsass, Diana. *Miss Mary Bobo's Home Cooking: Traditional Recipes from Lynchburg, Tennessee.* New York: New American Library, 1984.
Whet your appetite with these 120 Tennessee recipes passed down through generations and preserved by Miss Mary Bobo, whose white-columned boarding house near the Jack Daniel distillery still serves amazingly good food.

Finger, John. *The Eastern Band of the Cherokees: 1819–1900.* Knoxville: University of Tennessee Press, 1986.
Finger tells how the Eastern Band avoided forced removal to Oklahoma, and provides anecdotal information that shows how Cherokees maintained their identity while adapting to encroachments.

Fradin, Dennis B. *Tennessee in Words and Pictures.* Chicago: Children's Press, 1980.
Take a look at the facts in a well-illustrated nutshell.

Harris, Bill. *Tennessee: The Volunteer State.* New York: Crescent Books, 1985.
Superb photography and anecdotal caption texts take the reader to the land of Andrew Jackson, the Grand Ole Opry, Jack Daniel's, Elvis Presley, and W. C. Handy, through caverns, mountains, and log cabins, to Cherokee villages and cotton fields.

Horn, Stuart. *Tennessee's War, 1861–1865.* Nashville: Civil War Centennial Commission, 1965.
Participants describe battles and warfare, and there are maps and illustrations.

Hurst, Jack. *Nashville's Grand Ole Opry.* New York: Harry N. Abrams, 1975.
This illustrated, coffee-table history of country music's home traces its roots from Elizabethan folk music to today's commercialized package, and offers detailed biographies of many important country music personalities.

Ingram, M. V. *Authenticated History of the Bell Witch*. Union City, Tenn.: Pioneer Press, 1974.
First published in 1894, this history of the Robertson County apparition known as the Bell Witch continues to inspire fear in local school children, perpetuating local belief in the ghostly legend.

Johnson, Mayme Hart. *A Treasury of Tennessee Churches*. Brentwood, Tenn.: J.M.P. Productions, 1986.
Tennesseans are proud of their religious heritage, as shown in this book of photographs, histories, and anecdotes from over two-hundred churches, synagogues and cathedrals, ranging from a 1783 log chapel, the oldest still standing in the state, to Episcopal carpenter gothic, to contemporary brick and steel, from the Appalachians to the Mississippi River.

Madewell, Terry. *Glory Holes: An Expert's Guide to Tennessee's Best Fishing*. Manning, SC: J.T. Publishing Company, 1986.
Chapters on every major lake and TVA reservoir, mountain stream, creek and river ensure that anglers get to the best fishing holes in the state.

Netherton, John. *Tennessee: A Homecoming*. Nashville: Third National Corporation, 1986.
Nearly 200 color photos of scenery, people, business, and wildlife with accompanying text take the reader from Mississippi cotton land through walking horse farms to Appalachian white water.

Patton, James Welch. *Unionism and Reconstruction in Tennessee, 1860–1869*. Gloucester, Mass.: Peter Smith, 1966.
This history of Tennessee during the Civil War and immediately afterwards deals with union sympathizers, and the generally easy Reconstruction period which the state enjoyed following Confederate defeat.

Rugby Recipes. Rugby, Tenn.: The Rugby Restoration Association, 1971.
Mouth-watering, inspirational recipes from the original British colonists, from today's residents, and from Tennessee's Cumber-

land Mountains include appetizers, pastries, entrees, breads, sal-
ads, desserts, and beverages.

*Seven Early Churches of Nashville: A Series of Lectures Pre-
sented at the Public Library of Nashville and Davidson County.*
Nashville: Elder's Bookshop, 1972.
A comprehensive history of the religious heritage of Tennessee's capital city, founded on Christmas Eve, 1779, this well-
documented book covers in great depth the pioneer days, the
growth of European settlement, and subsequent expansion.

Siler, Tom. *Tennessee Towns: From Adams to Yorkville.* Knoxville: East Tennessee Historical Society, 1985.
Every town and hamlet is listed, giving the origin of its name,
a brief anecdotal history, and details of some famous sons and
daughters.

Smith, Reid. *Majestic Middle Tennessee.* Gretna, Tenn.: Pelican
Publishing Company, 1982.
Discover over 120 antebellum plantation houses and churches
through photographs and anecdotal histories of their founding,
along with stories of the Civil War battles of Franklin and
Nashville.

Southern Arts and Artists

Bivins, John, Jr. *Two Hundred Years of the Visual Arts in North
Carolina: An Introduction to the Decorative Arts of North Carolina, 1776–1976.* Raleigh: North Carolina Museum of Art,
1976.
Bivins examines in detail the furniture, pottery, textiles, metal-
work, and painting that have flourished in North Carolina since
colonial days.

Bresenham, Karoline Patterson, and Nancy Puentes. *Lone Stars:
A Legacy of Texas Quilts.* Austin: University of Texas Press,
1987.
The official catalogue for the Texas Sesquicentenary Quilt Association traveling exhibition, this book illustrates over sixty
quilts in full color, all made between 1836 and 1936, with pho-

tographs of many makers, and descriptions of patterns, fabrics, and methods.

Carson, Jane. *Colonial Virginia Cookery*. Williamsburg: The Colonial Williamsburg Foundation, 1985.
These early recipes reflect not only the British cuisine from which they derive, but also the newfound ingredients of the eastern shore. While modern cooks could replicate these foods today, the recipes are not translated into contemporary equivalents.

English, Kathleen, and Alison Nicholls. *Christmas With Southern Living*. Birmingham, Ala.: Southern Living Magazine, 1988.
This annual publication documents holiday customs throughout the region, from hanging of greenery in Anglican churches to pageants in the Moravian communities of North Carolina, with recipes, arts and crafts instructions, and decorating tips from across the South.

Horwitz, Elinor. *Mountain People, Mountain Crafts*. Philadelphia: Lippincott, 1976.
Horwitz pays homage to Appalachian mountain folk artists and illustrates examples of toys, musical instruments, and domestic crafts.

Irwin, John Rice. *Alex Stewart: Portrait of a Pioneer*. Exton, Pa.: Schiffer Publishing Company, 1986.
A straightforward, sensitive story of a man whose people and way of life have passed. Stewart, born in 1891 in the East Tennessee mountains, tells the story of his life, his craftwork, and the ways of mountain folk.

King, Daisy, ed. *The Original Tennessee Homecoming Cookbook*. Nashville: Rutledge Hill Press, 1986.
From dinners in 18th-century mansions to the World's Largest Catfish Fry in the West Tennessee town of Paris, this book is a goldmine of over 3,000 recipes submitted by Tennesseans to provide a regional cookbook for the state's homecoming celebrations in 1986.

Made by Hand: Mississippi Folk Art. Jackson: Mississippi Department of Archives and History, 1980.
Mississippi folk artists have produced quilts and coverlets, de-

coy ducks and garden statuary, utilitarian furniture and wrought iron utensils, in addition to oil paintings and watercolors, all illustrated here.

Made in Tennessee: An Exhibition of Early Arts and Crafts. Nashville: The Life and Casualty Insurance Company and WSM-TV, 1971.
The catalogue of a traveling exhibition illustrates the proliferation of utilitarian and decorative arts in the Volunteer State since the mid-1700s.

Marshall, Lillian Bertram. *Cooking Across the South.* Birmingham, Ala.: Oxmoor House, 1980.
This collection of Southern recipes offers detailed instructions for the preparation of soups and stews, fish and shellfish, meats, poultry, and game, vegetables, breads, sweets, and beverages.

Mickler, Ernest Matthew. *White Trash Cooking.* Berkeley, Cal.: Ten Speed Press, 1986.
The southern peasant equivalent to Soul Food. The meals presented here make for entertaining reading, filled as they are with Southernisms and Southern ingredients, from 'gator tail and fried squirrel to catfish fillets and hush puppies.

Rubin, Cynthia Elyce. *Southern Folk Art.* Birmingham, Ala.: Oxmoor House, 1985.
This illustrated survey of pottery, painting, sculpture, decorated furniture, and textiles begins with earliest documentations and pieces, and progresses into the middle of the twentieth century.

Shuptrine, Hubert. *Home to Jericho: The South Beheld.* Birmingham, Ala.: Southern Living Books, 1987.
Ninety-one perceptive watercolor paintings of Southerners and their land, with text by the artist, this book represents some of the best in contemporary Southern art.

Wigginton, Eliot, ed. *The Foxfire Book.* Garden City, NJ: Doubleday, 1972.
High school students explore and write about the folkways surrounding them—hog dressing, log cabin building, faith healing, moonshining, and "other affairs of plain living."

Wilson, Sandy Tune, and Doris Finch Kennedy. *Of Coverlets.*
  Nashville: Tunstede, 1984.
  These researchers for the Tennessee Textile History Project
found, photographed, and documented over 1000 handwoven textiles, with anecdotal histories and information to enable the designs to be replicated.

Southern Life and History

Clinton, Catherine. *The Plantation Mistress: Women's World in
  the Old South.* New York: Pantheon Books, 1982.
  Behind the image of magnolias and leisure, most southern
women had active, working roles to play in estate management.

Foote, Shelby. *The Civil War: A Narrative,* 3 vols. Westminster,
  Md.: Vintage Books, 1987.
  Combining scholarship and narrative, this is a paperback reis-
sue of the 1958 original that came to be recognized as one of the
most accessible histories of the Civil War ever written.

Gamble, Robert. *The Alabama Catalog: A Guide to the Early Architecture of the State.* Tuscaloosa: University of Alabama Press, 1987.
  Gamble covers styles and history, county by county, from cabins
to early skyscrapers, churches, courthouses, mansions, and colleges.

Harwell, Richard B. *Confederate Music.* Chapel Hill: University
  of North Carolina Press, 1950.
  Harwell surveys the sheet music and popular songs published
in the South prior to its fall in 1865, relating them to the history of
the era, and including an exhaustive bibliography of publications.

Hightower, John M. *The Confederate Challenge.* Natural Bridge,
  Va.: Rockbridge Publishing Company, 1992.
  Eye-catching illustrations make this question-and-answer format entertaining as well as informative to the trivia buff who enjoys little-known facts, statistics, and behind the scenes tours.

King, Richard H. *A Southern Renaissance: The Cultural Awak-
  ening of the American South 1930–1955.* New York: Oxford
  University Press, 1980.
  King perceptively analyzes the phenomenal growth of literature
in the South, from Vanderbilt Agrarianism to Ambivalence to
New Outlook.

Thomas, Emory M. *The Confederacy as a Revolutionary Experience*. Englewood Cliffs, NJ: Prentice-Hall, 1971.
Thomas shows how conservative revolutions have a way of getting out of hand, transforming institutions they were meant to preserve, breaking traditions they wanted to save.

Vandiver, Frank. *Blood Brothers: A Short History of the Civil War*. College Station: Texas A & M University Press, 1992.
Dramatic in tone, and illustrated with maps and photos, this concise history of the war has a spicy delivery.

Wenberg, Donald. *Blue Ridge Mountain Pleasures*. Chester, Conn.: East Woods Press, 1987.
This A-Z travel guide suggests over 1500 places to visit and things to see and do from North Carolina's Grandfather Mountain to South Carolina and north Georgia.

Wertenbaker, Thomas Jefferson. *The Old South: The Founding of American Civilization*. New York: Cooper Square Publications, 1963.
Based upon the European ideals of scholarship and gentlemanly behavior, the Southern colonies of Britain strove to perfect their heritage of civilization.

White, Dan. *Kentucky Bred*. Dallas: Taylor, 1986.
An inside look at how the horse industry works in the Bluegrass State describes breeding, farm maintenance, racing, and historic moments.

The South in Drama and Poetry

Appalachian Autumn and Other Plays. New York: Scholastic Book Services, 1971.
With scope for fourteen actors, this drama about coal miners who dream of life outside, "Appalachian Autumn" by Earl Hamner, is one of four plays in this collection.

Richardson, Howard, and William Berney. *Dark of the Moon*, rev. ed. New York: Theatre Arts Books, 1973.
Originally called "Barbara Allen," this powerful, poetic play tells of the witch boy in the Smoky Mountains and of the human

girl who loved him, contrasting and fusing mountain revival religion with lingering beliefs in natural spirits.

Ryan, Abram Joseph. *Poems: Patriotic, Religious, Miscellaneous*. Baltimore: John B. Piet, 1880. (o.p.)
The author, known variously as Father Ryan or Poet Laureate of the Confederacy, is most remembered today for his powerful "The Conquered Banner," which is really a requiem for the Old South and of the men who fought for her. Over one hundred of his poems appear in this collection.

Tate, Allen. *Poems*. New York: Swallow, 1961.
This Vanderbilt Agrarian Movement poet writes of the marvels of man and nature.

Williams, Tennessee. *The Theatre of Tennessee Williams,* Vols. I–VIII. New York: New Directions Publishing Corporation, 1971.
All of Williams' plays in one similar format allows readers to compare and contrast his pictures of life in the steamy South.

Periodicals

The Confederate Veteran. Box 59, Columbia, Tennessee 38402–0059.
This glossy history magazine appears six times annually, and contains period photos and engravings, maps, and research about the War Between the States.

Southern Living. P.O. Box 28541, Birmingham, Alabama 35223.
A showcase for the region, *Southern Living* presents lively articles about travel, arts and crafts, and culture, Southern beauty spots and historic houses, liberally illustrated with color photos. There are book reviews of new books about the South.

For Further Information

The Appalachian Center for Crafts
State Route 56
Smithville, Tennessee 37166
Telephone 615-432-4111
This professional crafts center specializes in wood, metal, fiber,

glass, and clay, and teaches and exhibits fine arts skills in Tennessee and Appalachian traditions.

The Belle Carol Riverboat Company
106 First Avenue South
Nashville, Tennessee 37201
Telephone 615-244-3430
  Traditional 19th-century passenger steamboats ply the Cumberland as they once did, departing historic Fort Nashborough, a replica of the 1790s stockade that became Nashville.

Black Gnat
East Maine Street
Murfreesboro, Tennessee 37130
  This early 1700s log house is privately owned, but is open for guided tours to private groups who write ahead, and for bed and breakfast accommodation.

Cannonsburg Pioneer Village
South Front Street
Murfreesboro, Tennessee 37130
Telephone 615-893-6565
  Early Tennessee pioneer life is recreated in this living museum that includes log houses, forges, general store, one room school and church.

Cragfront
Route 25
Castalian Springs, Tennessee 37031
Telephone 615-452-7070
  Completed in 1802, this stone-built Federal-style mansion was the home of frontiersman James Winchester. The three-story house is completely furnished with period pieces and is open to the public.

Chamber of Commerce
Red Boiling Springs, Tennessee 37083
  Forty miles east of Westmoreland, this sulfur and mineral water spa town bubbles with natural springs. Beside its large, late-Victorian, Southern-style hotels, shops, restored houses and

churches winds Salt Lick Creek through wooded parkland. Write to the Chamber of Commerce for details of a walking tour of the area.

Rugby Historic British Colony
Rugby, Tennessee 37031
Telephone 615-628-2441
   About 70 miles east of Westmoreland is a rural British colony founded in 1880 by author Thomas Hughes (*Tom Brown's School Days*). Rugby lies on the Cumberland Plateau, with dramatic river gorges and nature trails in addition to the working Victorian village, Anglican Church, and Public Library with over 7000 Victorian books and periodicals. The colony failed because its founders spent their time writing poetry instead of growing vegetables.

Trousdale Place
183 West Main Street
Gallatin, Tennessee 37066
Telephone 615-452-7854
   A National Registered Historic Landmark 15 miles south of Westmoreland, this early 1800s house was the home of Governor Wiliam Trousdale, and contains period furniture, a Revolutionary and Confederate military library and museum, and a museum of county history, including artifacts from Westmoreland.

Wynnewood
Castalian Springs, Tennessee 37031
Telephone 615-452-5463
   This 142-foot long, two-story log stagecoaching inn was home to a mineral springs resort that had previously been a Native American village. One of the outbuildings was the doctor's office, and is preserved as it was in the late 1800s. It is open daily, April through October.

Chapter 3
Simple Gifts: A Shaker Festival

Perhaps no other American religious group captures the imagination as do the Shakers, or properly, the United Society of Believers in Christ's Second Appearing. Hounded out of England following persecution and imprisonment, founder Ann Lee and a small band of followers came in 1774 to America, where ridicule and persecution did not abate. A great religious revival swept through the U.S.A. in the early 1800s, however, and the Shakers rose to meet the challenge, attracting hundreds of converts who eventually banded together into celibate, prosperous, utopian communities from Maine to southern Kentucky. That they were people of great spiritual depth is seen in their reverence for the earth, for their own craftwork (which they would never have termed "art"), and for their daily creed of simple living. Today the Shakers are remembered for their exquisite, minimalist furniture, basketry, silk weaving, songs, and food (duplicatable today with the help of several good cookbooks). A few Shakers still live in New England; indeed, there have been recent converts, though the total number of believers has dropped from around 8,000 in the mid 1800s to less than 15 today.

A Shaker Festival can manifest itself along several lines; *music and dance* (the Shakers got their name from religious dancing); *American history* (they were conservationists, pacifist neutrals in the War Between the States, and the first to sell seeds in packets commercially); *art* (their "simple" architecture is admired today for its strength and beauty; their furniture sells for thousands of dollars); or *commerce* (they integrated mass production techniques of "the world" into their manufacture and agriculture). An entire unit of study in school covering several grades could culminate in one Shaker Week, with food, drama, art, speakers, and, where possible, a visit to a Shaker site.

A Festival Display: Three Ideas

You Will Need:

Pencil, Pen, Ink, or poster paints
Sheets of white paper
Sheets of colored paper
Scissors
Craft Knife
Fixing Materials (Pins, staples, or glue)

In harmony with the simplicity urged upon the Believers by their philosophy, keep this display uncluttered. The first idea is a simple outline map of the eastern United States showing the location of the Shaker colonies, museums, and libraries. Refer to Van Kolken's *Introducing the Shakers* (see sources, p. 134) for help. Another idea is to copy a "Tree of Life" design, either by line drawing or scherrenschnitte. The "Tree of Life" is shown in most Shaker books since it came to symbolize the Shaker movement. Refer to the "Sources of Inspiration" at the end of this chapter.

To make a "Tree of Life" from cut paper, you will be using a centuries-old method from Poland, Germany, the Czech lands and other eastern European countries, known as scherrenschnitte, or scissor-cutting (Figure 22). Choose a large colored sheet of paper for the tree. The Shakers were not opposed to cheerful colors in their clothing, bed-linens, and paintings, so it is not necessary to use black or grey, although for the display board, these colors would be good choices.

First, fold the sheet of paper in half. Copy half the "Tree of Life" design on the paper in pencil, keeping the center of the tree on the fold of the paper. When the design is to your satisfaction, cut it out carefully through both thicknesses of paper, using a small craft knife or scissors. Unfold with care, and attach the Tree to background paper on the display area.

To avoid having a crease in the middle of the Tree, place the finished scherrenschnitte on an ironing board beneath brown paper, and iron it gently. Or, following the instructions in step one, place the scherrenschnitte Tree on another piece of paper, and use it as a template: trace around it, cut it out, and use the second Tree.

To involve students in the process, discuss with them the origins of the Tree of Life in the "spirit dreams" that some Shakers had from the middle of the 19th century until they were discouraged by the elders. Refer to Milton and Emily Rose's *A Shaker Reader* (see

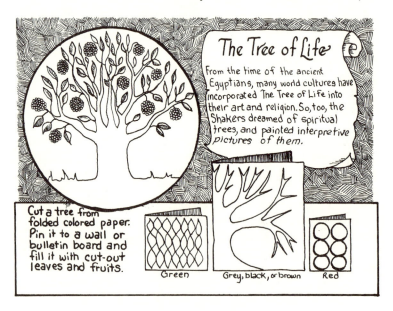

The Tree of Life

From the time of the ancient Egyptians, many world cultures have incorporated The Tree of Life into their art and religion. So, too, the Shakers dreamed of spiritual trees, and painted interpretive pictures of them.

Cut a tree from folded colored paper. Pin it to a wall or bulletin board and fill it with cut-out leaves and fruits.

Green   Grey, black, or brown   Red

Figure 22

Figure 23. Logo of *The Shaker Messenger* (courtesy of The World of Shaker)

"Sources of Inspiration") for a good illustrated introduction to the various kinds of trees that emanated from Shaker artists after what they felt were inspired dreams. Ask student artists to make small paper Trees of Life in scherrenschnitte, pen and ink, crayon, or other media for display throughout the school prior to and during the Festival. Display their work on a special "gallery" wall in a classroom, hallway, library, or foyer. After the Festival, consider sending some of the work to a Shaker museum or magazine.

A third simple, and evocative, motif is that used by *The Shaker Messenger,* a magazine devoted to scholarship and understanding of the Shaker movement (Figure 23). Their logo is a white picket fence, typical of many on Shaker properties, against a black background. Look through copies of the magazine and through Shaker books to find other items suitable for silhouettes: chairs, houses, Shaker bonnets, horses and wagons, barns, and other buildings, implements, or articles of clothing.

To make a fence for display, cut out the individual pickets from white paper, first making one to use as a template. Attach them to plain backing paper on the display area with pins or staples, adding finally the two horizontal cross pieces. Notice how *The Shaker Messenger* logo implies three-dimensionality with cut-out "shadows" beneath the two horizontal pieces.

Guest Speakers

1. *A living Shaker.* In New England, it is still possible to meet Shakers. While the Shaker brothers and sisters may be unable to

Create a Festival Ambience

Verses, Poems, Mottoes: Make a simple frame by over-lapping paper strips placed on the edges of artwork.

Pick up your crumbs, and, where you eat, Keep all things decent, clean and neat.

Cut a Shaker TREE of LIFE from paper for a main doorway.

Eat hearty and decent, and clearout your plate.

Make stand-up mottoes for desktops on card.

Copy SHAKER MOTTOES and rules for living on bookmarks, or display on walls.

Cut out a silhouette frieze of Shaker-style buildings to hang on the wall above eye level. Use dark paper.

WEAR 19TH C.- style clothing to school: long dress, shawl, bonnet, apron; collarless shirt, long-tailed coat, stovepipe hat, plain dark shoes.

DISPLAY A COLLECTION of Shaker-style boxes. See text for instructions on making a facsimile.

Drape checked woolen blankets over chairbacks and tables.

(sidebar, right:) at end of chapter. Where to find Shaker mottoes? Sources

Figure 24

travel to *your* festival, it is possible to arrange group visits to their colonies. Write first to:

The Director
Sabbathday Lake Shaker Community
Sabbathday Lake, Maine 04274.

2. *A Shaker museum curator or staff member.* Contact one of the museums or libraries on page 122ff. to see if they could supply a guest speaker or a lecture illustrated with slides, books, and artifacts.

3. *A Shaker collector or historian.* Contact an author through his or her publisher (see the list of sources beginning on page 130). Shaker museums may also be able to recommend local historians who would like to share their enthusiasm and knowledge with your school. Write to the editors of *The Shaker Messenger* for help in locating a historian near you.

4. *An artist or crafter in the Shaker tradition.* While by no means definitive, this list of artisans known for the quality of their work in the Shaker style should help locate one who would speak or share catalogues or photos of his/her work for display.

Barratts Bottoms, Chairmakers
Rt. 2, Box 231, Bower Road
Kearneyville, West Virginia 25430

Cabin Crafters
S.R. North
Shipshewana, Indiana 46545

Dana Robes, Wood Craftsman
POB 707
Lower Shaker Village
Enfield, New Hampshire 03748

Donald Mack, Wood Crafter
R.R. 11, Box 494-A
Pawling, New York 12564

John McGuire, Basketmaker
c/o Schiffer Publishing Company
West Chester, Pennsylvania 19380

Orleans Carpenters
70 Rock Harbor Road
Orleans, Massachusetts 02653

Shaker Traditions
817 Dempster Street
Evanston, Illinois 60201

Geoffrey Gale, Instructor in Design
49 Grasmere Road
London N10 2DH, England

5. *A cook.* Find a local cook who would like to experiment with Shaker recipes, then demonstrate the preparation of one or two items during the festival. Include some recipes to be made by children, if possible. For recipes, refer to the list of sources on page 131–133.

6. *A tailor or seamstress.* Engage a local person to make an item of Shaker clothing based upon old photographs or drawings from the list of sources on page 131. A local museum might be willing to loan items for a lecture-demonstration. A museum would certainly encourage supervised young artists to sketch items of clothing while they were touring the facility.

Projects

1. *Seminars and discussions.* These discussions may take place in conjunction with a guest speaker or demonstration, or alone, and can be geared for different ages and abilities. They may be held in a classroom as part of a small group's study, or in a public arena such as the library or assembly room, with an audience composed of several classes. A topic of interest for lower and middle schoolers is Shaker dress. Assignment: Compare the Shaker way of dress with that of groups today who dress in particular ways: the Amish,

Hassidic Jews, Muslim women, Christian monks and nuns. Discuss why dress is considered important among these people and religious groups. What does dress symbolize, both for those who practice the religion and for outsiders?

Other topics can include "The Revival of Interest in Shaker Furniture"; "The Gift to Be Simple—What Does It Mean?"; "Shaker Celibacy—Why Did They Do It?"; "Shaker Worship Services—Music and Dance." Teachers may suggest themes for written projects that could easily be presented as a seminar in a public reading. A perusal of Shaker books will offer many other points for discussion.

2. *A community service project.* Organize and carry out a group service project to show how cooperation worked for the good of all in the Shaker community. Divide into teams with "elders" and "eldresses," "houses" or families, and separate sections for boys and for girls, according to Shaker philosophy. Each homeroom could become a Shaker "house" or family (often named after the geographical position within the community, such as North Family, or Center Family); each family can then elect an elder and an eldress as leaders, and decide on the community service project:

a. Litter clean-up on campus or in town.
b. Gardening and tree planting.
c. Painting or redecorating a room using some Shaker motifs or designs with stencils.

You Will Need:
Boiled Linseed Oil (from decorator's supply shop)
Craft Knife
Pencil and ruler
Old rags
Stiff manila-type paper
Sponge or stencil brush
Water- or oil-based paints
Water or turpentine for cleaning up, depending on choice of paint

To make a stencil, first find a simple Shaker-like symbol, such as a house, flower, or implement. It could be a leaf from the Tree of Life, or a Shaker woman's bonnet, or a barn. Draw the design simply on manila folder paper. Brush boiled linseed oil over the paper and let it dry, wiping off any excess oil with a cloth. Then use an artist's knife to cut out the design. When the stencil is thoroughly dry, hold it flat against the wall, wooden floor, desk, or other item to be decorated. Using a sponge or stenciling brush, dab paint over the stencil. Carefully lift off the stencil from the surface. Rinse the paint from the stencil paper, dry with a cloth, and repeat the pattern elsewhere, preferably in a line that follows the architectural details of the room, such as the ceiling, picture rail, baseboard, or doorframe.

d. Visiting elderly people, either in their own homes or in a nursing facility. Contact the supervisor of local social services, a church, or a nursing home for information about how to proceed with visits that could include offering small gifts of food, periods of reading aloud, or sharing artwork.

Shaker Art Projects

1. *Build a model of a Shaker village.*

What You Need:

For Paper Village

Paper
Pencil and ruler
Felt-tip pens or crayons
Stick glue
Papier mâché for base (optional)

For Wooden Village

Wood block scraps
Sandpaper
Paint
Tempera or
    Latex emulsion or
    Acrylic
Paint brushes
Varnish
    Acrylic or
    oil-based

Study photographs of Shaker buildings in the sources listed on pages 131–133. Draw barns, houses, meeting houses, ice-cellars, and other buildings. Make them three-dimensional by following instructions in Figure 25. When an entire village is ready, display

Build a Shaker Village

As Shakers grew in numbers, they moved into communal farms, which by the 1870's were well organized, prosperous, and industrious. Buildings were sturdy and graceful, though devoid of extra frills of pure ornament. If a gable or a gatepost were too decorative, it would have to come down. These utilitarian houses, barns, and workshops have a stark beauty that attracts many visitors today. Refer to the sources at the end of this chapter for photos and drawings of Shaker buildings. Make a table-top Shaker village using the photographs as inspirations. Light card or even typing paper will work.

One-dimensional facade

1. Draw the facade only. Use a ruler for accuracy.
2. Draw a base, followed by a
3. back support.
4. Cut on solid lines. Fold where indicated.
5. Glue the tab and stick it to the back of the facade.

base
← fold

cut to here
Tab
glue
back brace
← fold
← fold

Base and **back brace** MUST be same width.

base
← fold
cut to
Tab
glue
back brace
fold
← fold

Shaker dwellings often have two front doors. Why? So that men could use one, and women the other, proceeding into a hallway with separate stairs to their separate rooms on the top floors. Meeting houses also had separate sides.

---

three-dimensional facade

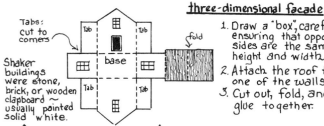

Tabs:
cut to corners

Tab   Tab

base

fold

Shaker buildings were stone, brick, or wooden clapboard ~ usually painted solid white.

Tab   Tab

1. Draw a "box", carefully ensuring that opposite sides are the same height and width.
2. Attach the roof to one of the walls.
3. Cut out, fold, and glue together.

hands to work, and hearts to God. — Mother Ann Lee

Figure 25

it on a window ledge, a table, or on a realistic farm terrain built up with folded newspaper and papier mâché.

Alternatively, ask a wood shop for off-cuts and scraps. Find house-shaped pieces. Prepare them for painting by sanding to remove rough edges. Use acrylic, tempera, or latex paints, and coat with non-gloss varnish. To make them look old, sandpaper away the paint on the top of the roof and along edges. Add a bit of red paint to the varnish to give them further "antiquing."

2. *Draw Shakers in costume to show what they wore.* Write down the names of various items of clothing with which most people are not familiar today.

3. *Paint a portrait of yourself or a friend in Shaker costume,* or dress up your school photograph with Shaker dress. Place your photograph under a piece of paper. Trace around your head and shoulders. Remove the photograph from beneath the paper, and draw Shaker clothing, including bonnet or hat, to fit the outline of your head. Cut out the face so that the photograph will show through the drawing when you place it beneath.

Put your portrait in a frame. Select a piece of stiff card slightly larger than your finished portrait. Place your portrait in the center of the paper and trace lightly around it. Remove the portrait. With a ruler, draw lines just inside and parallel to the "box" that you drew around the portrait. Cut out the hole for your portrait, and tape your picture in place within the frame.

4. *Make profile silhouettes* of members of your family or of friends. Place a bright lamp on a table and ask the subject to sit between it and a large piece of paper fixed to the wall. Trace around the shadow of the subject's profile. Cut out the paper. Silhouettes are traditionally cut from black paper. To keep pencil marks from showing, display the reverse of the silhouette by gluing it to a sheet of paper of contrasting color.

Another method for making silhouettes takes a bit longer, but enables you to cut out small shapes that are more suitable for home display, and more nearly like early silhouettes in Europe and colonial America. Take photographs of your friends in profile against a plain light wall. When the photos are developed, cut out the person in the picture, glue the cut-out to plain paper, and take a photocopy. Fill in the photographic image with a black felt-tip pen.

Display small silhouettes in picture frames, or glue them to a backing sheet of plain paper.

5. *Make a Tree of Life,* described earlier.

6. *Make a map of the Shaker colonies.* Include geographical features, other towns and cities, agricultural and manufacturing products, railroads, and other features that show economic or political boundaries, or that contrast modern development with Shaker farm land. Refer to Van Kolken and other "Sources" at the end of this chapter.

7. *Make a Shaker storage box.* These stacking boxes were made of wood to store seeds, buttons and sewing materials, herbs, and other household items. Like Russian stacking babushka dolls, they were made in "families" so that empty, smaller boxes would nestle inside larger ones, saving storage space. Today, old Shaker boxes are worth a lot of money. Even good reproductions of these simple boxes are not cheap. Students can make a paper version (Figure 26) that is reasonably sturdy, with potential for individual attention in decoration and finish.

These boxes will make a colorful display, and can be used at home for storing coins, desk paraphernalia, or jewelry.

What You Need:

Corrugated cardboard	Ruler
Pliable stiff card	Tape Measure
Craft knife	Clothes pins
Glue	Paper clips
Cellophane Tape	Varnish (optional)
Acrylic Paint	
Paintbrushes	
Wallpaper or Giftwrap	
Wallpaper paste (optional)	

Step-by-Step Procedure

a. *Make an oval bottom.* It should be about 8 inches (20 cm) long and 5 inches (12.5 cm) wide. Draw it carefully on the corrugated cardboard, and cut it out with an artist's knife. Alternatively, trace

Build a Shaker Box

1. Make an oval (or round) bottom. Cut the bottom from heavy corrugated cardboard.

2. Make a top. Trace around the bottom you have just made, making the top slightly larger all around. Fold the tabs up.

Tabs

oval or circle

3. Tape measure the circumference of the bottom. From a piece of card cut the sides of the box, longer than the circumference, and about as high as the diameter.

omit
omit

Shaker boxes have tonque overlaps. To simplify, omit the cutouts, leaving one tonque.

4. Wrap the side panel around the base, having first applied white glue to the tabs, all around the edge of the base, and to the inside of the tonque.

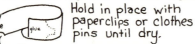

glue   glue

Hold in place with paperclips or clothes pins until dry.

Tape the side to the bottom.

5. Repeat steps 3 and 4 for the top piece to make a lid; but the rim should be comparatively shallow.

6. Paint the outside of the box and lid a bright color. Paint the inside another color, or line with wrapping paper, cut to size by tracing, and glue in place.

7. Apply a protective coat of clear polyurethane varnish.

Figure 26

around a large saucer or a small wastepaper basket to make a less authentically-shaped round box.

(You may make *tabs* at intervals on both the bottom and the top, scoring them on one side so they may be folded to glue to the side piece; alternatively, make tabs for the side in step c below to glue onto the bottom oval.)

b. *Make an oval top.* Trace around the bottom piece which you have just made, making this top piece *slightly* larger all around. This will enable it to fit easily onto the side of the box when it is assembled.

c. *Tape-measure the circumference of the base.* Shaker boxes were not very tall. Choose a piece of stiff card about six to eight inches (15 to 23 cm) in width, and about three inches (8 cm) longer than the circumference of the base. Make the sides of the box from this card, long enough to wrap around the bottom piece, leaving a rather large overlap. Shaker boxes were made with two "tongue" overlaps. You may make yours like this, too, or make only one "tongue" by tapering the side piece to the center with scissors.

(Skip to procedure g, below. On the reverse side of the decorative lining paper, trace around the lid, bottom, and side of the box. Set the lining paper aside.)

d. *Apply glue sparingly to the inside of the tongues.* Gently bend the sidepiece around the bottom oval. With a friend's help, tape and glue the side to the bottom. Press the tongues into place, folding them under the bottom oval. Attach a clothespin to the join until the glue has dried securely.

e. *Make the side of the top piece* just as you did for the bottom of the box. The side of the lid should be much shallower, however, so use stiff card that is only about an inch (3 cm) wide. (Skip to procedure g, below, and on the decorative lining paper, trace around the side of the lid. Set aside.) Secure this sidepiece to the lid with tape and glue. Clothespin or paperclip the overlapping join until it is dry.

f. *With fairly dry acrylics or tempera, paint the box one solid color.* Avoid very wet paints which may make the paper warp.

When the paint is dry, apply a second coat to cover if necessary. Decorate further by sponging on a light covering of a complementary color, or by painting a border around the side of the lid.

g. *Line the inside of the box with decorative paper* cut carefully to size by tracing. Cut the decorative paper as high as the width of the side of the box, and just slightly longer than the inside circumference. When cutting these out, leave a few tabs along the bottom edge to help secure the paper in place. Attach the paper with glue or wallpaper paste. Cover the inside bottom of the box and the inside of the lid by tracing their shapes on the reverse of the decorative paper. Glue these pieces on after you have attached the side covering.

Optional: protect the boxes from handling and dust by applying a coat of varnish. Allow twenty-four hours drying time before attempting to attach the lid to the bottom piece. Varnish may darken the paint.

8. *Make a Shaker Quilt Wall Hanging.*

What You Need:

Two sheets (8 x 8 inch; 20 x 20 cm) diffently colored construction
   paper (or wallpaper or giftwrap), per person
rulers
scissors
newspapers
large roll of butcher paper for backing

First, the leader (art teacher, craft leader, or supervising adult) needs to get a backing sheet ready. Determine the expected number of participants. If there are twenty "quilters," the backing sheet could be five blocks wide and four blocks deep, or two blocks wide and ten blocks deep. If there are uneven numbers, eager students can make extra blocks to fill in the gaps. (To make a much larger wall hanging, ask students to make three or four blocks each; enlarge the backing sheet accordingly. Or join the work of several small groups together to make one large hanging.)

Each person is given two squares of paper. Each square should be of a different color or design. Set one square aside. On the other square, measure to find the center line between top and bottom, or fold the paper in half, creasing to find the center line. Then, repeat on the other side, so that the paper is divided in half from top to bottom, and from side to side. Finally, cut along the lines to get four squares.

Next, on two of the small squares, draw a diagonal straight line from one corner to the opposite corner. Cut along those lines to create four triangles. Each artist should now have four triangles, two small squares, and one large square.

On the one large remaining square, follow the above procedure to make a grid of four squares—BUT DO NOT CUT THEM OUT. Using the cut-out triangles and squares, try to create different geometric patterns, placing them in the quartered grid of the large, uncut square. Use as many or as few of the cut-outs as you wish. After exploring the many design possibilities, select one and leave it on display on the work surface.

Look at the geometric arrangements that other people have done. Decide on one pattern, either by drawing names out of a hat or by nomination and vote, to use to create the wall hanging. Each participant then glues his or her pieces onto the large square according to the chosen plan. Then the leader and young artists assemble the squares on the backing sheet, gluing them in position. When dry, the wall-hanging will be a focal point in a hallway, classroom, or in the library.

As an alternate arrangement, students may glue their own favorite geometric design in place on their second sheet. The leader can then glue them onto the backing sheet. Students can comment on which quilt they prefer if there is time to make *both* quilts.

Prepare Shaker Food

As a special treat during the Simple Gifts Festival, have some Shaker cookies on hand. The festival organizers can bake them at home, or, for students' participation, encourage group cookery as a special event during the celebrations. Organize a parent volunteer to lead a cooking project with a class or a few interested students. The following recipes are reprinted, with kind permission of the authors, from *The Best of Shaker Cooking,* by Amy Bess Miller and Persis Fuller, of Hancock Shaker Village in Massachusetts. Consult this marvelous book to find out how to make over five hundred other delicious foods. Full details can be found in the list of sources beginning on page 130.

Rose Water Cookies

What You Need to make 6–7 dozen cookies:

1 cup butter	1/2 cup chopped orange or lemon peel
1 cup sugar	pinch of salt
2 eggs	1/2 cup raisins (plus extra raisins)
2–3/4 cups flour	
1 tsp baking soda	
1/2 tsp cream of tartar	
2 Tbsp rose water	

mixing bowls
spoons
cookie trays, greased

What You Do:

1. Preheat oven to 375 degrees F (190 C).
2. Cream together in a large bowl the softened butter and sugar.
3. Beat the eggs until fluffy; then add them to the creamed mixture.
4. Sift together the flour, baking soda, and cream of tartar. Add this to the creamed mixture, and blend well.
5. Add the rose water, chopped citrus peel, salt, and measured raisins to the batter, and blend well.
6. Drop this mixture onto a greased cookie sheet in spoonfuls. Press a single raisin into the center of each dropped cookie.
7. Bake in the oven for about 20 minutes.

Mother Ann's Birthday Cake

What You Need to Make One Cake:

1 cup best unsalted butter	2 tsp vanilla
2 cups sugar	12 eggwhites, beaten

3 cups flour, sifted

1/2 cup cornstarch

2 tsp baking powder

1 cup milk

1 tsp salt

peach jelly

icing (your choice)

mixing bowls

spoons

electric mixer

sifter

3 square 3 x 8 inch cake tins

1. Preheat oven to 350 degrees F (180 C).
2. Beat the softened butter and sugar into a smooth cream.
3. Sift the dry ingredients together.
4. Blend small amounts of flour mixture into the creamed mixture, alternately with small portions of milk. Beat well after each addition.
5. Add the vanilla, and stir it in.
6. Add salt to the beaten egg whites, and lightly fold this into the batter mixture.
7. Divide the cake batter among the three greased cake pans.
8. Bake for 25 minutes. When cool, remove cakes from pans and fill between layers with peach jelly and cover the cake with any delicate icing.

Mother Ann's birthday fell on February 29, so it was usually celebrated on March 1 by the Shakers. The above cake was served at supper, following the afternoon meeting commemorating the life of the Shaker's beloved founder, Ann Lee (1736–1784). The original recipe reads: "Cut a handful of peach twigs, which are filled with sap at this season of the year. Clip the ends and bruise them and beat cake batter with them. This will impart a delicate peach flavor to the cake."

Serve a Shaker Supper

For a celebration supper or a special school lunch during the Festival, organize a potluck Shaker meal. All meals should be prepared from a Shaker recipe book. To prevent overloading in one area, ask cooks to sign up for a particular dish before the event.

This will ensure a balanced table. If a fee is charged for the Shaker meal, proceeds could either offset costs involved in food purchase and preparation, or go towards funding a speaker or new library materials on the Shakers, or they could even be forwarded to a Shaker community or museum as a contribution to restoration projects.

Decorate the dining area with the Wall Hanging Quilt, the Trees of Life, the model villages, the silhouettes, and the Shaker clothing. Follow the meal with Shaker songs and a demonstration of Shaker dance by a school group.

Sing a Shaker Tune

The Shaker melody "Simple Gifts" has passed into the American folk consciousness. It has been used by classical composers such as Aaron Copland ("Appalachian Spring") and by Christian hymn writers ("Lord of the Dance"). We can use it, too, in praise of books and reading for this Shaker Festival (Figure 27) by using the melody for these words:

1. Read a book in the morning,
    Read a book at noon,
    Read a book when the evening star is winking at the moon!
    Read a book when you're working,
    Read a book at play,
    Read a book right now,
    For it makes the day!

2. Read a book upon waking,
    Read a book before you sleep,
    Read a book in the evening when into your bed you creep,
    Read a book when eating breakfast!
    Read a book while sipping tea!
    Read a book right now from the li-bra-ree!

Chorus

Books, books fit in so perfectly!
Read them in the evening; there's no need to watch tv!
You may read them in the garden,

Figure 27

> You may read them by the street,
> Take a book with you—
> They are such a treat!

"Simple Gifts," which can, of course, be sung to its original words, is the most famous Shaker melody, but there are many others. Refer to Edward Andrews' *The Gift to Be Simple* in the list of sources for further words and melodies.

A Shaker Dance

Shakers earned their nickname from outsiders' observations that their worship services consisted of quaking and shaking. By the 1790s, Father Joseph Meacham (1742–1796) had instituted an orderly alternative to the individual dancing. With men on one side of the meeting house, facing the women on the other, worshippers would symbolically "gather" and "bestow" God's blessings with the palms of their hands while moving in a simple backward and forward step. The Shakers would dance to unaccompanied singing. A Shaker dance can be learned fairly quickly, and would be a good "event" for the Simple Gifts Celebrations, either as a rehearsed performance, a participation workshop, or a combination of both. Refer to Leslie's *Dancing Saints* and Rose's *A Shaker Reader* for ideas.

Visit a Shaker Site

If you live close to a Shaker colony, museum, or library, consider organizing a group outing to see the buildings, eat the food, observe Shaker furniture in its proper settings, and wander about the farmlands with a knowledgeable guide. This list will help with such a visit:

Delaware

The Henry Francis du Pont Winterthur Museum, Winterthur 19735. Shaker storage walls, woodwork, furniture, baskets, and other Shaker items are displayed in a recreated living and storage room. Reservations required. Admission fee. Telephone (302) 656–8591.

Kentucky

The Kentucky Museum, Western Kentucky University, Bowling Green 42101. South Union community Shaker furniture, tools and crafts, such as quilts, as well as much other Kentuckiana, displayed in a well-designed modern museum. The campus also has three restored log dwellings nearby which are open to the public. Telephone (502) 745–2592.

Shakertown at Pleasant Hill, Harrodsburg 40330. A restored Shaker village of twenty-seven buildings with original furniture, costumes, shops, and artifacts. Crafts demonstrations. Riverboat cruise at Shaker Landing on Green River. Overnight accommodation and Shaker dining are available in this finest remaining Shaker site in the South. Admission fee. Telephone (606) 743–5411.

Shakertown at South Union, South Union 42283, fifteen miles west of Bowling Green. Though part of the site is occupied by a Roman Catholic monastic order, the 1834 Centre House is completely restored, and contains a fine exhibition of furniture, baskets and boxes, silk fabric (made on the site), and other textiles in original settings. There is an annual Shaker Festival in early summer, with an outdoor musical drama and food. Shaker meals may be enjoyed in the Shaker Tavern, a Southern Renaissance boarding house about two miles from the site. Admission. Telephone (502) 745–2592.

Maine

Shaker Museum, Sabbathday Lake Shaker Community, Poland Spring 04274. This 1793 Shaker village, still inhabited and farmed by Shakers, is open in summers, with a gift-shop stocking Shaker items open all year. Extensive collection of Shaker manuscripts for the researcher. Telephone (207) 926–4597.

Massachusetts

Boston Museum of Fine Arts, 465 Huntington Avenue, Boston 02115. A Shaker room with furniture and artifacts. Open

Tuesday–Sunday, 10–5, but closed some holidays. Free for children under 16. Telephone (617) 267–9300.

Fruitlands Museums, Rte. 110, Harvard 01451. The Shaker House is one of five museums in this cluster. It contains furniture, clothing, textiles, household paraphernalia, along with a large collection of manuscripts for the serious scholar. Open from the end of May to the end of September, Tuesday–Sunday, 1–5. Admission fee. Telephone (617) 456–3924.

Hancock Shaker Community, U.S. Rte. 20, Pittsfield 01201. Restored Shaker village of seventeen original buildings, including the famous Round Barn. Shaker furniture, clothing, industrial tools, and household objects. Open from June 1 to October 31 daily, 9:30–5. Admission fee. Telephone (413) 443–0188.

Massachusetts Historical Society, 1154 Boylston Street, Boston 02215. Research collection of books, pamphlets, and manuscripts. Apply to the Librarian. Telephone (617) 536–1608.

New Hampshire

Canterbury Shaker Museum, East Canterbury 03224. About fourteen miles northeast of Concord. Restored village founded in 1792 open from May 25 to the third Saturday in October. Tours every hour on the hour from 9 to 4. Visits from Labor Day to October 12 are by prior appointment only. Closed Sunday and Monday. Admission fee. Telephone (603) 783–9822.

New York

New York Public Library, 5th Avenue and 42nd Street, New York City 10018. Collection of manuscripts and Shaker publications. Apply to executive officer, research libraries administrative office. Telephone (212) 790–6254.

New York State Library, State Education Building, Washington Avenue, Albany 12224. Important holdings of Shaker manuscripts, pamphlets and books. Closed weekends. Apply to chief librarian of readers' services. Telephone (518) 474–7451.

Shaker Museum, Old Chatham 12136. Seventeen miles from Albany, this is the largest of the public Shaker museums with over 18,000 objects on view: furniture, crafts, inventions, clothing, fabrics, complete shops and industries. Shaker books and manuscripts available to the scholar. Open May 1–October 31 daily, 10–5.30. Admission fee. Telephone (518) 794–9105

Ohio

Dunham Tavern Museum, 6709 Euclid Avenue, Cleveland 44106. There is a Shaker room, recreated to show how a Shaker family would have lived. Open all year, except Mondays and holidays, 12.30–4.30. Telephone (216) 431–1060.

Golden Lamb Hotel, 27–31 South Broadway, Lebanon 45036. Ohio's oldest inn, the Golden Lamb is handsomely furnished with antiques, some of which are Shaker. There is an authentic Shaker bedroom and pantry, and a Shaker dining room for the public. Free. Telephone (513) 932–5065.

Kettering-Moraine Museum, 35 Moraine Circle, Kettering 45439. Along with general local history there is a Shaker room dedicated to the Watervliet Shaker community. Limited opening times. Free. Telephone (513) 299–2722.

Ohio Historical Society Library, 1982 Velma Avenue, Columbus 43211. Manuscripts, books, and pamphlets. Apply to the librarian. Telephone (614) 469–2064.

Shaker Historical Society, 16740 South Park Boulevard, Shaker Heights 44120. Shaker furniture, crafts, and industries, mainly from the North Union Shaker community. Some manuscripts for the scholar. Open Tuesday–Friday, 2–4; Sunday, 2–5.

Warren County Historical Society, 10825 East Boulevard, Cleveland 44106. Shaker furniture, crafts, industries, and inventions displayed in the Shaker Room. Here is deposited the world's largest and finest collection of Shaker books and manuscripts for research purposes. Open Tuesday–Saturday, 10–5; Sunday, 2–5. Closed on national holidays. Admission fee. Telephone (216) 721-5722.

Pennsylvania

Philadelphia Museum of Art, Benjamin Franklin Parkway at 26th Street, Philadelphia 19130. Shaker furniture and artifacts given in the spring of 1977 by Mr. and Mrs. Julius Zieget and Marcia Zieget. Apply at main desk for admission daily, 9–5, except holidays. Admission fee except on Sunday mornings and Mondays. Telephone (215) 763–8100.

Vermont

Shelburne Museum, U.S. Route 7, Shelburne 05482. Seven miles south of Burlington, this small museum houses Shaker artifacts in a Shaker shed from the Canterbury, N.H. community. Open May 15-October 15 daily, 9–5. Admission fee. Telephone (802) 985-3344.

Wisconsin

Milwaukee Art Center, 2220 North Terrace Avenue, Milwaukee 53202. Various opening times depending upon the season. Telephone (414) 271–3656 or 271–9508.

State Historical Society of Wisconsin, 816 State Street, Madison 53706. Collection of manuscripts. Opening hours vary with the academic year, but are generally Monday–Friday, 8am–10pm, and Saturday 8–5. Telephone (608) 262–9590.

England

The American Museum in Britain, Claverton Manor, Bath BA2 7BD. Just over two miles from the center of historic Bath, the American Museum houses twenty galleries of (largely New England) Americana, with a Shaker room of furniture, fabric, and household paraphernalia. There is a magnificent rosery, a herb garden, and gift shop. *It encourages school visits.* Admission fee. Telephone (0225) 60503.

Shaker Shop, 25 Harcourt Street, London W1H 1DT. Centrally located between Oxford Street and Marylebone Road, this warm and inviting shop displays high quality reproduction Shaker furniture and household equipment, along with books, providing first-hand opportunities to examine Shaker style. Free. Telephone (0171) 724-7672.

Other Religious Groups: Comparative Study

There are other Christian religious communities that are either indigenous to the United States (or were successfully transplanted there) that could inspire a local festival, such as:

The Mormons (The Church of Jesus Christ of Latterday Saints)
The Disciples of Christ (Church of Christ or Christian Church)
The Amish
The Mennonites
The Moravians, and other groups who have influenced local culture and social patterns.

Naturally there must be lines drawn between festivals which create appreciation for American history and cultural development, and events whose main purpose is proselytization. It should not be the intent in any secular setting to win converts, but to increase awareness of the contribution made to society, scholarship, craftsmanship, music, the arts, and culture by these groups.

As part of this Shaker Festival, or as part of a similar period of specialization, students can compare the ways that various religious groups do things. From basic beliefs to the actions that are based upon them, each group offers a glimpse into a peculiar way of living. Several ways exist to gather and present this information in interesting formats.

First, and perhaps most obviously, students may study in-depth one religious group (Disciples of Christ or Cumberland Presbyterians, for instance; or another group, such as Sikhs, Hindus, Jehovah's Witnesses, or Muslims). The result could be a research paper, a story in journalistic style, or an illustrated bulletin board. An oral report should also be part of the project, delivered in a seminar or to a class.

Second, students may use the many history books now available on the development of religions in the United States and elsewhere to draw up a chart which compares the way people of different creeds do things. The chart may also be filled in while listening to or observing the visual results of the more intensive research outlined above. Items to look out for include things which may have passed into the general cultural life of a region, such as the music and Christmas foods of the Moravians in North Carolina; things which groups share in common with others, such as use of historic creeds, belief in certain sacraments, or observance of particular holidays; things which they alone practice, such as forbidding use of instrumental music. Students may also find out which groups support schools, universities, and hospitals; which participate in organizations such as the World Council of Churches; which groups include famous writers, artists, or musicians.

Third, students may find recorded or printed music peculiar to certain groups to listen to, to play during a seminar or study period, and to comment upon. The Roman Catholic and Anglican (Episcopal) Churches have a long tradition of liturgical music, including such varied composers as Claudio Monteverdi, William Byrd, and Benjamin Britten. Lutherans claim Johann Sebastian Bach as their own. The Mormon Tabernacle Choir is world famous. But what of the musical traditions of other groups, such as the Amish, the Mennonites, and the Disciples (who divided over a musical issue).

Fourth, students may look for examples of art produced by certain religious groups, not necessarily for purposes of devotion. Amish quilts are growing in fame in Pennsylvania, Ohio, and other places where their colonies are prospering. Moravians hold a specially-designed star in esteem during their Christmas celebrations. But what is the view of these and other groups on the use of art in their architecture and worship? Which groups would place a crucifix or a statue in their buildings? Which groups would not?

In any of these activities, students should learn to appreciate others' points of view, based upon an understanding of the historical development of religious ideas and the evolution of belief. The following two formats (Figures 23 and 24) can help students organize their findings as they research. Sources of information on comparative religion (see pp.135–36) will be helpful.

Figure 28

Name of
Group _____

1. Where did this group originate? Who were the founders?
2. Are there any special initiation rites or procedures required for membership?
3. Does the worship follow a set procedure (liturgy)? What type of music is used?
4. Are there any special art forms connected with this group, such as specific symbols or logos, domestic crafts, church furnishings? What is their feeling about religious art?
5. What special holidays, if any, does this group observe?
6. Does this group support specific charitable institutions, schools, hospitals, or other subsidiary organizations?
7. Are there other religious groups similar to this one?
8. What special characteristics make this group different from all others?
9. Is there a particular creed to which this group adheres?
10. What famous or historical people have been members of this group?

Figure 29

Comparison Chart
Religious Groups: The Way People Do Things

Use this chart to compare or contrast the ways that different religious groups practice their faith through beliefs, worship, and special observances. Take only brief notes.

Names of Religious Groups

Activities and Observances				
Founders				
Number of Members				

Location of Headquarters				
Publications				
Holidays Observed				
Special or unique art forms associated with this group				
Special musical forms or composers associated with this group				
Is this group famous for any unique or special characteristics?				

Sources of Inspiration: Books About the Shakers

Andrews, Edward Deming. *The Gift to Be Simple: Songs, Dances, and Rituals of the American Shakers*. New York: Dover, 1967.
   This authoritative account of Shaker music includes the texts and melody lines of nearly 100 songs, with illustration of ring, wheel, circular, hollow square, and other dances, and is prefaced with a clear and informative Shaker history.

———. *The People Called Shakers: A Search for the Perfect Society*. New York: Dover, 1953.

An illustrated history of the Shaker utopian movement, this book offers a broad spectrum of information for the history student.

Brewer, Priscilla. *Shaker Communities, Shaker Lives.* Hanover, NH: University Press of New England, 1986.
Through the lives of individual Shakers, the reader gleans an understanding of the movement's philosophy, work ethic, and community organization.

Carr, Sister Frances. *Shaker Your Plate: Of Shaker Cooks and Cooking.* Sabbathday Lake, Maine: United Society of Shakers, 1985.
The Shakers loved to eat well, and regarded it as a sin to leave any remnants on a plate. This book provides historic Shaker recipes and insights.

Dewhurst, C. Kurt, and others. *Religious Folk Art in America— Reflections of Faith.* New York: E. P. Dutton, 1983.
This book examines the spiritual emphasis in not only Shaker work but in art from many American religious sources, placing pieces in historic and social perspective.

Faber, Doris. *The Perfect Life: The Shakers in America.* New York: Farrar, Straus, and Giroux, 1975.
The struggles of the founders and followers of the Shaker communal societies overcame the opposition of neighbors and governments.

Gordon, Beverly. *Shaker Textile Arts.* Hanover, NH: University Press of New England, 1980.
Famed for their growth of silkworms and sheep, the Shakers also wove silk, cotton, and wool into handsome fabrics.

Handberg, Ejner. *Shop Drawings of Shaker Furniture and Woodenware,* 3 vol. Stockbridge, Mass.: The Berkshire Traveller Press, 1977.
Drawings by a master joiner of cupboards, chests, log baskets, long case clocks, and other handsome pieces from the Shaker heritage.

Horgan, Edward R. *The Shaker Holy Land—A Community Portrait*. Boston: Harvard Common Press, 1982.
Horgan depicts the history, beliefs, and society of Shakers in Harvard and Shirley, Massachusetts, from the 18th century to the present.

Jekis, Marguerite. *The Standard Book of Quilt Making*. New York: Dover Press, 1949.
Considered by many to be the best, most thorough coverage of the subject, this book provides step-by-step patterns, photos, and instructions for over 100 traditional and unusual quilts.

Lipman, Jean, and Tom Armstrong, eds. *American Folk Painters of Three Centuries*. New York: Hudson Hills Press, 1980.
Covering the 18th–20th centuries, the book includes extensive coverage in text and illustrations of Shaker artist Hannah Cahoun (1788–1864), whose visions produced the Shaker Tree of Life.

Mastin, Bettye Lee. *A Visitor's Guide to Shakertown*. Lexington: Richard S. Decamp, 1969.
This is a fully illustrated guide to the Shaker community of Pleasant Hill, Kentucky, with a history of each building and a guide to Shaker crafts and surrounding geography.

Meader, Robert I. W. *Illustrated Guide to Shaker Furniture*. New York: Dover Press, 1972.
A prolifically illustrated history of wardrobes, tables, chairs, work benches, desks, beds, and other items of graceful, utilitarian woodwork, it is ideal inspiration for bulletin board designs.

Miller, Amy Bess, and Persis Fuller. *The Best of Shaker Cooking*. New York: Collier Macmillan, 1970.
Here are over 500 authentic recipes from 19th-century Shaker farm kitchens, including soups, fish, poultry, meat, vegetables, cakes, pies, wine, ices, and other delicacies.

Moriarty, Kathleen, and Mary Taylor. *A Shaker Sampler*. Old Chatham, NY: The Shaker Museum, 1981.
This is an A-Z coloring book, based on Shaker designs and history, with text by Moriarty and line drawings by Taylor. Included are a Tree of Life, inventions, farm implements, and costumes.

Neal, Julia. *The Kentucky Shakers*. Lexington: University Press of Kentucky, 1982.
Neal shows how Southern converts differed from those in northern climes, their attitudes to slavery and the Civil War, their cooking, government, and architecture.

Patterson, Daniel W. *Gift Drawing and Gift Song*. Sabbathday Lake: The United Society of Shakers, 1983.
Shakers did not paint or sing to beautify their environment, but to glorify God and to interpret messages from Mother Ann and the Deity. This is a concise history.

Pierry, Caroline, and Arthur Tolve. *The Shaker Cookbook: Recipes and Lore from the Valley of God's Pleasure*. Bowling Green, Ohio: Gabriel's Horn Publishing Company, 1984.
Here are 192 pages of original recipes updated for modern use, with historical lore and drawings.

Rose, Milton C., and Emily Mason Rose. *A Shaker Reader*. New York: Universe Books, 1975.
Based on periodical articles from the 1930s to 1970s, this book covers the history, philosophy, architecture, furniture, crafts, and mystique of the Shakers, in text and illustration.

Sprigg, June. *Shaker Design*. New York: Whitney Museum of American Art, 1986.
The catalog of an extensive Shaker exhibition in the Whitney Museum shows why Shaker goods have such modern appeal.

———, and David Larkin. *Shaker Life, Work and Art*. New York: Stewart, Tabori, and Chang, 1987.
Author June Sprigg has lived with the Shakers since 1972. More than 200 full-color photographs from New England and Kentucky colonies' furniture, houses, and farms make this lovingly written book, which includes interviews with living Shakers, a very important source.

Tolve, Arthur, and James Bissland, III. *Sister Jennie's Shaker Desserts*. Bowling Green, Ohio: Gabriel's Horn Publishing Company, 1983.
A collector's item, this small book contains—in her own handwriting—the treasured dessert recipes of Shaker Sister Jennie

Wells. Recipes are translated into modern equivalents for use today.

Van Kolken, Diana. *Introducing the Shakers: An Explanation and Directory*. Bowling Green, Ohio: Gabriel's Horn Publishing Company, 1985.
Why are they called Shakers? How did they earn their living? This book handily reveals all, with photos, maps, and original drawings.

Shakers in Fiction

Giles, Janice Holt. *The Believers*. Boston: Houghton Mifflin, 1976.
In this agonizing story of a strange ordeal, Rebecca follows her husband Richard into the land of the Shakers where husband and wife must live apart.

Leslie, Ann George. *Dancing Saints*. Garden City, NY: Doubleday, 1943.
A young boy, separated from his sister and brother, is taken in by a declining Shaker community.

McCollough, Robert W. *Me and Thee*. New York: Lothrop, 1937.
Kate, a young Shaker girl, has to decide whether she will follow the world, and human love, or follow the Believers.

Yolen, Jane. *The Gift of Sarah Barker*. New York: Viking, 1981.
This novel tells the story of Shaker teenagers Sister Barker and Brother Abed, who meet and fall in love, risking their places in the only home they have ever known.

Periodicals and Articles

Andrews, Edward D. "Shaker Inspirational Drawings," *Antiques,* vol. 48, no. 6 (December 1945), pp. 338–341.

The Shaker Messenger. Post Office Box 1645, Holland, Michigan 49422-1645.
This quarterly contains scholarly articles based on continuing research. There is artwork, newly published original Shaker mu-

sic, listings for handcrafts and antiques, and a calendar of events. See Figure 23.

Books on Comparative Religions

Backman, M. V., Jr. *Christian Churches in America: Origin and Beliefs,* rev. ed. New York: Charles Scribner's Sons, 1976.
This comprehensive guidebook relates history, development, and distinguishing peculiarities of twenty religious groups in the U.S., including a section on Christian churches of American origin.

Dolan, Jay P. *The American Catholic Experience.* Garden City, NY: Doubleday and Company, 1985.
Following the 500-year evolution of immigrant, urban Catholicism into its position as the largest religious body in the U.S. today, this book provides insights into a much-changed organization.

Ferguson, George. *Signs and Symbols in Christian Art.* New York: Oxford University Press, 1982.
With illustrations from Renaissance artists, this handbook reveals in detail the origins of symbols found in many Christian religious buildings today.

Hudson, Winthrop. *American Protestantism.* Chicago: University of Chicago Press, 1969.
This 190-page comparative history evaluates the development of Protestant America as a mirror of U.S. culture.

Kern, Louis J. *An Ordered Love: Sex Roles and Sexuality in Victorian Utopias: The Shakers, the Mormons, and the Oneida Community.* Chapel Hill: University of North Carolina Press, 1981.
Kern comments on the sexual sublimation and fulfillment among the early utopian groups. His observations on the celibate Shakers is of special interest.

Parrinder, Geoffrey, ed. *World Religions from Ancient History to the Present.* New York: Facts on File, 1983.
Twenty-one well-illustrated chapters survey religions past and present in the contexts which formed them, from ancient civiliza-

tions around the globe to contemporary Judaism, Jainism, Islam, Christianity, and Buddhism.

Rice, Edward. *American Saints and Seers: American-born Religions and the Genius Behind Them.* New York: Four-Winds Press, 1982.

The author conveys the unique spirit of several U.S. religions: the Shakers, Mormons, Christian Scientists, Pentecostals, American Indian religions, Muslims, and others. The Shaker chapter gives an excellent, sensitive protrayal not only of Mother Ann and her immediate followers, but also of the group up to the present day.

Rosten, Leo. ed. *Religions in America.* New York: Simon and Schuster, 1963.

Rosten gives facts about beliefs and practices, membership statistics, clergy salaries, and holidays, including Christian churches, Jews, and Jehovah's Witnesses.

Chapter 4
Reach for a Star: A Festival of the Zodiac

Reach for the Stars

She loves me, she loves not . . . daisy petals fall to the ground as a youngster seeks to find his true love. Spin the bottle...claim a kiss. Spin a knife on the kitchen floor . . . who will die first? Spot a falling star, and make a wish. Childhood games to predict the future originated in the unlettered days of prehistory, when, as in ancient Babylon, people believed that messages could be read into certain rituals. Similar superstitions—walking under ladders, throwing salt over the shoulder, breaking mirrors, finding four-leaf clovers, first-footing on New Year's Day in Scotland—began so long ago that they have passed into the common experience of shared folklore.

Chief among the message-bearers in ancient Babylon was the moon, which changed faces every night. High in its entourage were the five planets visible with the naked eye, each of which directed the life of the king. The Egyptians and the Greeks extended their study of the stars, or astrology, to encompass not just the king and his court, but every human being. Faith in astrology continued to grow, along with superstitions about natural phenomena, from thunder and lightning to strong winds, frosts, and floods, until in the Middle Ages the Church prohibited the arcane study of the stars while permitting its use in art and literature provided it was seen through Christian interpretation. Later, the Arabians reintroduced pure astrology to Europe, where it has more or less flourished ever since, though few today treat it seriously.

One of the most popular columns in many daily papers and monthly household magazines is that written by a regularly employed astrologer. People are interested in the future, so the horoscope provides a few minutes' diversion, no more serious than that of the schoolboy plucking petals from a daisy in search of his true love. At any rate, horoscope "forecasts" are, by their nature, so general that in effect they are little more than intriguing pastimes, providing some humor during the busy day.

A festival of the Zodiac can encompass several programs of emphasis:

(1) it can study ancient cultures and beliefs, such as those of the Tigris-Euphrates valley, Egypt, or China;

(2) it can "test" various methods of telling the future, from tea leaves to horoscopes, asking students to decide if these methods are really valid, or whether, as in the symbolic paintings in Waltham Abbey, England, the future always remains a closed book;

(3) it can cover a study of symbolic art;

(4) it can help children determine if their personality traits fit in with those of other people with the same star sign, and if such signs really determine or limit paths of action;

(5) it can contrast astrological theories with currently held scientific opinion;

(6) it can open forums for discussion about the objections of religion to astrology and other forms of soothsaying (to many, astrology is still controversial);

(7) or it can simply be a short and enjoyable celebration of a folkloric and journalistic phenomenon to which many people refer daily.

Since the zodiac is essentially concerned with time, the festival could occur near the end of the school year when students and teachers look back upon goals and achievements. Similarly, it can be held near the beginning of a school year—what do the stars hold in store? Or the teacher could turn a bulletin board display into a day's mini-festival at any time, highlighting special books on time, astrology, and ancient history, along with photocopied craft activity sheets for students to take home.

A Star-Studded Display

Cut stars from shiny paper, or cover cardboard stars with aluminum foil. Suspend them at different heights from the ceiling in front of the display board. Enlarge simple line drawings of zodiacal symbols and place them around the edge of the display board. A title such as "What Is Your Star Sign?" or "Astrology—What's in It for Me?" will spark interest.

Obviously, the focus of the festival will determine the theme of the central display. Stars have been, however, potent symbols throughout history, and symbolize hope, scholarship, pinnacles of achievement, and light. To call attention to ancient cultures, cover the display board with dark blue paper. Cut out a silhouette of a representative structure, such as the pyramids of Giza, and place one cutout white star on the background sky. In ancient Christianity, the zodiac was represented by the Labors of the Twelve Months, based largely on the agricultural cycle. Around the edges of the blue sky, place silhouettes of these monthly Labors, referring to works such as Hall's *Dictionary of Subjects and Symbols in Art*. A star festival also goes hand in hand with a study of space exploration or science fiction. Dot the blue background with several white stars of different sizes, and hang three-dimensional stars in front from the ceiling.

Use other star projects (see p. 150ff.) to make display items to attract attention to books, guest speakers, or other festival activities from cookie baking to art projects.

Guest Speakers

1. Invite the astrologer from a local newspaper or magazine to speak about how he or she writes the horoscope. What training is involved in becoming an astrologer? How much of the horoscope is pure invention?

★ Create a Festival Ambience ★

Fly a Flag!

MOBILIZE readers by suspending paper stars, comets and moons from wire, dowels, or coat hangers.

ZODIAC symbols can read when you paint them onto squares of old cotton sheets or paper. Hang them from broom handles, dowels, or on walls...

Put Puns on Posters to attract readers to books, magazines, CD's...

ARIES	Ram home a few facts with these great new Encyclopedias
TAURUS	It's no bull! These biographies are bound to intrigue.
GEMINI	Double the fun this weekend! Take home TWO paperbacks.
CANCER	There's no need to be CRABBY with these tapes to enjoy.
LEO	Want something to ROAR about? Just glance at our art books.
VIRGO	GO for a quiet read in the study corner now.
LIBRA	Having WEIGHED the choices, which thriller will you read next?
SCORPIO	Don't get STUNG by ignorance. Pick up a free Study Guide.
SAGITTARIUS	Fly straight as an arrow to these archery books.
CAPRICORN	Boredom got your GOAT? Let it go with reading.
AQUARIUS	All washed up? Thirsty!? This shelf is for you!
PISCES	There's nothing FISHY about these new compact discs!

Is your Library or Classroom upstairs?

Then turn the steps into The Stairway to the Stars with posters, directional arrows and mobiles.

STAIRWAY to the STARS! Find Something CELESTIAL in the LIBRARY!

STARS

Figure 31

2. Ask someone to talk about fortune telling through crystal balls, tarot cards, dice, or tea leaves. The person need not be a practitioner, just someone who can talk about it entertainingly and educationally.

A feature of many school Halloween parties is the fortune-teller, usually a parent or teacher willing to assume a gypsy identity for an hour or two in a tent or booth in which he or she reads palms, tea leaves, or cards. Using the same dramatic device, engage a parent, a colleague, or a student to "tell fortunes" as part of the festival. Set up a tent in the classroom or library, or set aside a small room. Dress the astrologer or fortune-teller exotically, and have fun.

3. Bring in a magician to perform some slight of hand. Children themselves often enjoy learning and performing magic tricks for their friends. Organize a student magic show to complement that of a professional magician.

Tell the story of *Jack, the Beanstalk, and the Magic Beans.* Make the beanstalk grow magically by turning old newspapers into a telescoping vine.

What you need:

Four complete sheets of newspaper
Tape or stick glue
Scissors

What you do:

1. Lay the sheets of newspaper end to end horizontally, and tape them together to make one long rectangle.

2. Roll the paper up loosely, leaving a space in the middle big enough to insert your thumb. Tape one end of the roll together where the last sheet of paper overlaps the others.

3. Placing the scissors on the untaped end, cut halfway down the side of the roll. Then make two more identical cuts, evenly spaced around the side of the roll.

4. Reach inside the cut end, and grasp a few of the strands of paper, carefully pulling up to make a beanstalk about four feet (1-1/4 meters) high.

Practice before performing the trick in public, for it doesn't always work smoothly the first time. Provide extra sheets of newspaper and scissors for students to try making their own magic beanstalks after the story.

Star Searches:
Activities Relating to the Star Signs

1. Compare the Papers

Read the daily or weekly horoscopes in several newspapers or magazines for the same time period. Do the predictions match, contradict, or in any way relate to each other? Students could make a simple chart for their own birthdays to help make the comparisons and draw conclusions. Following the name, birthdate and star sign, students can list each publication, and make notes about predictions in various categories.

Name——————— Birthday——————Star Sign—————

PREDICTIONS

Name of Publication	Name of Astrologer	Predictions
1.———————	—————	
2.———————	—————	
3.———————	—————	

Conclusions: Do the papers say the same things? Are the predictions simply good advice that anyone could follow? Should I base my actions on these horoscopes?

---

2. A Dramatic Assembly Program

To create an hour-long theatrical presentation based upon the signs of the Zodiac, ask different classes to find songs, poems, or legends that relate in any way to the theme. Or, instead of classes, ask groups of students with the same star sign to work together.

Here are some suggestions for readings, improvisations, and songs appropriate for small groups, for outdoor games, and for performance in public. Use your school library as a resource for finding other materials. Brainstorm with students to get ideas for other performance items that can be tied in to Zodiac starsigns, such as improvisations based on current films or popular music.

Aries, The Ram, March 21–April 19

a. Sing with appropriate actions "Old Dan Tucker," who rode "our darby ram down the hill. If he hadn't got up, he'd laid thar still."

b. Act out a version of "Three Billy Goats Gruff."

c. Read the story of Joshua who blew a ram's horn trumpet when he marched around the walls of Jericho.

Taurus, The Bull, April 20–May 20

a. Read the legend of the Minotaur and the Labyrinth of King Minos. Improvise the story. Write a poem based on the Minotaur.

b. Read *Ferdinand the Bull*.

Gemini, The Twins, May 12–June 21

a. Write a story about twin brothers or twin sisters who use their identical appearance to outsmart their teacher, each taking time off from school without anyone knowing. Ask students to think about the actual results of such a caper.

b. Organize a parade of twins in school.

Cancer, The Crab, June 22–July 22

a. Hold a crab race in which participants have to walk on all fours, face up. The race can be run backwards or forwards.

b. What does it mean to be "crabby?" Improvise short skits about crabby people and how to deal with them.

c. Schools near the shore or a marine aquarium can observe crabs in their habitat, draw pictures of them, and learn about their life cycles.

Leo, The Lion, July 23–August 22

a. Read the story of Androcles and the Lion or of St. Jerome and the Lion. Improvise parts of the story.

b. Discuss the lion as King of the Forest. Read parts of *The Wizard of Oz* and watch the Judy Garland film of that name. Perform scenes from the show.

Virgo, The Maiden, August 23–September 23

a. In medieval legend, because of her purity, only a maiden could catch a unicorn. Maidens were often in distress, too, held against their will in castle towers. Act out a story in which a damsel is rescued, saved from a dragon, or lives happily ever after, such as "Sleeping Beauty" or "Snow White." Act out the capture of a unicorn.

b. Read the legend of St. George and the Dragon, and of the princess whose country was saved when the hero conquered the wild beast.

c. Act out a story of *A Damsel in Control!* Modern girls can be what they want to be. Improvise the story of a woman who rescues a man in distress. Reverse one of the old tales so that it is the *prince* who falls asleep and is rescued by the princess.

d. Find out about an "iron maiden" from medieval history. Why was this implement of torture called a "maiden?"

Libra, The Scales, September 24–October 21

a. Read the story of Archimedes who, while taking a bath, discovered a great law of physics, that a floating body loses in weight an amount equal to that of the liquid displaced. So excited was he that he ran through the streets shouting "Eureka!"

b. Make up a play for the end of school in which the teacher weighs the good deeds and the not-so-good deeds of his or her students on a giant scale.

c. As part of a regular health check, weigh every student, and discuss the ratios between weight, height, age, and activity.

d. Improvise a story about someone who can't make up his or her mind. Two or more people can take part in this tale of a Libran who has to weigh all the possibilities before reaching a decision.

One person starts by saying, "I think today I'll take a walk, because it's so sunny and warm". The next person counters with, "On the other hand, it might get too warm, so I'd better stay right here." The next person continues, "On the other hand, I brought my ice pack, so I can stay cool." "On the other hand, the ice pack might melt." The story goes on and on until a decision is made.

Scorpio, The Scorpion, October 22–November 21

a. Find out where scorpions live and how they protect themselves. Learn why human beings are rightly wary of scorpions.

b. Find out about the kinds of venom which certain creatures produce. Which venoms are most powerful? Do scientists use any venoms for worthwhile projects?

Sagittarius, The Archer, November 22–December 21

a. Listen to or play the "William Tell Overture" by Rossini. Read the folk tale and improvise the story.

b. Participate in an archery competition.

c. Find out about long bows, cross bows, and Native American bows and arrows.

Capricorn, The Goat, December 23–January 20

a. Read the story of "Three Billy Goats Gruff" and perform it.

b. Buy goat's milk and compare it in a taste test with cow's milk. Provide unmarked glasses of each type of milk to a random group and see if people can tell the difference between the two.

Aquarius, The Water Carrier, January 21–February 19

a. Sing songs about water, such as "Michael, Row the Boat Ashore," "Roll, Jordan, Roll," "Way Down Upon the Swanee River" and "Old Man River." Learn some sea chanteys and try to dance a hornpipe.

b. Bring water to a parched land in an improvised drama, having first experimented with bean seeds, some of which have been allowed to grow and flourish in water, some of which have been refused sufficient water. What is the effect of water on life?

c. Dramatize parts of folk legends, novels or short stories that relate to the theme of water, such as *Tom Sawyer, Huckleberry Finn,* or *Mike Fink.*

Pisces, The Fish, February 20–March 20

a. Set up an aquarium.

b. Read the story of Jonah and the Whale, and the story of Pinocchio.

c. Make paper fish to hang from the ceiling to accompany an improvisation on the theme of fishermen's tales. People who like to fish are often good-naturedly accused of stretching the truth about their catches, changing small catfish into great channel churners. Hang the paper fish from a pole and line, and improvise stories that begin with, "The fish I caught was so big that . . . " The next person continues with, "That's nothing. The fish I caught was so big that . . . "

3. Star Sign Language:
Same Sign, Same Characteristics?

In a classroom, library, gymnasium, auditorium, or lunch room—anywhere there is sufficient wall space—mark out areas into the twelve signs of the Zodiac. From a book on astrology, write down some of the general character traits of people born under the various signs; write at least two positive aspects, and one or two negative. Post them along with artistic representations of the signs of the Zodiac (made by students). Separate the spaces with borders of paper or string.

Ask students to bring in photographs of themselves, or take individual pictures at school, to place within the display, showing which people share the same star sign. Students can each make a star frame (Figure 33) for their photographs. Dramatize the display during an assembly or storytelling session by asking students to read some of the character traits of the signs. Then have everybody stand beneath the appropriate star sign.

Points to discuss or write about: (a) Am I really like the character described for my star sign? (b) Am I like all the other people in my class or school who share my sign? (c) Why are people born under this sign supposed to have these traits and behave in this way? (d) Are star signs important enough to rely on them for decision-making?

4. Award Star Readers

Set a time limit, such as three to four weeks (or less if there is a chance of waning enthusiasm), and award *Stars* to readers who can (a) read the most books; (b) design a superb book jacket based on one of the books; (c) dress believably as a character from a book; (d) memorize a speech or segment from one of the books; (e) write a short play script based on one of the books; (f) paint a mural; (g) build a model; (h) persuade others to read through personal enthusiasm; or (i) act in other ways to promote reading.

Stars can be awarded in several ways. Traditionally, teachers give stars to students when they complete a project successfully. Often the stars are placed on a class chart posted conspicuously on the wall. *Star-shaped cookies* (see page [161]) are also appropriate. Make *Star medals* from colored poster board, to be worn Olympic style. Give certificates with a big *Star Reader* design at the top, with calligraphy and art work reproduced on the school's copy machine. Cut out big stars and glue students' portrait photographs to them; post them on a bulletin board.

Another Star Reader program involves a memory quiz. Assign a set group of books which every person who wants to participate has to read. By a given date, all participants must have read them all.

With other teachers who have also read the books until they are "experts" about characters, plot, setting, and use of language, devise a long set of questions to test readers' knowledge. Hold a *Star Reader Quizathon* in the school auditorium or in a large classroom or library. Preliminary play-offs can be held in classrooms prior to the big event so that only winners of small competitions take part. Award prizes to the students who can answer the most questions correctly. Ask publishers, bookstores, record stores, or other businesses to donate prizes for the Star Readers. Every participant should, however, be given a certificate or consolation prize.

A Zodiacal Publication: Reading "Predictions"

"Predict" reading trends within a humorous booklist brochure. Arrange the brochure according to the signs of the Zodiac. Make forecasts about which books will be popular with Librans, Aquarians, Sagittarians, etc. Using this format, and keeping the tongue firmly in cheek, write a prediction for each star sign, followed by annotations of selected book titles. Read horoscopes in the papers to gain familiarity with astrologists' jargon, and lace your predictions with words such as *planet, ascendant, star, solar* and *influence*. The books recommended for each star sign can be a selection of new acquisitions on any topic, seasonal, biographical, fiction, or highlights from the library collection. To provide balance, offer each star sign a sprinkling from several categories.

Teachers, too, can spice up their classes' writing and recreational reading programs with a list of *Star Favorites*. Ask students to write short annotations of their favorite books, available either in the school library or in bookstores. Divide students into a publication team to assemble the reading list according to the zodiac, and publish it on the photocopier. Give away free copies at the library circulation desk, at bulletin boards, or at the school reception area.

Capricorn: December 23–January 20

Because of your general high spirits, Capricorns will be drawn to read many of these books, especially during long starlit evenings when homework is finished under the influence of scholastic motivation.

Aquarius: January 21–February 19

As the planets continue to circle Sol, chief star in our system, Aquarians will lose no time in checking out these books from the paperback racks. Some Aquarians will also join Sagittarians in reading recipes from the cookbook collection in preparation for a special birthday.

Pisces: February 20–March 20

There's something fishy going on, Pisceans, so to help you take advantage of the expected fine weather, make sure that you are among the first to check out these books to get new ideas for fashion, gardening, and sports.

Aries: March 21–April 19

Arians will have to act quickly if they expect to get their hands on these books, because Taurans and Leos will also find them popular, especially around the first week of February.

Taurus: April 20–May 20

Taurans will find themselves on the horns of a dilemma as they search through these titles. Some Taurans will find themselves unable to decide immediately, but most will rely on their determination to choose a book that fits their mood.

Gemini: May 21–June 21

Gemini falls under the influence of fiction as publishers continue to produce outstanding novels and short stories such as these. Confluence of asteroids near Mars will result in more hours spent in reading. Gemini students also know that though books may look alike, they can't judge them by their covers.

Cancer: June 22–July 22

No longer will Cancerians be content merely to while away evenings watching the moon pass through its phases, for they know that this reading list was designed to help them achieve their potential in the liberal arts.

Leo: July 23–August 22

Known for their great strength of character, Leos will lead the way not only in schoolwork, but also in recreational and educational reading, finding that high grades come from daily application and reading. Watch out for those Librans, though, who will also find these books appealing and could use their sense of harmony to talk you out of your favorite book so they can read it themselves.

Virgo: August 23–September 23

Though it pays to be cautious, Virgoans need not fear collision with an asteroid while looking over these books for some weekend reading, especially if they browse with a Sagittarian or Aquarian.

Libra: September 24–October 21

Because of rising planetary interference with television reception throughout this area, Librans will turn in increasing numbers to books over the next few weeks. Popular among Librans will be the following titles, chosen from among the new books in the school library.

Scorpio: October 22–November 21

Stung by reports of a new super strain of pop quiz about to erupt all over school, Scorpio readers will fling themselves into extra reading, knowing that only with knowledge will they be empowered to meet the challenge.

Sagittarius: November 22–December 21

As the moon exerts its influence over tides across the eastern coasts of America, Sagittarians can relax with a selection of books from this chart, but they shouldn't put off making their selections for too long since Pisceans often enjoy the same reading materials.

Stellar Art Projects

Stars are popular decorations at any time of year, and as art projects, they fit in perfectly with this festival. Students can make four-, five- and six-pointed starts to use as badges, picture frames, and three-dimensional hanging ornaments for the festival display area. These can be brought out again in winter to decorate the holiday tree. The librarian, classroom teacher or art specialist may want to make large versions of these stars to award to star readers; as attention-grabbers, they can be suspended from the ceiling on varying lengths of thread or fishing line, above book displays or in front of the bulletin board.

What You Need:

Assorted Paper
   Art room craft paper
   typing paper
   gift wrap
   brown grocery bags
   thin card
Pencils
Rulers
Scissors

For 3-D stars:
Papier Mâché
   newspapers or paper towels torn into small strips
   white glue or wallpaper paste
   mixing bowls
String or flexible wire
Stapler
Paint
   tempera
   acrylic
   gold or silver spray
Paint brushes
Wiping cloths or tissues

How to Make a Four-Pointed Star (Figure 32)

This is the simplest of the stars to make. Each student needs one *square* sheet of paper and a pair of scissors. There are only five steps involved.

1. Fold the paper in half.
2. Fold it in half again.
3. The closed corner of the folded sheet is the center of the paper. Fold the paper in half diagonally on the closed corner.
4. Cut through all the layers of the paper. The angle of slant will make spiky or squat stars. A steep angle will make sharp points, while a slight angle will make a fat star. Experiment to make several four-pointed star shapes.
5. Unfold the cut paper to reveal the star.

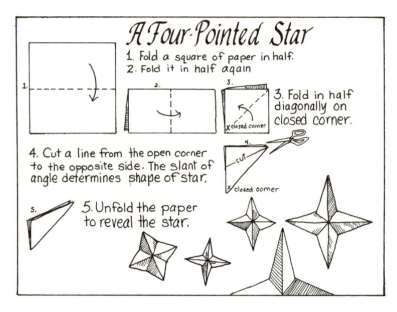

A Four-Pointed Star

1. Fold a square of paper in half.
2. Fold it in half again
3. Fold in half diagonally on closed corner.
4. Cut a line from the open corner to the opposite side. The slant of angle determines shape of star.
5. Unfold the paper to reveal the star.

Figure 32

How to Make a Five-Pointed Star (Figure 33)

Students need a rectangular sheet of paper 8 by 10 inches (20 by 25 cm). The rectangles always have to be in this 4 by 5 proportion. Students will also need a ruler and a pencil. There are six steps to follow.

1. Fold the paper in half by bringing the short ends together. Crease well along the fold.
2. Measure the short left edge and mark the *middle* with a pencil. Bring the right bottom corner to the pencil mark, and make a sharp crease.
3. Fold the right edge over to the left, and made a sharp crease.
4. Fold the remaining left edge over to the right, and crease. The paper should now look something like a flat ice-cream cone.
5. Cut along an angle from the right edge to the corner marked with a star. You can vary the degree of angle to make sharp or fat stars.
6. Open out the paper to reveal the star.

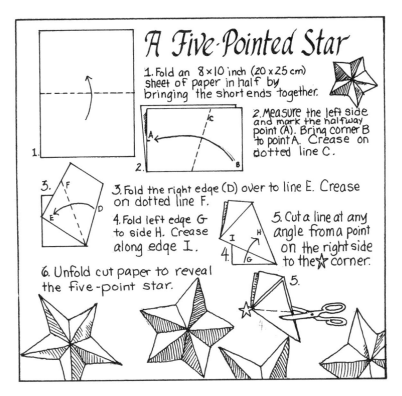

A Five-Pointed Star

1. Fold an 8×10 inch (20×25 cm) sheet of paper in half by bringing the short ends together.

2. Measure the left side and mark the halfway point (A). Bring corner B to point A. Crease on dotted line C.

3. Fold the right edge (D) over to line E. Crease on dotted line F.

4. Fold left edge G to side H. Crease along edge I.

5. Cut a line at any angle from a point on the right side to the ★ corner.

6. Unfold cut paper to reveal the five-point star.

Figure 33

How to Make a Six-Pointed Star (Figure 34)

Students will need a *square* of paper, a pencil and a ruler. There are six steps to follow.

1. Fold the square in half on the diagonal.
2. Find the middle of the folded edge. This should be exactly beneath the point of the triangle. Mark the spot with a pencil.
3. Fold the triangle into equal thirds. First, fold the right corner over to the left, using the pencil mark as the bottom of the crease. Then fold the left corner over. Before creasing firmly, slide the paper around until the edges align. Then crease.

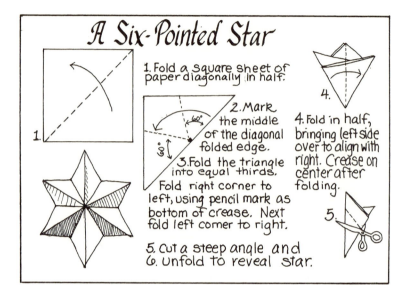

Figure 34

4. Fold the paper in half, bringing the left side over to meet the
   right.
5. Cut an angle. The steeper the angle, the sharper the star.
6. Unfold the paper to reveal the star.

How to Make 3-D Hanging Stars (Figure 35)

What You Need:

One cut-out *thin card* star of student's choice
Drawing paper
Pencil
Glue
Papier Mâché
String or wire
Stapler
Brushes
Paint
Wiping cloths or tissues

How to Make 3-D Hanging Stars

Cut out a Star. Then...

1 Make "mountain folds" along all the points, working from the outside to the center. Crease "valley folds" along the lines between the points.

2 Rest the crisply folded 3-D star on thin card. Trace the outline while holding the star in place with your free hand.

Cut out the traced star. **3** Staple and glue a short loop of string to one of the points on the traced star. This becomes the top of the star.

Trace and cut out...

4 Glue the 3-D star to the base.

5 Apply papier mâché to the whole surface of the star, beginning at the edges, which should be linked with strips of papier mâché. This will bind both stars securely.

6 When the first layer has dried, apply up to four more papier mâché layers, allowing each to dry before adding another.

7 Finally, paint the dry 3-D star with acrylics or tempera. Spray with metallic paints, or "antique" by wiping off a still-wet second coat of complementary color. Paint faces or patterns.

Figure 35

1. Make *mountain and valley folds* on the star. A mountain fold is made by pinching the paper together from above the crease. Valley folds are made by pinching the paper together from below the crease. Crease mountain folds along all the long points, and valley folds on the creases in between.

If the card is too stiff to crease easily or without damaging the star, score along the back of the fold lines. This will mean scoring on the front of the star for the mountain folds, and on the reverse of the star for the valley folds.

After making the first mountain fold, proceed to the valley fold on its immediate left. Press the crease carefully to the center of the star. Then holding the mountain fold between the thumb and fore-finger, bring the next point alongside, pressing both mountain folds together.

Repeat this process until all the mountain and valley folds have been done.

2. Place the cut-out star on drawing paper or thin card, and trace around it. Cut out the second star.

3. Staple and glue a folded piece of string (or wire) on one of the points of the flat star. This will become the top of the completed star.

4. Glue the edges of the two stars together, effectively giving the folded star a flat back, or base.

5. Options:

A. Make an identical folded star to glue onto the other side for a completely contoured star.

B. Make a smaller folded star to glue onto the back, letting the flat star create a border or frame.

C. Make a smaller star with a different number of points to glue on the back, letting the flat star create a border or frame.

6. Dip the torn paper strips into the white glue or wallpaper paste, and one by one fix them to the star, completely covering the sur-face one layer deep. Begin by covering the glued join between the two stars.

7. Add one or two (or more) papier mâché layers: the more layers, the sturdier the finished product. Dry completely between layers, and before painting. Though the star will be sturdy, handle carefully when painting to avoid puncturing or denting the surface.

8. Paint the stars, either with solid colors or with imaginative designs, such as geometric stripes, stylized faces, or scenes. Spray solid colors with gold or silver paint for highlights. To give depth and an antique look, paint complementary colors onto dried paint surfaces, and wipe off gently with a tissue or rag.

Putting the Stars to Work

Swinging Star Signs (Figure 36)

Figure 36

Call attention to special book collections in the library or classroom with swinging star signs.

What You Need:

Five-point star templates
Lightweight card
Glue
Double-sided tape
Scissors
Pencils

Use five-point star templates to cut stars from lightweight card. Glue a star to a narrow strip of the same card. To make the strip of card flexible, run the edge of the scissors gently down its length once or twice. Glue a second star to the other end of the strip, but on the side opposite to the first one.

Put tape or Blu-Tak on the connecting strip behind one of the stars and attach it to the top of the bookshelf. The swinging star should now be facing forward. If the connecting strip is not flexible enough, bend it slightly in your hands.

Cover the stars with aluminum foil, gift wrap, or colored paper. Write the names of authors, titles, or book categories on the stars. Attach Swinging Star Signs to the display board, the library circulation desk, or anywhere else that needs an attention getter.

Star Picture Frames

Feature photographs of star readers, or of students in each of the signs of the Zodiac, inside paper frames (Figure 37).

What You Need:

Star templates large enough to cover photograph
Colorful paper
Pencil
Scissors
Ruler
School portrait photograph

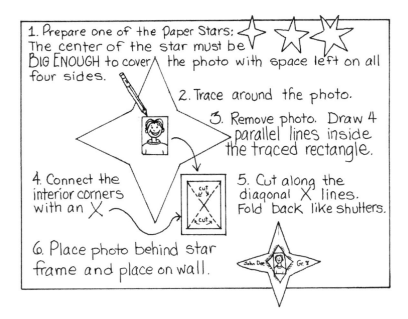

1. Prepare one of the paper Stars: The center of the star must be BIG ENOUGH to cover the photo with space left on all four sides.

2. Trace around the photo.

3. Remove photo. Draw 4 parallel lines inside the traced rectangle.

4. Connect the interior corners with an X

5. Cut along the diagonal X lines. Fold back like shutters.

6. Place photo behind star frame and place on wall.

Figure 37

1. Trace around the template, and cut out a flat star from selected paper.

2. Turn star face down and place photograph on center of star. Lightly trace around the edges of the photo, and set it aside.

3. With a ruler, draw parallel lines about 1/8-inch (4 cm) inside the lines drawn in step 2.

4. With a ruler, connect opposite corners of the box with a line. With scissors or craft knife, cut along the diagonal lines. This creates four triangles.

5. Fold the four triangles back to make shutters.

6. Tape the photograph behind the opening and display.

Taste Treats: Zodiac Cookies

Making the Templates

Early in the morning or the day before baking the cookies, help students make templates. Give participating students a piece of paper on which to design cookie templates: stars, simplified signs of the Zodiac, or other representative shapes such as hearts, circles, or squares. Students will need:

Paper
Pencils
Scissors
Stiff card

1. To make a symmetrical design, fold a piece of paper about three inches square (8cm) in half, and draw on half the shape (Figure 34). Cut out the design and open up the paper. This works well with hearts and geometric shapes.

2. To make stars, follow the procedures outlined in Figures 32–34 but use proportionally smaller sheets of paper. To make five-pointed stars, keep the rectangles of paper in ratios of 4 by 5. Give students, therefore, a piece of paper measuring 10 by 12.5 cm (about 4 by 5 inches).

To make four-pointed or six-pointed stars, start with a square of paper about 12 by 12cm (or 5 by 5 inches), and proceed as in Figures 32-34.

3. Reusable, more durable cookie templates can be made by tracing around the paper cutouts onto stiff card. Cut around the design with scissors. Whether using paper or card templates, students should write their names clearly on them to help identify ownership of cookies when they come from the oven.

Making the Cookies

Because the dough needs to chill in the refrigerator before rolling out and cutting, the recipe may be prepared in stages, either on one day, or spread out over two or three. Day 1 (or early in the morning), prepare the templates; Day 2 (or early in the morning), mix the ingredients and chill; Day 3 (or late in the school day), roll out and prepare the cookies. Depending upon the size of the templates, this recipe makes up to 40 cookies. Several student teams working at once can make separate batches. Parent volunteers could also make the dough at home, and bring it to school for students to roll, cut, and bake. Teachers, librarians, or parents could also prepare them at home beforehand, and give students a Zodiac cookie at the checkout desk or as a special treat at

snack time. But to give students a chance to participate fully, prepare as much of the recipe at school as possible. The cookies will
keep in an airtight container for a few weeks.

What You Need:

1/3 cup softened butter or margarine
1/2 cup dark brown sugar
1/3 cup runny honey or molasses
1/3 cup maple syrup
1 egg
1 tsp vanilla essence
1 tsp ground cinnamon
1 tsp ground ginger
1/2 tsp allspice
4 cups flour
4 tsp baking powder

Mixing bowls and containers
Electric mixer
Spoons
Sifter
Waxed paper or large zip-lock food bag
Rolling pin
Extra flour for work surface
Small kitchen knife
Spatula

Mix butter and brown sugar in a large bowl, creaming together
well. Add honey (or molasses) and maple syrup, egg, vanilla, and
spices. Blend well and beat with electric mixer until fluffy.

Sift flour and baking powder together. Gradually add the flour
mixture to the liquid, and stir. Toward the end, carefully washed
hands may be used to give the ingredients their final hefty mixing.

Roll the batter into a ball. Wrap it in waxed paper (or put it in a
large, zip-lock plastic bag) and chill it in the refrigerator for about
two hours (or longer).

When ready to bake, preheat the oven to 350 degrees F (180 C.).
Cut the dough ball into quarters. Roll out each quarter on a floured
surface to about 1/8-inch (1/2 cm) thick. Use the templates by

placing them one at a time *as near the edge of the dough as possible to avoid waste.* Cut around the templates carefully with a small kitchen knife and lift them off the work surface with a spatula.* Place on cookie sheet, two inches (5 cm) apart. Bake from 8 to 10 minutes. Cookies should be golden brown and firm. Remove from cookie sheet and cool on a flat surface.

*Note: To hang cookies as decorations, pierce the top of the cookie with a drinking straw prior to lifting from the work surface. Insert a ribbon, string, wire or Christmas ornament hanger after the cookie is baked and cooled. Hang them from bare tree branches in a vase or from a clothesline strung across the room. Intersperse them among paper stars in front of the festival display.

Sources of Inspiration: Books About Astrology

Aylesworth, Thomas G. *Astrology and Foretelling the Future.* New York: Franklin Watts, 1973.
Find out how to prepare a horoscope. Foretell the future by reading the stars, tea leaves, and tarot cards.

Branley, Franklyn. *Age of Aquarius—You and Astrology.* New York: Crowell, 1979.
Branley reviews the zodiac, discussing the symbols and their significance, and testing personality traits and characteristics assigned to people born under different signs.

Cope, Lloyd. *Your Stars Are Numbered.* Garden City, NJ: Doubleday, 1971.
A combination of astrology and numerology, with some philosophical concepts that probably wouldn't stand up under close scrutiny, this book is by a convinced believer.

Dean, Dinah. *The Christian Symbolism of the Zodiac.* Waltham Abbey, England: Holy Cross Abbey, 1989.
The author explains the significance of the signs of the zodiac in medieval churches, and in particular the ceiling paintings on the Abbey Church of the Holy Cross in this town just north of London.

Eisler, Robert. *The Royal Art of Astrology.* London: Herbert Joseph, 1946.
Eisler feels that astrology is a hopelessly confused affair, full of self-contradiction and of no possible use. His history of the system is, nevertheless, quite objective, especially as he traces the use of zodiacal symbolism in literature.

Gallant, Roy A. *Astrology: Sense of Nonsense.* Garden City, NJ: Doubleday, 1974.
Investigate the history, art, and growth of astrology, and decide whether or not it is true.

Garini, Eugenio. *Astrology in the Renaissance.* New York: Arkana, 1990.
Rather than replacing superstition immediately, the growth of Renaissance scientific exploration fused new knowledge based on observable facts with that of astrology. Garini uses the example of Galileo, who was refuted by the church because he contradicted accepted beliefs in astrology and centricity of the earth.

Gettings, Fred. *The Secret Zodiac: The Hidden Art in Medieval Astrology.* New York: Arkana, 1987.
The author interprets the zodiacal art in the 13th-century Italian Church of San Mineato, Florence, the last surviving ecclesiastical structure designed by architects with astrological knowledge, and relates it to Christian meaning.

Gleadow, Rupert. *The Origin of the Zodiac.* New York: Atheneum, 1969.
Gleadow is an astrological practitioner, so this book is an authoritative account from the inside, covering birth signs especially well.

Hall, James. *Hall's Dictionary of Subjects and Symbols in Art,* rev. ed. London: John Murray, 1992.
While not specifically about the zodiac or stars, this reference work of art symbology does contain concise histories of the use of star signs in ancient Christian and other art.

Hone, Margaret. *The Modern Text-book of Astrology*. London: L.
  N. Fowler, 1968.
  Hone helps searchers discover zodiacal roots and offers help in
  preparing a personal horoscope.

Huntley, Janis. *The Elements of Astrology*. London: Element
  Books, 1990.
  A practicing astrologer with 25 years of experience introduces
  and interprets the Zodiac.

Jones, McClure. *Cast Down the Stars*. New York: Holt, Rinehart,
  and Winston, 1978.
  Two sorcerers and starcasters confront evil to avoid the destruction of their civilization in this young adult novel.

Kenton, Warren. *Astrology: The Celestial Mirror*. London:
  Thames and Hudson, 1974.
  Do the stars influence life on earth, determining character traits,
  and guiding human beings into inevitable futures?

Le Gette, Bernard. *Numera: The Craft of Numerology*. London:
  Pan Books, 1976.
  Find out the numerological significance of names and identities
  in this ancient practice, rooted in over 4000 years of history.

Leo, Alan. *The Complete Dictionary of Astrology*. Rochester,
  Vermont: Destiny Books, 1989.
  This reference work of terms and concepts necessary to an understanding of astrology offers charts to the signs, and astrological meanings of planets.

McIntosh, Christopher. *The Astrologers and Their Creed*. London: Arrow Books, 1971.
  McIntosh believes that the zodiac *does* influence destiny,
  though his account of astrology and those who developed it does
  not preach or try unduly to persuade.

MacNeice, Louise. *Astrology*. Garden City, NJ: Doubleday,
  1964.
  Written by a non-believer in the astrological system, this book
  nevertheless provides tables and charts for those who wish to

make their own horoscope, information on the development of astrology, and detailed descriptions of signs, houses, and the zodiac.

Oken, Alan. *As Above, So Below: A Primary Guide to Astrological Awareness.* New York: Bantam, 1973.
Oken argues that the stars *do* determine events on earth, and sets out to convince the reader of this certainty.

Schwartz, Alvin. *Telling Fortunes, Love Magic, Dream Signs, and Other Ways to Learn the Future.* Philadelphia: Lippincott, 1987.
Students can play games based on traditional beliefs, popular sayings, and superstitions rooted in folk interpretations of natural phenomena.

Seymour, Percy. *Astrology: The Evidence of Science.* New York: Arkana Books, 1990.
The debate over astrology continues with Dr. Seymour's conclusion that there is something, after all, to the influence of the stars, and that individuals are attuned to specific solar symphonies.

Walters, Derek. *Chinese Astrology.* London: Aquarian Books, 1992.
Walters traces the history of Chinese astrology through texts written over 2000 years ago to the work of contemporary eastern astrologers.

Periodical Articles

Cohen, David. "Is Astrology Scientific?" *Science Digest,* 61:30–32, February 1967.

Dixon, J. "Follow Your Star." *Holiday,* 54:32–33, July 1973.

"The First Whole Earth Horoscope." *Esquire,* 79:144–145, January 1973.

"How Much Can Your Horoscope Really Tell You" *Ebony,* 41:74 ff., April 1986.

Rathgeb, M. M. "Do-It-Yourself Astrology: The Chart That Helps You Plot the Right Career/Right Life For You." *Mademoiselle,* 86:3–96, March 1980.

Van Horne, H. "Is Astrology Nonsense?" *Redbook,* 130:20 ff., January 1968.

Chapter 5
Valentine's Day: A Festival of Friendship

Hail, Bishop Valentine,
  whose day this is,
All the air is thy diocese.
—John Donne
  (1571?–1631)

Valentine's Day is forever linked with the billing and cooing of lovebirds. In fact, as early as Chaucer's time in England, birds were thought to begin mating on February 14, a belief perpetuated in rural English folklore to this day. Yet this special day of love has a sinister history.

No one knows when Valentine's Day came to be associated with *l'amour,* for the original Valentine (who may have been up to three different people), was a third-century clergyman, martyred, after much torture, on February 14, which happened to be the eve of the Roman feast of Lupercalia, a celebration in honor of the goddess Februata Juno, a patroness of young people of marriageable age. The day was originally celebrated to appease the god Luperus, or Wolf Killer, with animal sacrifices designed to inspire the god to keep the wolves away from the sheep until next year.

The day was one of great rejoicing. Luperus was honored with blood sacrifice; Lupera (mythic wife of Luperus, and the she-wolf who suckled Romulus and Remus, founders of Rome) was praised in song and dance; and Februata Juno was worshipped by putting the names of marriageable girls into a Love Urn. Local lads would each draw out a name in a sort of mating lottery. The festival came to Britain with the Roman occupation, and was adopted readily by the natives.

When Rome, and then England, converted to the new Christian religion, the Church Fathers shrewdly retained many of the old pagan holidays, changing their names and natures in order to keep them as Christian feasts. Lupercalia, a very popular holiday, was put back a day to coincide with the martyrdom of St. Valentine. The old customs remained, albeit sanitized. Up to the present century, British lads and lasses drew each other's names from a box and were then expected to treat their "Valentine" to surprises and gifts until the next year's "dating game."

In England, where the American concept of Valentine's Day originates, cards are still traditionally sent, but anonymously, as part of the intrigue of love. Children's book illustrator Kate Greenaway (1846–1901) helped popularize Valentine's cards with her highly successful illustrated greetings in the latter half of the nineteenth century. Shakespeare's Ophelia (*Hamlet,* 1603), mentions a playful practice still humorously perpetuated in British folk custom. According to tradition, the first person an unmarried girl sees on February 14 will be her true love:

> Good morrow! 'Tis St. Valentine's Day
> All in the morning betime,
> And I a maid at your window
> To be your Valentine.

In Wales, young men give their sweethearts wooden love spoons as a sign of betrothal. Carved by hand when winter evenings draw in, these spoons usually include several heart shapes or lover's knots intermingled from the basin up to the tip of the handle. And in America, greeting card companies and chocolate manufacturers do a roaring trade. It must be said, however, that the sending of Valentine's cards, chocolates, and flowers is no longer taken as seriously as it once was. Today they are mere tokens of esteem, and provide adults with an amusing way of keeping in touch with friends, and school children with another excuse for a few hours away from classwork.

This festival of friendship and love, based on folklore and literature, and appropriate for upper, middle and high school students, may easily be a one-day event, but with prior work required on the part of participating musicians, artists, and dramatists. The books chosen to illuminate the festivities represent the themes of love, friendship, and kindness in poetry, fiction, and non-fiction.

A Valentine's Display

A simple red heart, cut from construction paper, on a background of white captures the traditional Valentine mood. Jazz it up with a border of stain ribbons, or with rows of tiny red hearts, also cut from construction paper. Look through a dictionary of quotations for a pithy saying about love, the human heart, or Valentine's Day to write calligraphically inside the large heart.

Other, more elaborate, displays can recall the origins of the celebrations. Draw a rustic teenage couple, based on illustrations in Victorian American or English books, holding hands over a love urn or Valentine lottery box (Figure 39). Use an opaque projector to enlarge a photograph of a snarling wolf. Trace it, enhance it with felt-tip outline, and place it on the bulletin board, along with cut-out letters that read, "What does a wolf have to do with Valentine's Day?" At the bottom, in small letters, invite people to come to a fifteen-minute lecture in the library on the origins of Valentine's Day, during which you reveal the answer, offer appropriate books to read, and entice the wary with Valentine's Cookies.

A humorous Valentine's display can instruct the untutored in the fine art of writing love letters (Figure 40). A simple title, such as "How to Write a Love letter," will attract attention. Write the letter expansively on a large sheet of butcher paper, and attach it to the display like a scroll, pinning it several inches from the top and bottom so the overhang will curl. Be very didactic. Write the mushiest, corniest letter you can think of. Then, in the best professional manner, write criticisms and instructions on 5 x 7 note

An Ancient Valentine Custom

On the Display show a boy and girl selecting a card from a Love Urn.

1. Have all boys (or girls) put their names in a box to be selected by a member of the opposite sex who then has to give him or her a gift, such as a Valentine card, on February 14.

~ OR ~

2. Make it a Friendship Box in which all names are put in together. Boys and girls draw names at random in order to be the Secret Pal who provides good deeds and small gifts leading up to February 14

LOVE URN

Whose Name Will You Choose

A Renaissance-Inspired Bulletin Board Research Game

1.
Offer a prize to the first student who can translate the Latin phrase, widely popular in the 16th century.*

2.
Offer a prize to the student who can explain the symbolism of the flaming heart.*

Design Hint:
Cut flames from yellow and orange paper in small segments.

Glue them to back of a red heart.

Amor Vincit Omnia

* Love conquers all * Flames = Burning Love!

Figure 39

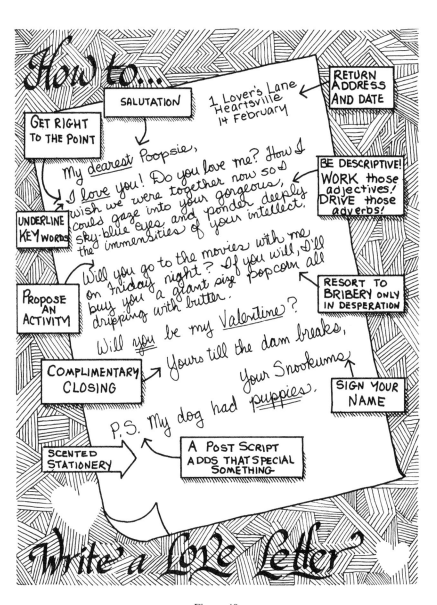

Figure 40

cards, and attach them to the display, using red twine to connect them to specific parts of the letter.

Valentine Games to Play

"Adam and Eve"

Adam and Eve is a game for all ages. It builds trust (since players are blindfolded) with good humor, and helps shy youngsters join in without feeling pressured. The object of Adam and Eve is for one player to catch another, using a set formula of words. Since the players' eyes are closed, they must rely on the sound of their partner's voice and foot movements, either to escape or to catch. Players left remaining in the circle must hold hands to prevent Adam and Eve from getting outside. Not only is this a safety measure, it also confines the game to a tight area. Although this is primarily a game for fun, Adam and Eve can be used by the teacher to show children something of what it is to be without sight.

How to Play

1. Set the scene by gathering up to twenty players into a large circle. Tell them this is how Adam and Eve went looking for each other back in the Garden of Eden, and that since there was so much thick vegetation, they had to keep calling and calling or they would never find one another.

2. Players stand in a circle, just close enough to hold hands loosely. The leader, who does not play, asks all people in the circle to close their eyes, having explained that he or she will walk around and through the circle, touching lightly *one boy's forehead* (Adam), and *one girl's forehead* (Eve). The leader must use subtlety so that no one knows who has been selected. One ploy is to whistle, sing or talk while choosing the couple.

3. The two players having been chosen, *the leader asks everyone except Adam and Eve to open their eyes*. It is more fun if the other players can refrain from laughter at this stage, for Adam and Eve

Create a Festive Ambience

Put up Posters or Photos of Great Movie Heart Throbs. Promote their biographies: Rudolph Valentino, Mae West, Clark Gable, Sophia Loren, Harrison Ford...

Valentine Mobiles
Cut out 2 paper hearts with slits. Slip hearts together and suspend on a string.

WEAR VALENTINE RED ALL WEEK

IF MUSIC BE THE FOOD OF LOVE, GO FOR NOSTALGIA

Designate Monday 1940's Day, Tuesday 1950's Day, and so on until the Festival is over. Play the *MUSICAL HITS of the DECADES* daily at lunch. Invite teachers and students to bring their meals to the music! Ask colleagues, students, and parents to lend recordings of their favorite sounds of yesterday.

DANCE OF THE DECADES! FUN

Find dancers to demonstrate those Steps of the Decades, from waltz, jitterbug, and *The Twist* to the mashed potato and the hand jive!

Attach red and white paper hearts to wire or sticks. Display in vases with cut-out green paper tulip leaves.

GIVE AWAY CHOCOLATE KISSES: SWEETS FOR THE SWEET!

Figure 41

should not know each other's identity. Any talking or laughter in the circle will help Adam and Eve to eliminate known voices from their guesswork.

4. The leader asks Adam and Eve to spin around three or four times, just to disorient them slightly within the circle. At the same time, the leader may ask the circle to take five or more quiet steps (giant steps, scissor steps, baby steps, one leg hops) to the left, or to the right, to further confuse Adam and Eve. This maneuver also lets younger players work off a bit of energy.

5. The object of the game is for Eve to find Adam or vice versa. Eve asks out loud, *"Adam, where are you?"* His response must always be, *"Over here, Eve."* She moves toward the sound of his voice, while Adam begins to move away from the sound of hers. The chase is on! She asks the question repeatedly, and he must answer her each time, until she catches him.

Adam and Eve may disguise their voices for more fun and surprises, adding "sweetheart," "darling," "honey," or other terms of endearment to the question or response.

6. A "catch" doesn't count unless Eve has a firm grip on Adam, or vice versa. Players may open their eyes when the catch is made, or, for further fun, they may explore one another's faces with their hands before opening their eyes to determine who their partner is. After opening their eyes and discovering their mate, Adam and Eve return to the circle, and the game starts over again, the leader selecting new players.

7. *Variations:*
   a. Adam may chase Eve.
   b. Play *"Farmer Brown"* by choosing a "farmer" to find his "animal." The farmer calls the name of any animal he or she chooses, such as "Where are you, sheep?" or "Where are you, rhinoceros?" The response is an approximation of the animal's sound, which may be a firm "baaaa," a squawk, a chirp, a growl, a howl, or a hoot. This variation is good in same-sex groups or if young-sters seem reluctant to enter into the Valentine spirit of Adam and Eve.

c. The leader may place a blindfold over Adam and Eve if it becomes difficult for players to keep their eyes firmly closed.

d. For much more hilarity, instead of questions and answers, Adam and Eve have to make loud, exaggerated kissing sounds by smacking their lips. They move toward the sounds to catch and identify each other. Start the game by asking everyone in the circle to practice their kissing sounds out loud; then move around the circle to "test" each potential player's osculatory decibels out loud.

"Sweetheart"

The object of Sweetheart is to form couples through skillful observation of a ball being passed behind the backs of players. Recorded music may be played to establish a rhythm.

How to Play

1. An equal number of males and females is required, up to five to ten of each, seated (or standing) alternately, boy-girl-boy-girl. They should face into the center of a tight circle, shoulders almost touching, their hands behind their backs.

2. One player becomes the "sweetheart," and goes into the middle of the circle. A group leader may determine each new sweetheart, or a clockwise rota may be established before play starts.

3. Then those in the circle have to pass a small ball (ping-pong, tennis, or jack ball, or an apple or orange) from one to another, trying not to let the sweetheart see who has it.

4. The sweetheart may guess aloud at any time the identity of the person with the ball. If the choice is correct, the sweetheart and chosen one become a pair and retire from the game to have refreshments, watch the others, or read a book. If incorrect, the sweetheart changes places with the wrong guess, and the "wrong" player becomes the sweetheart. (Variation: give the sweetheart three chances before trading places.)

5. The circle becomes tighter as each couple leaves.

Hint: Practice passing the ball or fruit before play starts so players can get the hang of it. Good players can disguise their possession of the ball by moving constantly, not just when they have the ball. Recorded music will help all players develop rhythmic shoulder and body movements to help trick the sweetheart.

Valentine Art Projects

"Love Lanterns" (Figure 42)

For a light touch, illuminate a special table, desk, or library circulation area with a Love Lantern during the Valentine Season. Observe safety precautions with live flames at all times, especially with the paper and wooden Love Lanterns, which should be lit only when adults are in the room. Never leave Love Lanterns alone when candles are burning.

Type One: A Pumpkin

As a table or shelf display, use a *pumpkin* to make a Love Lantern (Figure 42). Cut away a cap from the stemmed top of the pumpkin, and remove all the seeds. Then, instead of carving a jack-o-lantern face, cut out a series of hearts around the side of the pumpkin. Place a small candle inside, and replace the top.

These Love Lanterns can be made by each class in the school as a group project so that every room has one, or they can be made in one craft period by a select group to place in the library. Ask a local farmer for contributions of pumpkins, or shop around in the supermarket. After Valentine celebrations, give the pumpkins away to cooks for use in soups, pies, and breads.

Type Two: Votive Lights

What you need:

Paper Lanterns

Art paper or thin card
Pencils
Scissors and craft knife

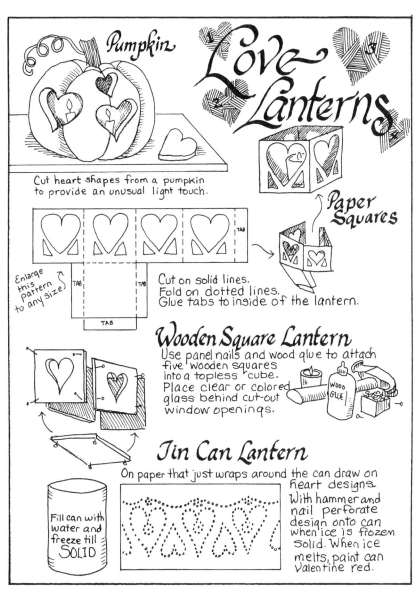

Pumpkin

Love Lanterns

Cut heart shapes from a pumpkin to provide an unusual light touch.

Paper Squares

Enlarge this pattern to any size.

TAB

Cut on solid lines.
Fold on dotted lines.
Glue tabs to inside of the lantern.

Wooden Square Lantern

Use panel nails and wood glue to attach five wooden squares into a topless cube.
Place clear or colored glass behind cut-out window openings.

WOOD GLUE

Tin Can Lantern

On paper that just wraps around the can draw on heart designs.

With hammer and nail perforate design onto can when ice is frozen solid. When ice melts, paint can Valentine red.

Fill can with water and freeze till SOLID

Figure 42

Glue
Colored cellophane or tissue paper
Votive candle in glass holder

Wooden Lanterns

Plywood sawn into five equal squares
Electric jigsaw or fret saw
Small panel nails
Hammer
Sandpaper
Paint or varnish
Paint brushes
Optional clear or colored glass panels

Love Lanterns can also be made of wood or paper. For paper lanterns, cut out a strip of four squares, leaving a tab at one end, and attaching another square of the same size to the bottom of one of the strip squares. The size of the squares is up to the maker. They may be large enough to surround a small votive light safely, or they can be several inches bigger, to accommodate more than one candle. Make another square for the bottom, adding tabs on all four sides. Draw a heart inside each of the four squares and cut them out with an artist's knife or sharp scissors. The adult may wish to enlarge the design in Figure 42 to give to each student, or use this project to teach measurement skills. Glue colored cellophane or tissue inside each of the four squares.

Score along the line between each of the four squares and the tab. Bend the squares into a box shape. Apply glue to the tabs. Glue the tabs to the inside of the box. Insert the votive candle *inside its glass holder* and the love lantern is ready to work its magic by providing an appropriate ambience for Valentine giving.

To make these lanterns from wood, proceed as above, except make each square separately, and leave off the tabs. Sand the rough edges from the squares. Make the lantern openings as ornate as you wish: a simple heart; or a combination of doves, ribbons, and hearts; or a tracing of a scherrenschnitte design. Or use an electric drill to perforate the design as if it were punched paper.

To assemble the squares, drive a panel pin into the top and bottom of the side of each square deep enough to secure it in place without coming out the other side.

Apply wood glue to all surfaces that will touch. Form a box, and press the squares firmly together. Fit the bottom square in place. With a hammer, drive the panel pins in firmly. Hammer extra pins in place along the bottom of the squares.

Paint the wooden lantern red, or stain it with lightly tinted varnish. Use colored glass votive candle holders. Never burn while unattended.

Type Three: A Tin Can

What You Need:

Empty metal cans
Water and freezer
Paper
Pencil
Hammer
Large nail
Paint
Brush

Yet another Love Lantern can be made from an empty tin can. Fill the can with water, and place it in the freezer until the ice is firm. Meanwhile, draw heart designs on a piece of paper the height of the can, and just long enough to overlap when it is wrapped around.

When the ice is solid, tape the paper firmly on the side. Turn the can into a lantern by hammering a large nail at regular intervals along the heart design which you drew. When you have finished, allow the ice to melt away. Paint the outside of the can with bright red enamel paint. When it is dry, place a small candle inside a glass votive holder, or make certain that the tin Love Lantern is on a coaster or cloth to protect table surfaces from scorching.

Valentine and Friendship Cards

A couple of weeks before the Festival, using paper and other materials at hand, make Valentines to give away or to display. Older students can begin a pen-and-ink project a few days before February 14, first drawing a heart outline, and then filling it with fantasy creatures, Chinese-inspired ying-yang, British paisley, flowers, or other designs. These may be colored in with paint or ink. Middle schoolers can make linoleum block prints in about two intensive hour-long sessions.

For a more permanent Valentine, and one that can be worn on a string around the neck, use paper templates to draw heart shapes on plywood. Cut them out with a power saw, drill a hole in the top, sand, and stain with red varnish. Thread a string through the hole and hang them from a bare branch to make a Valentine tree.

The Literature of Romance

Some of the following literature-based activities are suitable for oral or visual festival displays and seminars; others are meant for individual learning experiences. Festival organizers can determine which will make appropriate seminars or lectures, and which can be turned into displays or bulletin boards.

"Romantic Reactions"

What funny things people do when they fall in love! They forget where they are. They daydream in class. They walk straight into lamp posts. Explore with students the funny things people/characters in books do when they are in love. This could result in a list: "100 things to do to get the attention of someone you like (as demonstrated in literature)." It could be set up this way:

The Action	From the Book
(Examples:)	
1. Karen wears a "hands off" tee-shirt to school so the guys will notice her.	*Bus Ride,* by Marilyn Sachs (E. P. Dutton, New York, 1980).
2. Deedie Wooster sticks Joey Falcaro with a pencil when he calls her by a nickname she thought he'd never use again.	*Where Has Deedie Wooster Been All These Years?* by Anita Jacobs (Delacorte Press, New York, 1980).

3. Adrian wants to find Pandora 3-dozen red roses but his bank account is nonexistent.	*The Secret Diary of Adrian Mole aged 13 3/4,* by Sue Townsend (Methuen, London, 1985).
4. Marcus uses all kinds of excuses to get his mother's car to take Wendy out.	*I Love You, Stupid!* by Harry Mazer (Thomas Crowell, New York, 1981).
5. Avie writes love letters she never mails.	*Summer Girls Love Boys,* by Norma Mazer (Delacorte Press, New York, 1982).

Love Poetry Projects

A Traveling Collection

Place an equal number of library poetry books into a set of brightly colored boxes, one for each classroom or group involved in the festival. Rotate the boxes from class to class for set periods (from one to two periods to half a day or longer)l. This provides every class or group with access to every book, the limited time period providing impetus to peruse them.

Because most school libraries will have only a few anthologies of love poems, include not only love poetry collections, but poems of every variety. Decorate the boxes with colored paper, Valentine wrapping paper, or with paper hearts. Appoint a special "Cupid" from each class to rotate the box to the next station at an appointed time.

Activities for Poetry Appreciation (Middle School and Up)

Beginning

Project One: The Neglected

What do poets write about? From an examination of the poetry book collections students can see that poets write about nature, about friendship, about the world around them. But there are some things that poets rarely touch upon. With students, come up with a list of items that poets have neglected, such as spark plugs, deflated footballs, and dust rags. See how many objects the group can name before running dry. In a mini-seminar find out why these objects are so unattractive to poets.

Ask students to bring in one example of a thing about which poets never write, either from the list made in class or from items found at home. Place these objects on a convenient table. Then make this assignment: either alone or with a partner write a short verse or poem about one of the objects on the table. Give it a title: "Ode to the Wastepaper Basket" or "Nails Without Hammers." Provide pieces of card or paper for the poems to be copied on and attached to the objects about which they were written.

Project Two: Colors

Ask the group to think of colors: red, cinnamon, orange, purple, yellow, and so forth. Divide into mini-teams with two or three students per color. Their task is to come up with at least twenty items that are normally found in their color group. Ask each team to read its list to the class, who may be able to add other items. The final assignment is to write a descriptive sentence about each of the words in the list. One word in the sentence has to be a noun, and one has to be an adjective. The object of this exercise is to find out how poets use description to form images with words.

Example: *Green*

Green is a glistening, wet frog on a lily pad.
Green is a wide, freshly-mown lawn.
Green is a cool Key Lime pie.
Green is the jealous glower on a jilted lover's face.

Ask the group to cover a cardboard box or tube with paper in the color they chose. Write the descriptive sentences on strips of paper and put them in this container. Random choices of strips can be arranged into "free verse" poems, hymns to color, or paeans to colorful description. The colored containers also make an attractive display, especially if attached to a poster inviting passersby to create poems by selecting sentences from the boxes.

Project Three: Feelings

Choose several love poems from the anthologies to read aloud. Provide copies for students so they can follow easily, or read aloud together. Discuss the way love poets write about human emotions: embarrassment, passion, desire, gratefulness, or grief. Then ask students to think about (or write down) their reactions to these questions:

  i. How do you feel when you get a Valentine?

  ii. How do you feel when your boyfriend/girlfriend telephones when you are doing homework?

  iii. How do you feel when you send a Valentine?

  iv. How do you feel when your boyfriend/girlfriend looks at someone else?

  v. How do you feel when you see your boyfriend/girlfriend across a crowded hallway in school?

  vi. How would you feel if your girlfriend/boyfriend told you she/he didn't care for you anymore?

Finally, ask students to choose the question(s) and response(s) of their choice to enlarge into a serious or humorous poem or verse which they may or may not decide to share with others.

Going Further

Project Four: What Is Love?

Find out what poets have said in their definitions of love. First discuss allegory and metaphor. Keep a chart, either as the class discusses poetry or as a homework assignment, such as:

Love Defined	Poet and Poem	Source
1. Love is a universal migraine, a bright stain on the vision	Robert Graves, "Symptoms of Love"	*Penguin Book of Love Poetry*
2. Love is a careless child	Sir Walter Raleigh, "Walsingham"	*Penguin Book of Love Poetry*

Love Defined	Poet and Poem	Source
3. My Luve's like a red, red rose that's newly sprung in June	Robert Burns, "O My Luve's Like a Red, Red Rose"	*Poetry Festival*
4. . . .love like thunder . . .	Betsy Hearne, "Spring"	*Love Lines*

Project Five: Love Described

In poetry find phrases that, instead of defining, *describe* love. Discuss how the language of poetry implies more than it states. Think about the pictures which poetic language paints. Make a chart like this:

Description	Poet and Poem	Source
1. Secret galaxy of my love	Miklos Radnoti, "Hesitating Ode"	*Love Is Like The Lion's Tooth*
2. My beloved is like a roe or a young heart	Song of Solomon	*Bible*
3. O it's I'm sick and very very sick, And 'tis a' for Barbara Allan	Anonymous, "Bonny Barbara Allan"	*Penguin Book of Love Poetry*
4. Love may be blind	Robert Graves, "Down, Wanton, Down"	*Penguin Book of Love Poetry*
5. Love is likened to vertigo induced by looking down from a skyscraper	Anthony Hecht, "Going the Rounds"	*Penguin Book of Love Poetry*

Projects Six to Ten: Working Poetically

Six: Copy a favorite love poem in calligraphy.

Seven: Illustrate a scene, metaphor or emotion from a poem.

Eight: Rephrase a love poem in prose. Compare the results. Which form seems more evocative, alluring, or transcending the limits of language?

Nine: Memorize and speak a love poem.

Ten: Identify poetic techniques in particular works. Learn to recognize and practice these techniques: simile, metaphor, alliteration, onomatopoeia, repetition, richness of vocabulary and image—to find out what makes the loveliness of love, the dogginess of dogs, the owliness of owls.

Other Creative Writing Projects

1. Write a song, using a traditional or currently popular song as a model. Base your song on a tune you know, or write the melody yourself. Create a comedy by making the words come alive with the sound of sickly-sweet love, or tell of a lover who was jilted.

Seek help from the music department in setting love poetry to the rhythmical accompaniment of percussion. Ask a music teacher to help set poems to music.

2. Compose a poem about your best friend. Tell why you like your friend. What qualities does your friend have that make you want to be a friend, too?

3. Compose a poem about a loved pet. Use the poetic devices of simile and metaphor (activity ten above). Describe the appearance and character of the pet.

3. Present a researched paper or report on artist Kate Greenaway, including her involvement in the greeting card industry; famous lover Casanova; St. Valentine; Robert and Elizabeth Barrett Browning; William Shakespeare; or another famous person associated with love or Valentine's Day.

4. Write and/or perform with peers a short play about love, friendship, or growing up.

Stories to Read Aloud

Listeners of all ages will enjoy a well-read story. In addition to the well-known fairy tales, try these short pieces of fiction that will be appreciated by adults as well as middle and high school students.

Benson, E. F. *Lucia's Progress*. London: Black Swan, 1984.
Chapter 12 of this volume of the Mapp and Lucia novels tells how the reluctant Georgie finally proposes marriage to Lucia, leader of Tilling society. Benson's books prove easy to read aloud since individual chapters may be excerpted and enjoyed as vignettes.

Brown, George MacKay. *A Calendar of Love and Other Stories*. London: The Hogarth Press, 1967,
"A Calendar of Love" follows the lives of three Orkney Islanders: the fisherman Peter; the pub owner Jean; and lonely crofter Thorfinn Vik. Both Thorfinn and Peter love Jean. The story reveals the agonies of adult emotions in the Calvinist islands north of Scotland.

Bowen, Elizabeth. *The Demon Lover and Other Love Stories*. Harmondsworth, Middlesex: Penguin, 1966.
"The Demon Lover" is a very short horror story. Mysteriously and inexorably a widow's childhood sweetheart keeps a rendezvous they agreed upon long, long ago.

Mazer, Norma Fox. *Summer Girls Love Boys*. New York: Delacorte Press, 1982.
This contemporary series of short stories about teenage boys and girls makes for exciting read-aloud sessions.

Waddell, Martin. *Can't You Sleep, Little Bear?* Illustrated by Barbara Firth. London: Walker Books, 1988.
Not all love stories are about "romance." This is a warm-hearted picture book about the love of a parent for a child.

Widle, Oscar. *The Happy Prince, and Other Stories*. London: J. M. Dent and Sons, 1968.
"The Happy Prince" is a story of kindness and self-sacrifice. A gilt statue in a town square and a tiny swallow deny themselves in order to relieve the squalor and misery around them.

Creative Drama

Read the stories of "The Frog Prince," "Sleeping Beauty," or "Beauty and the Beast." After reading or telling one of these familiar tales, give students five minutes to plan an improvisation, then ask them to retell the story in action and dialogue. Help them out by filling in some of the narrative or by side-coaching. Encourage shy students to participate by giving them silent roles as inanimate objects. Students may need to be assigned roles by the teacher to avoid conflict. Or, if the group is large, divide it into small mini-teams, each of which will devise its own interpretation of the tale.

Ask middle schoolers to improvise upon the themes of "my first date," "the balcony scene from Romeo and Juliet," "boy takes girl to soda shop for a milkshake," or "great movie love scenes."

The Lovemakers' Almanac

Using poetry from anthologies and other books, the drama leader and students select material for a fifteen- to thirty-minute show. The Valentine theme provides a convenient umbrella for works on friendship, the family, and love by authors as varied as Silverstein and Shakespeare, and as different as comedy and tragedy. Some students may read monologues; others will read duologues. Some poems should include all the actors and actresses in "choral reading," with appropriate movement and choral sound effects.

For variety, intersperse dictionary definitions of love, friendship, dating, spooning, sweetheart, and related synonyms. Include mini-biographies of famous lovers in history, theatre, or films. Sing a current pop song. Include an instrumental introduction or interlude.

Bear in mind that copyright laws permit use of material for curricular or educational purposes, but often not for fee-paying audiences. Check with the copyright holder if in doubt.

Allow sufficient rehearsal time to make the show a success. This may require only a few hours after school for an eager, talented group, or a semester project for a drama, English, or library class.

A presentation of this sort can "travel" to various classrooms as well as performing in a central location, such as the school auditorium, the library, or the piazza in the local shopping mall.

Songs to Sing

Valentine's Day is a perfect time for digging out the old folk songs, such as:

Johnny Has Gone for a Soldier
Black Is the Color of My True Love's Hair
Froggy Went a-Courtin'
Scarborough Fair
Barbara Allan
Mairi's Wedding
My Bonny Lies Over the Ocean

These can be used either for a concert or to round off a story-telling session, followed by cookies.

The Food of Love: Valentine Cookies
(Makes 70–80 cookies)

What You Need:

1 cup butter, melted and cooled	1/2 tsp nutmeg
1 cup sugar	1 egg
1/2 cup molasses, warmed	1/2 tsp vanilla essence
1 tsp cloves	1 tsp baking soda
1 tsp ginger	3 Tbsp water
1 tsp cinnamon	3 cups all purpose flour

ungreased cookie sheet
mixing and measuring bowls
spoons
electric mixer
heart-shaped cookie cutters or cardboard templates

Ten minutes before baking, heat the oven to 350 degrees F (180 C).

Cream together the butter and sugar. Blend in the warmed molasses, all the spices, and the egg.

Stir together the vanilla, soda, and water. Add to the batter and whisk for ten seconds on lowest setting of the electric mixer.

Gradually add the flour, stirring until it is well blended. Chill the dough for at least two hours, or until firm. Roll it out thinly on a surface lightly dusted with flour and spices. For hard cookies, roll the dough very thin. For soft cookies, roll it thicker, up to one-third of an inch. Cut with a heart-shaped cookie cutter, or draw a sharp knife around a cardboard heart template. Leave minimal gaps between cut-outs to avoid waste.

Bake on a cookie sheet for 10–12 minutes, or until golden.

A Hearty Idea: Go to Press

To accompany the Valentine celebrations, provide free booklists, not just to be taken away by browsers, but also to be placed in teachers' mail slots, sent home to parents, or placed in the local doctor's waiting room. Books in the bibliography do not have to relate to love or romance. Include a broad spectrum of choice with short annotations, call numbers, and other pertinent information, the object being to attract readers to the library.

Using paper suitable for your word processor and photocopier, list the books alphabetically by author and/or divided into subjects, typing them lengthwise in columns so the bibliography can be folded like a book for distribution.

The cover needs a catchy title, such as *Here's a Hearty Idea: Give Yourself a Good Read! For Valentine's Day and Every Day!* Or how about *Books You'll Just Love*? Brainstorm with students to find corny puns on the Valentine theme, using the words *love, heart, hug,* or *kiss.*

The Puberty Blues: A Comedy

The Puberty Blues is a comedy about the teenagers of Peasdale High School, home of the mighty Peasdale Worms, and the best school in all of Love County, where teens are growing up, breaking free, and falling in love. *The Puberty Blues* grew out of improvisations in the author's eighth grade drama classes at the American School in London.

The play, which takes about twenty minutes to perform, requires minimal sets to create the illusion of school classrooms, a living room, and a sports stadium. These can be created with chairs or theater boxes which the characters move into position at the beginning and end of each scene. To create the alien creature, stuff a knee sock with rags. The cheerleaders may use pompoms.

The Cast

There are twenty-two speaking parts, some of which may be doubled up. There are four non-speaking roles.

Narrator
Herman Nuttley, a weakling
Tracey, a very smart girl
Jocko, a tough guy
Linda Toast, a "with-it" teen
Melba Toast, her mother
Clarence Toast, her dad
Gilbert Toast, her younger brother
Mrs. Gladys Cuticle, a teacher
Mr. Inkington, the principal
Clint, new boy in town
Cheerleaders:
  Peggy, Chase, Jessie, Meredith
Prehistoric Family, non-speaking:
  Mother, Father, teenage boy, teenage girl
Medieval Family:
  Mother, Father, Gwendolynn (their daughter), Walter (Gwendolynn's suitor)
1950s Family:
  Tommy, Peggy, Mother

Musical Opening

The play opens as the cast comes on stage briskly. A piano plays the "alma mater" vamp until the cast assembles in a semi-circle in the center of the stage and sings:

> What always brings a tear to my eye?
> You guessed it—Peasdale High.
> What always makes me want to cry-high?
> You got it—Peasdale High.
>
> "Forward" ever be our watchword.
> "Conquer and Prevail."
> Hail to thee, our Alma Mater,
> Peasdale High, all hail!

Alma Mater

To avoid the cast going on and off stage constantly, those not in a particular scene should quickly turn their backs to the audience and sit down. They must remain motionless throughout scenes in which they are not required.

Scene One: A Science Class

NARRATOR: Peasdale High School was an ordinary school, at least on the surface. No one suspected that underneath a surface of calm normality there lurked teenagers—trying to break free!

HERMAN: (Carrying books) Gosh, Linda! Won't you come to the worm races with me?

NARRATOR: A typical example of a Love County teenage boy. Interested in science, in athletics, and the American dream.

(At the word science, Herman strikes "thinker" pose; athletics, a muscle pose; American dream, a faraway look.)

LINDA: Oh, uh . . . like, I'm washing my hair all weekend, Herman. Too bad, maybe next time.

HERMAN: Aw, ok. I'll ask you when the Regional Championships are in Peasdale next summer.

(Teenage jock enters and knocks Herman's books onto the ground. He forces Herman to give him his lunch money.)

JOCKO: Ok, Herman! Hand over your pocket money. Now!

HERMAN: But Jocko! It's my lunch money! And my money for Saturday night's worm races over at the stadium!

JOCKO: (takes Herman's notebook) And what's this! I told you to *type* my homework! Mrs. Cuticle will know this ain't my handwriting.

HERMAN: Oh, she's so blind she can't even see you guys playing cards in class.

JOCKO: Next time, type it, birdbrain. (Jocko grabs Herman's collar.)

HERMAN:	Roger, dude, over and out.
JOCKO:	And don't call me Roger! (Jocko struts off.)
NARRATOR:	Who would believe such crass and unwholesome behavior could happen at ordinary little Peasdale High? But wait! It gets worse!
HERMAN:	Oh, no! I gave Jocko my science homework! What'll I do? (Tracey enters.)
TRACEY:	Hi, Herman. Going to the worm races on Saturday?
HERMAN:	(absentmindedly) Huh? Yeah, I guess so. (He fumbles in his homework.) I'll just use this old homework from last week. If I tear holes in it, maybe Mrs. Cuticle won't see the difference.
	(Herman and Tracey circle stage to join other kids at back. Mrs. Cuticle moves down front, and rest of cast forms classroom, either in rows of chairs which they bring with them, or seated on the floor. The class is fairly chaotic. Jocko, Linda, and one or two others are playing cards fairly obviously.)
MRS. CUTICLE:	Ok, kids, put away your cards. It's time to begin.
JOCKO:	But Mrs. Cuticle! We're testing different brands of cards to see how friction . . .
MRS. CUTICLE:	Oh, all right. I'm glad to see you've finally taken an interest in math and science. You should do well in the science fair.
TRACEY:	Do you want our homework now, Mrs. Cuticle?
LINDA:	Shhhhh!
JOCKO:	Quiet, Tracey!
Others:	(ad lib) Shhh! Don't remind her! Good grief, Tracey.
JOCKO:	I've got mine, Mrs. Cuticle!
HERMAN:	What am I going to do! I wish I was big and strong and I'd show that Jocko a thing or two!
MRS. CUTICLE:	(She has been walking among students, collecting homework papers.) Herman! Where is your homework?
HERMAN:	Uh . . . my dog . . . my dog ate it.

LINDA:	You don't have a dog, stupid!
HERMAN:	It was the . . . the neighbor's dog.
MRS. CUTICLE:	Likely story, young man.
HERMAN:	But see, here it is: all chewed up!
MRS. CUTICLE:	This is a disgrace! Peasdale High expects more of its students than this! Herman, you are to report to me after school for special detention!
HERMAN:	But . . .
MRS. CUTICLE:	But me no buts! Why couldn't you turn in work like Jocko? Answer me that!
JOCKO:	Yeah, Herman!
HERMAN:	Mrs. Cuticle, I want to see the Worm teams this afternoon! They're practicing for the big meet on Saturday!
LINDA:	Who cares? Count me in on the next poker game, Jocko.
MRS. CUTICLE:	Are you *sure* this is for a math project?
TRACEY:	Here's *my* homework, Mrs. Cuticle. It's perfect, like all my work. *And* I don't play cards in class. I'm going to tell the principal.
	(Tracey leads off, followed by all others, taking their chairs with them. Set up scene two with Melba and Linda. Melba is seated stage left.)

Scene Two: The Toast House

LINDA:	(Entering) Hey, Mom. It's me, I'm home.
MELBA:	About time, too! I expected you *three hours* ago! *Where have you been!* I'm surprised you even bothered coming home! It's almost 9:30, and a school night, too!
LINDA:	Oh, is it? Well, you see, I've been working on this science project. The science fair is . . .
MELBA:	Don't give me any of your lame excuses, young lady! Your homework must be done right here in this house from now on. I suppose you stopped by to see the rehearsals for the school play, watch the worm races, and then save a few minutes to . . . to!

LINDA:	To what, Mother?
MELBA:	To make out with that Jocko Sloat!
LINDA:	Mother! How did . . .
MELBA:	And as for those other hooligans you call friends!
LINDA:	Mother, this is so . . .
MELBA:	Don't get smart with me, young lady!
LINDA:	Mother, I don't . . .
MELBA:	How dare you talk back to me!
LINDA:	Mom, I . . .
MELBA:	And don't you have a big science test tomorrow?
LINDA:	Yes, I do, but . . .
MELBA:	Then why aren't you cramming for it?
LINDA:	Because I'm here listening to you! You're talking nonsense!
MELBA:	Nonsense, is it, when you and some local thug are out necking in the shrubbery!
LINDA:	But! . . .
MELBA:	Go to your room, Linda Toast, and don't show your face until you have learned some respect for your mother!
LINDA:	Why don't you ever listen to me? Just because I happen to like Jocko very much— why, I'd do anything for him! He cares about me a great deal!
MELBA:	Oh, yeah? And who pays your bills, missy? Did Jocko pay for that new dress last week? Did Jocko pay to have your orthodontistry mended when you bit into that chocolate bar? And who pays for your Clearasil, huh?
LINDA:	Mom, you are so—so—domineering! You wouldn't care if I dropped dead! You wouldn't care if I . . .
MELBA:	To your room, this instant!
LINDA:	No!
MELBA:	Linda Marie Toast, you are grounded! Just wait till your father comes home!

(Cast gathers in two tight rows center stage as piano begins introduction to "Alma Mater." They sing verse two.)

Who's the greatest team in ta-hown?
You guessed it—Peasdale High!
We're the greatest thing since sliced bread
Here at Peasdale High.

"Forward" ever be our watchword,
"Conquer and prevail."
Hail to thee, our Alma Mater,
Peasdale High, all hail.

(Everyone leaves except cheerleaders, who
begin a silent routine stage center.)

Scene Three: Cheerleading Practice

CHEERLEADERS: Pea! Pea! Peasdale High!
We're the best, and we'll tell you why!
Gooooooo, Peasdale!
Yaaaayyyyy!

PEGGY: Well, girls, let's do that again. Only this
time, Jessie, try to keep your pom-poms out
of my face for once, OK?

Jessie: I can't help it, Peggy. It's just so thrilling to
be on the Peasdale High cheering squad af-
ter all that heartbreak.

CHASE: You mean after your zits cleared up?

JESSIE: Yeah. I still have a few, see?

MEREDITH: Yuck, that's revolting! Don't you wish you
had nice smooth skin—like mine?

JESSIE: Oh, you girls are so cool. I'll never be able
to catch up with you. I mean, I've never been
on a real date before. I'm just hoping that
some of the guys will notice me in this neat
cheerleading outfit and ask me out.

MEREDITH: You mean that's all cheerleading means to
you, kicking your heels up in the air and trying to catch a man?

CHASE: Cheerleading is a way of life, Jessie.

JESSIE: I know that. I mean, everyone looks up to me,
now that I wear the Peasdale Beige and Mauve.

PEGGY: Matches your zits.

JOCKO:	(casually strolling up) Mind if I watch, girls?
JESSIE:	Oooh, Jocko! Watch this! (She does a big routine, twirling about and kicking.)
JOCKO:	Great, kid! Say, what's your name? (Jocko tick-les her under the chin. Peggy snatches his hand away.)
PEGGY:	Don't mind her, Jocko, honey. Come on, girls, let's get this cheer ready for the big worm race! A-one, a-two, a-one, two, three!
CHEERLEADERS:	Pea! Pea! Peasdale High! Peasdale Caterpillars, go, fight, win! Kick 'em where it hurts! Hit 'em in the shin! Gooooo, Caterpillars! Yaayyy, Peasdale!

(Cheerleaders and Jocko leave together. Melba and Clarence set up the Toast home. She is seated, sobbing. He stands beside her.)

Scene Four: The Toast House

MELBA:	Oh, Clarence, at last you're home! (She dries a tear, but continues to sniffle.)
CLARENCE:	What's wrong, Melba honey? You seem upset.
MELBA:	Upset! I should say so! Linda came home three hours late after necking in the shrub-bery with that ill-mannered Jocko Sloat!
CLARENCE:	Well, gosh, Melba, kids have to go some-place. Remember how it was when you and I were young?
MELBA:	Clarence! She's our only daughter! She's turning out to be a bad egg, just like your side of the family!
CLARENCE:	Well now, Melba, she's just feeling her oats.
MELBA:	Feeling Jock's oats, more like it.
CLARENCE:	Where is she now?
MELBA:	In her room. I sent her up there to . . .

| CLARENCE: | I'll see her later. I'm starved, Melba. What's for dinner? |

Scene Five: The Toast House

NARRATOR:	Later that week, Linda came home from school to a very cold welcome. Her loving mother was polishing her nails over a cold martini when the kids came in from Peasdale High.
LINDA:	Hi, Mom.
MELBA:	Hello, darling. What did you get on that science test?
GILBERT:	(tauntingly) Yeah, Linda, what did you get?
LINDA:	Well, uh . . . I am . . . I gotta go do my homework. (She starts to run off.)
MELBA:	Get back here, young lady!
GILBERT:	(mockingly) Get back here, young lady!
LINDA:	It was all Mrs. Cuticle's fault!
MELBA:	Out with it!
LINDA:	Ok, Ok! I got an F!
GILBERT:	(singsong) You got an F! You got an F!
LINDA:	Mom, tell him to go away!
MELBA:	Go to your room, Gilbert! Now, what do you mean, you got an F? I thought you and Jocko had been studying every night at the library. (Gilbert moves a few paces away, but stays to listen.)
LINDA:	No, not studying exactly. You see, his brother is in the navy, so Jocko got us tickets—to the submarine races!
MELBA:	(shouting) Young lady! There are no submarines within a thousand miles of here! And anyway, you were in your room all evening after supper last week!
GILBERT:	She wasn't in her room, Mom!
MELBA:	What! What does your brother mean, not in your room?
GILBERT:	She snuck out the window and went to the party. With Jocko!
LINDA:	You promised you wouldn't tell, you little creep!

MELBA: A party! You went to a party on a school night!? Young lady, that's it! You're grounded!

LINDA: Big deal!

MELBA: You bet your makeup bag it's a big deal! Get to your room this instant! March!

GILBERT: She'll just crawl out again, Mom!

MELBA: Not after I superglue the window shut, she won't!

GILBERT: Way to go, mom! That'll fix her!

MELBA: You, too, buster! Go to your room! Don't your teachers ever give you any homework?

(Melba grabs Linda and Gilbert by the ears and marches them into a space, stage center. They both sit down, grumpily. Melba paces in front of them.)

NARRATOR: That night, Linda sat alone in her prison-like bedroom. Outside the hallway, her mother paced up and down like a soldier to make sure she couldn't escape.

LINDA: Oh, this is just awful! What will the other girls think if they find out Mom grounded me! What will Jocko do? He might even ask some other girl out to the submarine races instead of me! This is just the uncoolest thing that's ever happened! When I get my hands on that Gilbert Toast, I'll tear him limb from limb!

(Toast family clears stage, and cheerleaders come on, doing a silent cheer as narrator speaks.)

Scene Six: At Cheerleader Practice

NARRATOR: Later that week, the whole school was getting ready for the big Worm race. The whole gang was revved up—even the teachers were excited. The cheerleaders were practicing when Tracey and Herman finished their homework and started out for the stadium.

CHEERLEADERS: Yayyyy, Peasdale!

PEGGY: Now, one more time. The whole cheer needs
                 more enthusiasm, know what I mean? Our
                 Worm team means a lot to Peasdale, and we
                 want to keep the trophy! So let's hit it!
MEREDITH: Ok, Peggy, let's go!
CHASE: Yeah, we'll show 'em!
JESSIE: I'm not sure I got it.
PEGGY: For goodness' sake, Jessie, will you just pay
                 attention for once? It's not hard, you know.
                 Come on, girls, let's do it for Jessie.

                 (Jessie sits this one out and watches the other
                 three.)

THE THREE: Earthworm, roundworm, fishingworm, too!
                 The Peasdale Worms are better than you!
                 Caterpillar, ringworm, glow-worm, glow!
                 The Peasdale Worms are anything but slow!
                 Yaaayyy, Peasdale!
JESSIE: I think I got it!
PEGGY: OK then, let's try it once more! With oomph!
CHEERLEADERS: (Repeat the cheer above. Tracey and Her-
                 man walk by.)
TRACEY: Gosh, Herman. I never knew a Worm race
                 could be so exciting!
HERMAN: I'm so glad you said you'd go with me, Tracey!
TRACEY: Oh, yuck, Herman! There's that Linda!
HERMAN: And who's that with her? I heard she was
                 grounded!

                 (Cheerleaders, Tracey and Herman, and rest
                 of group form busy hallway at Peasdale
                 High School. Much confusion as kids try to
                 find their first period class.)

                 Scene Seven: New Kid in School

NARRATOR: Next morning, just as the Peasdale High
                 boys and girls move sleepily down the cor-
                 ridors of their alma mater, a new student
                 tries to join the in-crowd.

CLINT:	Excuse me. Could you tell me which way is room 5-a? (No response. Everybody rushes past without even looking at him, pushing and shoving.) Say, uh, is this the way to . . .
MRS. CUTICLE:	Out of my way, young man! I'm late to my first period class!
CLINT:	Oh, excuse me, Miss . . . ?
MRS. CUTICLE:	Cuticle. Gladys Cuticle. Teacher of romance literature, good grammar, effective study skills, and science. Now out of my way.
CLINT:	But I'm new here and . . .
MRS. CUTICLE:	Then try to make some friends! That shouldn't be too difficult! Peasdale is renowned for its friendly students! Run along now and I'm sure somebody will help you.
CLINT:	I've tried, honest, but nobody will . . .
JOCKO:	Outa my way, kid! I'm late for Cuticle's science class.
LINDA:	Say, you're new here, aren't you?
CLINT:	Yeah, I just moved here from . . .
PRINCIPAL:	What are you kids doing out here in the hall at this time of day! Detention for all of you!
JOCKO:	Hey! Not fair, man! I was just trying to give Linda the kiss of life and this creep comes along and . . .
LINDA:	Oh, Jocko, you're so masculine!
CLINT:	Honest, sir, I'm new today! I don't know where to . . .
PRINCIPAL:	Silence, all of you! Meet me in my office this afternoon, immediately after school!
LINDA:	But the Worm races! We can't miss the Worm races!
PRINCIPAL:	The Worm races? Of course you can't miss the Worm races! Nothing can keep a Peasdale student from supporting our team!
CLINT:	Thanks, Mr. Inkington!
PRINCIPAL:	Just stay out of my way, kid—and try to make some new friends, ok?

(Everyone sets up the Cuticle classroom quickly.Clint sits on front row, stage left. Peggy sits front row, stage right.)

Scene Eight: Mrs. Cuticle's Class

NARRATOR:	Later that day, in Mrs. Cuticle's science class, the new boy makes contact for the first time.
PEGGY:	Did you see that cute new boy over there? I think he just winked at me!
CHASE:	What, with those zits all over your face? Don't be stupid. Nobody was winking at *you*!
MEREDITH:	Yeah, I mean, Peggy, like at the submarine races? Any boy could read Yucksville in braille all over your face.
PEGGY:	Honestly, you girls treat me so mean, and after all the cheers I've taught you, too. My zits are getting better every day, honest they are!
NARRATOR:	Across the room, the new boy *is* winking like mad! But not at Peggy! He's spilled chemicals in his eye during a science experiment!
CLINT:	Man, this hurts!
MRS. CUTICLE:	You!
CLINT:	Yes, ma'am?
MRS. CUTICLE:	Stop those contortions! What do you think this is, anyway? Peasdale High has standards that you are obviously not used to!
CLINT:	I just spilled acid on my desk, and the fumes are hurting my eyes. It's nothing important.
MRS. CUTICLE:	Peggy, come over here and help this new boy clean up. And Jocko, put those cards down this instant!
JOCKO:	But we haven't finished our experiment, Mrs. Cuticle.
PEGGY:	(she has moved beside Clint.) Hi! I'm Peggy. Head of cheerleading and Most Popular Girl at Peasdale High. You sure are cute.
CLINT:	Thanks. I'm Clint. I'm new in town, and this is my first day at Peasdale High. I hear the Worms are a mighty team!

PEGGY:	Gosh! Clint, have you got a girlfriend?
CLINT:	Why, no. I left my girl back in my old school.
PEGGY:	I know you don't know me, but would you be *my* boyfriend?
CLINT:	Why, sure! Wow!
PEGGY:	Would you like to take me out Friday night?
CLINT:	Gosh, yes! But I promised Mom I'd help her unpack the china Friday. What about Saturday night?
PEGGY:	What about my house? (She makes a big deal of dropping her notebook.)
CLINT:	Great. Don't you live at 5407 Lookout Drive?
PEGGY:	Why, yes! How did you know?
CLINT:	You just dropped your notebook. It's there. On the front cover. (He hands notebook to her.)
PEGGY:	By the way, my parents are out of town for the weekend, so after the worm races . . .
CLINT:	Great. Maybe you can help me catch up on all I've missed. I mean, I'm new and all, and . . .
PEGGY:	Say no more. See you Saturday night at six.
NARRATOR:	Mrs. Cuticle was right about some things. Peasdale students *are* friendly. But some are friendlier than others.
	(Students move back, and face away from audience. Prehistoric parents and teens prepare to mime their scene.)

Scene Nine: Times Past

NARRATOR:	Yet, things haven't really changed all that much over the centuries. Back in pre-historic times of dinosaurs and gigantic creepy-crawlies, teenagers were even then trying to break free!
	(Prehistoric father pounds his chest, groans and grunts, and indicates to prehistoric mother

that he is hungry and that she must do some
thing about it. Wife mimes that she is fed up
with doing as he says. Teenage son, mean
while, hits teenage girl over the head with
club, puts her over his shoulder, and drags her
home. Father pats son on back. Mother helps
girl down, and they all swagger off, apelike.)

NARRATOR: In the dark ages, teenage lovers in medieval Europe had the same problems as kids do today.

(Medieval mother and Gwendolynn appear,
ballet-like, on stage right, as if peering down
through castle window.)

MOTHER: Gwendolynn, thou art grounded.
GWENDOLYNN: But, faith, Mother! Wherefore art thou so
sorely vexed with me, thine only daughter?
MOTHER: Outrageous wench! Didst thou not plant
thine ruby lips upon the cheek of that foul
swain Walter last night, and beneath my
very window?
GWENDOLYNN: Yes, good my mother, I can not lie. Kiss him
I did, and would do so again, didst thou not
forbid me!
WALTER: (as if from a distance, *sotto voce,* beneath
castle window.) Gwendolynn, Gwendolynn!
Come into the garden, fairest damsel!
GWENDOLYNN: (Running to window, one hand on her heart,
the other cupped to her ear.) Walter, Walter!
Wherefore art thou, Walter? Speak softly, else
my good mother wilt hurl at thee a cooking pot.
WALTER: What, my lovely?
GWENDOLYNN: Alas, I am grounded!
WALTER: Dost mean that thou hast been planted like a
bean in the sod?
GWENDOLYNN: Nay, Walter! Worse! 'Tis the latest slang!
To be grounded verily puts me out of com-
mission! I shall be a virtual prisoner in the
castle tower of my sire.

WALTER:	But forsooth, fair Gwendolynn! For why hast this been visited upon thee?
GWENDOLYNN:	Because—and 'tis but a trifle of my mother's—because thou and I wert seen necking in the shrubbery.
MOTHER:	Gwendolynn! Thy father approaches! Remove thyself from yonder window. And stop muttering to thyself!
FATHER:	My dear wife! (She curtsies low, and he plants his cheek against hers briefly.) And darling Gwendolynn, apple of thy father's eye! (Gwendolynn curtsies.)
MOTHER:	She doth have a worm at her core! I have caught her embracing Walter beneath thy very window!
FATHER:	What? Thou art grounded for a fortnight!

(Gwendolynn throws a kiss to Walter from the window, and the parents each grab one of her ears and march her away. Walter runs back to join others, facing rear of stage. Set up 1950s scene with Tommy and Peggy.)

Scene Ten: 1950s

NARRATOR:	Even as time marched on, teenagers and parents still could not get their acts together. Here we are in the 1950s.
TOMMY:	Hey, Peggy, guess what? We just got a TV! Wanna come over and watch "Howdy Doody"?
PEGGY:	Swell, Tommy! And then could we go out for a cruise in your souped up 1949 Ford, maybe do some drag racing over on the main highway, and then take in a hamburger with double fries over at the Dairy Queen so everybody can stare at us with envy?
TOMMY:	You bet, Peggy Sue! But wait a minute! Here comes my mother!
MOTHER:	Young man, just what do you think you're up to?

PEGGY: Oh, hello, Mrs. Strathclyde.

MOTHER: And as for you, young lady, you should be
                    home helping your mother peel potatoes.
                    Tommy! Come home this minute! You have
                    homework to do.

TOMMY: But—Peggy and I are gonna watch "Howdy
                    Doody"!

MOTHER: Don't be silly. This television thing will
                    never catch on anyway. So don't waste your
                    time. Now march!

                    (Mother leads Tommy off stage right, hold
                    ing one of his ears. Peggy leaves opposite di
                    rection, depressed.)

                    Scene Eleven: Alien Beings

NARRATOR: Today, all is not as it seems in Peasdale.
                    Look! Up in the air!

                    (Cast turns around as they speak, points up
                    into the air, amazed.)

TRACEY,
LINDA, AND
JESSIE: It's a bird!

MELBA,
MRS. CUTICLE,
AND PRINCIPAL: It's a plane!

                    (Piano sounds opening chord of "Alma
                    Mater." Entire cast forms two tight lines
                    stage center, and sings:)

                    What's that up there in the sky-high?
                    Over Peasdale High?
                    Alien beings flying by-high!
                    You know we wouldn't lie!

                    Moving earthward, over Peasdale,
                    From beyond Time and Space.

Creatures from another planet!
Out to get the human race.

(Cast turns abruptly to face rear wall, leaving Herman to set up his telescope down center stage.)

NARRATOR: As Peasdale slept, no one knew that Love County was being invaded by a horrible force from beyond the galaxy. No one, that is, but Herman, who was doing a science experiment with his telescope.

HERMAN: Jeepers! That looks like a flying saucer! Just like in the comic books! I wonder if I ought to phone Mrs. Cuticle? (More and more excited) My gosh, it's landing in the back yard! The door is opening! Holy catfish! There are strange and horrible beings inside! They're crawling and squirming down the gangplank! And—they're looking at me!

NARRATOR: What was Herman to do? What would you have done? Should he phone Mrs. Cuticle? Can he protect Tracey from this unknown alien invasion?

HERMAN: Well, I guess the fate of Peasdale is in my hands! I'm not very brave. But I'm going down to meet these space creatures and see what it is they want!

(Herman gathers up telescope and leaves de terminedly.)

Scene Twelve: The Worm Races!

NARRATOR: Today is the biggest day in the sports calendar of Peasdale High! The fans are gathering in the stadium for the Worm Races. So it's not surprising that Linda is most upset.

LINDA: (angry, sobbing, and very emotional) This is just great! Today the worm races are on, and here I am *grounded* in my room! I just want to die!

NARRATOR: Meanwhile, back at the stadium, the crowds are pouring in.

CLARENCE: Well, Gladys. I'm certainly glad you introduced me to the thrill of Worm racing again. (He tries to put his arm around her waist, but she removes it haughtily.) Why, I haven't been to the Worm finals since I was a senior at Peasdale myself.

MRS. CUTICLE: Don't you try to sweet talk me, Clarence Toast! I'm here to enjoy the Worm races, not let you talk me into giving your daughter an A. She's flunking, you know.

CLARENCE: It's all because of that Jocko Sloat. He's a bad influence. Great guns, Gladys! There's my wife, Melba!

MELBA: So! Linda was right! You *are* at the Worm races with Gladys Cuticle! Are you trying to persuade Mrs. Cuticle to give her an A? I'm just glad Linda is not here to witness this!

CLARENCE: Linda! What are you doing here? I thought you were grounded!

LINDA: I am. But the worm races are important to me! I'd just die if I couldn't be here. Oh, hi, Mrs. Cuticle.

MELBA: Jocko! I knew it!

JOCKO: What'd I do? I'm just here for the Worm finals. Oh, hey, Linda! Wanna play some cards before the races start?

MRS. CUTICLE: How proud you both must be! Those darling children, always working on their science projects!

PEGGY: Everybody ready?

CHEERLEADERS: Worms in the pen?
The race has nearly started,
And who's gonna win?

(Everybody gets into stadium formation to simulate the Worm Races. Cast forms large football-shaped oval on their knees, facing in toward center of formation. Principal Inking ton should be at rear of oval, facing audence. When characters speak, they rise up slightly, to face audience. They pass a stuffed sock clockwise around the floor, hand to hand, to simulate Worm Race. Mrs. Cuticle can carry the worm in her handbag until time to release it for the race.)

EVERYBODY:	Pea, Pea, Peasdale High! Pea, Pea, Peasdale High! Gooooo, Peasdale! Yaaayyyy!
INKINGTON:	They're off! The Peasdale Caterpillars are out in the lead! Yes, Worm Number Five is gaining over the Dumptown Grubs! And Peasdale wriggles down the stretch!
EVERYBODY:	Yaaayyyy!
INKINGTON:	But what's this? Worm Number Eight is rounding the bend . . .
EVERYBODY:	Gasp!
INKINGTON:	Worm Number Eight is out!
MRS. CUTICLE:	Leaping lizards! Somebody do something!
INKINGTON:	A pile-up in lane number seven! Worm Number Eight and Dumptown Number Six in a major bust-up! Medical aid is being rushed to the scene! (One cast member makes siren sound.)
CROWD:	Gasp!
JOCKO:	We're gonna lose!
LINDA:	What are we going to do?
INKINGTON:	Peasdale Caterpillars are crawling behind! Dumptown Grubs are inching ahead! Dump town is ahead in all ten lanes! And with ten seconds left to go in the first half, it is sad news for Peasdale!
EVERYBODY:	Ten, nine, eight, seven, six, five, four, three, two, one! Gasp!
PEGGY:	Come on, gang! We mustn't lose hope! Even though our Caterpillars *are* being trampled by that mob from Dumptown. Come on, let's give a cheer!

EVERYBODY:	(Half-heartedly, dispirited) Yay.
CLINT:	Come on, Peggy, cheer us up!
PEGGY:	Ready! Hit it!
CHASE:	We are the Worms!
JESSIE:	The Worms on Top!
CHEERLEADERS:	Peasdale Worms will never flop! Yaaayyy, Peasdale!
JOCKO:	Good try, girls, especially you, Jessie, but it just won't work. Our worms are too tired. And those Dumptown Grubs are ace, you have to admit.
MRS. CUTICLE:	Traitor! Jocko Sloat, don't let me ever catch you badmouthing our team like that again!
INKINGTON:	(Blows referee's whistle) Take your seats, fans, for the second half of today's championships! The Peasdale Worms . . .
EVERYBODY:	Yaaayyyy!
INKINGTON:	Versus the Dumptown Grubs!
EVERYBODY:	Sssssss/boooooo!
INKINGTON:	And they're off! Dumptown forges ahead in all ten lanes! Peasdale Number Seven is out! Dumptown is crawling ahead full steam! Peasdale Worm Number Three is out with a major tail sprain!
EVERYBODY:	Oh!
INKINGTON:	And with two minutes left to go, it seems that Peasdale may as well call it a day and admit defeat!
HERMAN:	(running on stage, holding stuffed knee sock aloft) Never! Here is the Worm to defeat all challengers! This Peasdale Worm will save the day!
EVERYBODY:	Yaaayyy!
HERMAN:	I have finally made contact with alien forces from beyond the galaxy!
EVERYBODY:	Gasp!
HERMAN:	They are a superior life form, with intelligence beyond that of even Mrs. Cuticle!
EVERYBODY:	No!
HERMAN:	And just because they look like worms is no reason not to listen to what they have to say!

In fact, I have here the Chief Galactic Battle Officer of the alien forces, and he volunteered to enter the Peasdale Worm Championships to show us that he and his fellow beings wish us only peace, harmony, and world understanding!

EVERYBODY: Yaaayyyy!

JOCKO: Put him in uniform!

PEGGY: Here, give him my sock! It's got a hole in the toe, anyway, and he'll look like a regular Peasdale Caterpillar! (They quickly put leg warmer over the stuffed knee sock.)

EVERYBODY: Yaaayyyy!

(In stadium formation, the cast passes the alien sock clockwise hand to hand, amid mounting excitement.)

INKINGTON: And they're off! The new Superworm is squirming along in lane five, fending off all the Dumptown Grubs! Look at him go!

EVERYBODY: Yaayyyy!

CHEERLEADERS: (This cheer runs as an undercurrent beneath the Principal's next lines, stopping when they start the cheer "kick 'em")
Go, fight, win! Go, fight, win!

INKINGTON: This is amazing! In all the annals of Worm racing here at Peasdale High, nothing can beat this! Look at that Worm go!

JOCKO: Greased lightning!

EVERYBODY: Yaaayyyy!

INKINGTON: There he goes into the final stretch!

EVERYBODY: Ten, nine, eight, seven, six, five, four, three, two, one!

INKINGTON: And he's in!

CHEERLEADERS: Kick 'em, womp 'em, stomp 'em in the ground! Peasdale Worms are the meanest ones around!

EVERYBODY: Yaaayyyy, Peasdale!

(Crowd lifts Herman up on shoulders of two tall boys. He is holding aloft the alien worm. The crowd is wild! They leave jubilantly.)

NARRATOR:	Gradually, the crowd thinned out. Some went to the Peasdale Pizza Parlor for a Four Seasons Special with thick, Chicago-style crust and extra cheese, with double mushrooms and sausage, for only three ninety-nine, and one slice free with the coupon from the weekly paper. Others headed for the submarine races up on Peasdale Ridge where the moon was shining as full as a new half-dollar. Herman went home a hero!

Scene Thirteen: The Hero's Revenge

HERMAN:	Gosh, Tracey, I thought we were gonna lose for sure.
TRACEY:	Yeah, Herman. That pile-up was scary! I nearly dropped my popcorn!
HERMAN:	Here, have some of mine.
TRACEY:	Oh, you're so sweet, Herman!
HERMAN:	Oh no! Here comes that Jocko Sloat! (Herman hides behind Tracey.)
TRACEY:	Herman Nuttley, what are you doing? This is no time for making out! Everybody will see!
JOCKO:	Hiya, Tracey. Have you seen that creep Herman Nuttley around here? He owes me five bucks from yesterday.
TRACEY:	Why, er, uh, no, Jocko. I haven't seen him. Hi, Linda. I thought you were grounded.
LINDA:	No sweat, Tracey. Want some licorice?
TRACEY:	Certainly not! I wouldn't want my mouth to taste like a prune when Herman kisses me!
HERMAN:	(Coming out from behind Tracey.) Gosh, Tracey, you want me to kiss you?
TRACEY:	Yes! I've loved you from the start of school! (They embrace tenderly. Jocko and Linda gape, amazed.)
HERMAN:	And as for you, Jocko Sloat! Take this! (Herman knocks Jocko to the ground with a punch to the jaw, and Linda runs away.)
TRACEY:	My hero!

HERMAN:	Shucks! (They hold hands. Peggy and Clint walk by.)
CLINT:	Wow, Peggy, did you see how Herman Nuttley knocked out Jocko Sloat after the Worm Race?
PEGGY:	No, but I heard. Pretty impressive, huh?
CLINT:	Yeah. Jocko is keeping pretty low these days.
PEGGY:	Embarrassed, I guess.
CLINT:	Like me.
PEGGY:	Whaddaya mean?
CLINT:	I'm—embarrassed. I want to—like hold your hand and stuff, but I'm afraid to.
PEGGY:	Afraid? Of little old me? Nonsense! (She grabs him. They hug.)
NARRATOR:	Peasdale High was an ordinary school. Underneath the surface, teenagers were trying to break free, and doing a pretty good job of it.
EVERYBODY:	(coming on, they get in the "Alma Mater" position)

What always brings a tear to my eye?
You guessed it—Peasdale High.
What always makes me want to cry-high?
You got it—Peasdale High.

Love has triumphed! Worms have conquered!
It's all turned out well.
Hail to thee, our Alma Mater,
Peasdale High, all hail!

The End

Sources of Inspiration: Books for a Valentine Festival

Sources for Poetry

Baker, Russell, ed. *The Norton Book of Light Verse*. New York: Norton, 1986.
　　Read especially the works of Christopher Marlowe. One of his most famous poems sums up Valentine's Day: "Come live with me and be my love . . . "

Betjeman, John, ed. *English Love Poems*. London: Faber and Faber, 1964.
Former poet laureate of the United Kingdom, Betjeman offers an anthology of poetry about love for God and man, for things and animals, by British poets from Chaucer to Richard Murphy.

Browning, Elizabeth. *Sonnets from the Portuguese, and Other Poems*. New York: Doubleday, n. d.
"How do I love thee? Let me count the ways." Her pen has given the English language many new ways of saying "I love you."

————. *Sonnets from the Portuguese: A Celebration of Love*. New York: St. Martin's Press, 1975.
Sonnet 43 is the most famous in this collection, which provides a handy pocket book of love lyrics.

Burns, Robert. *Poems and Songs*. London: Oxford University Press, 1971.
Read "My Love is like a red, red rose."

Byron, Lord. *Byron: Selected Poetry and Prose*. New York: New American Library, 1966.
See "She Walks in Beauty" for February 14.

Emerson, Ralph Waldo. *The Portable Emerson,* sel. by Mark Van Doren. New York: Viking, 1946.
"Give all to love," said this wise early American.

Farjeon, Eleanor. *The Children's Bells*. New York: Henry Z. Walck, 1960.
On February 14, read "Fair Maid of February" and "Good Bishop Valentine."

Johnston, G. B., ed. *Poems of Ben Jonson*. London: Routledge and Kegan Paul, 1971.
"Drink to me only with thine eyes, and I will pledge with mine" was Ben Jonson's message "to Celia."

Longfellow, Henry Wadsworth. *The Poems of Henry Wadsworth Longfellow*. New York: Random House, n.d.

"Hiawatha's Wedding Feast" would ideally be followed with festival Valentine cookies.

Love Is Like the Lion's Tooth: An Anthology of Love Poems. New York: Harper and Row, 1984.
Poems by Emily Dickinson, e. e. cummings, Robert Bly, and others probe this wonderful thing called love.

Millay, Edna St. Vincent. *Collected Sonnets*. New York: Harper and Row, 1988.
"Oh Think I Am Not Faithful to a Vow" catches Ms. Millay in a haughty mood.

Parker, Dorothy. *The Portable Dorothy Parker*. New York: Viking, 1973.
Parker was one of America's wisest and sagest writers. For her views on love, read especially "Plea," "News Item," and "Men."

Prelutsky, Jack. *New Kid on the Block*. New York: Greenwillow Books, 1984.
"My dog, he is an ugly dog" tells why a kid loves his pet: for all the right reasons.

Riley, James Whitcomb. *The Best Loved Poems of James Whitcomb Riley*. New York: Grosset and Dunlap, 1934.
Love, advises Riley, "While The Heart Beats Young."

Rossetti, Christina. *A Choice of Christina Rossetti's Verse*. London: Faber and Faber, 1970.
"My heart is like a singing bird."

Sandburg, Carl. *Honey and Salt*. New York: Harcourt, Brace, and World, 1963.
Read especially his poem, "Love Is Deep and Dark and Lonely."

Shakespeare, William. *The Sonnets*. New York: Signet, 1964.
"It was a lover and his lass, with a hey and a ho and hey nonny no" is a good contrast to "Shall I compare thee to a summer's day."

Stallworthy, Jon, comp. *The Penguin Book of Love Poetry.* London: Allen Lane, 1973.
English and American poetry for those in love or for those who wish they were.

Tennyson, Alfred. *Poems and Plays.* New York: Oxford University Press, 1983.
"Maud" is a lengthy poem about a lovely woman. Read parts of it, such as "O let the solid ground" and "come into the garden, Maud," which is also a fine song for Valentine's Day.

Whitman, Walt. *The Illustrated Leaves of Grass.* New York: Grosset and Dunlap, 1971.
Whitman sings in praise of beauty in the new land of opportunity that was his America. For Valentine's Day read especially his "Song of Myself."

Books About Romance Writers

Benet, Diana. *Something to Love: Barbara Pym's Novels.* Columbia: University of Missouri Press, 1986.
Criticism and interpretation of Barbara Pym's romantic novels from a scholar.

Biederman, Jerry. *My First Real Romance: Twenty Best-selling Romance Novelists Reveal the Stories of Their Own First Real Romances.* New York: Stein and Day, 1985.
Really, the title says it all.

Books Especially Right for Valentine Reading

Booher, Diana D. *Love.* New York: Messner, 1984.
Booher offers empathetic advice to teens about to embark on dating, romance, and lifetime commitments.

———. *Making Friends With Yourself and Other Strangers.* New York: Messner, 1982.
Feeling low and unloved? This book tells teenagers and others

how to fit in, how to make friends, and how to overcome rejection: a Valentine for one's self.

Harrowven, Jean. *Origins of Festivals and Feasts*. London: Kaye and Ward, 1980.
This useful book tells how to celebrate all the major Christian feasts, giving their history in England, along with old customs, games, and folk beliefs related to them. Her chapter on Valentine's Day describes how foods, greeting cards, and anonymous poetry came to be associated with the festival.

Stack, V. E., ed. *The Love Letters of Robert Browning and Elizabeth Browning*. London: Century, 1969.
How do they love each other? You can count the ways.

Staff, Frank. *The Valentine and Its Origins*. London: Lutterworth Press, 1969.
This concise, illustrated history of the holiday provides pre-Christian Roman myths, tales of early Christian martyrs, and stories of the excesses of love throughout the last two-thousand years.

Fiction for Valentine's Day

Appel, Benjamin. *Hell's Kitchen*. New York: Pantheon, 1977.
Growing up in the days of the New York gangs between World War I and Prohibition gives four tough kids a special link in friendship.

Bowen, Elizabeth. *The Demon Lover, and Other Stories*. Harmondsworth England: Penguin, 1966.
Tales of love as they are lived in the sophisticated world of London's West End and in other English places.

Bulla, Clyde Robert. *My Friend the Monster*. New York: Crowell, 1980.
Heroism is required of Prince Hal, whose extraordinary deeds must save his friend Humbert, a green monster, who lives beneath Black Rock Mountain.

Burch, Robert. *Wilkin's Ghost*. New York: Viking, 1978.
    Friendship in 1930s rural Georgia leads a teenager to stand up for a friend he believes to be innocent of theft.

Byars, Betsy. *The Pinballs*. New York: Harper and Row, 1977.
    Foster children and foster parents learn that love, friendship and care make lonely lives meaningful.

————. *Summer of the Swans*. New York: Viking, 1970.
    A teenage girl gains insight into the true nature of love when her mentally-handicapped brother gets lost.

Garfield, Leon. *The Book Lovers*. New York: Avon, 1976.
    A bashful young man falls in love with a young lady librarian and, unable to speak boldly, comes up with a novel idea: could she assist him in choosing an anthology of love scenes? He turns to the classics to woo her.

Giff, Patricia Reilly. *Love, from the Fifth Grade Celebrity*. New York: Delacorte, 1986.
    Casey Valentine is ecstatic over the reunion with her old friend Tracy, until Tracy proves more popular, and somewhat deceitful.

Greene, Constance C. *The Love Letters of J. Timothy Owen*. New York: Harper and Row, 1986.
    Determined to win Sophie's heart, 16-year-old Timothy sends her plagiarized love letters with humorous results.

Greenwald, Sheila. *Valentine Rosy*. New York: Little Brown, and Company, 1989.
    Fifth grader Rosy is not invited to popular Christi's Valentine Party, so she goes overboard in planning one of her own.

Karavasil, Josie. *Love You, Hate You, Just Don't Know*. London: Evans, 1980.
    This is a collection of pithy short stories about the effects of love.

Kerr, M.E. *Him She Loves?* New York: Harper and Row, 1984.
Sixteen-year-old Henry becomes the brunt of jokes in TV comedian Al Kiss's act because he fails in winning the love of Kiss's daughter.

—————. *I'll Love You When You're More Like Me.* New York: Harper and Row, 1977.
An undertaker's son and a teenage soap opera actress meet on a Long Island beach and learn about their feelings.

Klein, Norma. *Breaking Up.* New York: Pantheon, 1980.
Ali has to decide between her dad in California, her mom in New York, her best friend Gretchen, and the boy she loves.

—————. *Family Secrets.* New York: Dial Books, 1985.
A teenage couple discovers that her mother and his father have had an affair, and this leads to divorce, remarriage, and new relationships.

Marlin, Emily. *Taking a Chance on Love.* New York: Schocken, 1984.
Follow the cycles of love, its joys and disappointments in this psychological treatise that is both serious and entertaining.

Mazer, Norma Fox. *Someone to Love.* New York: Delacorte, 1983.
From different sides of the track, serious student Nina and dropout Mitchell enjoy the ups and downs of love.

Miller, Sandy. *Freddie the 13th.* New York: Signet, 1985.
The embarrassment of having fifteen siblings gives Freddie Oliver many problems.

Montgomery, L. M. *Emily's Quest.* New York: Bantam, 1983.
How to achieve success and find love on New Moon Farm? Ask Emily Starr. She's growing up there.

Norman, Philip. *Your Walrus Hurt the One You Love: Malapropisms, Mispronunciations, and Linguistic Cockups.* London: Elm Tree Books, 1985.
A hilarious journey through the surreal malapropisms of Eng-

lish speakers around the world, presenting a fund of mirth for jokes, public speaking, and puns.

O'Brien, Edna. *Some Irish Loving*. New York: Harper and Row, 1979.
An anthology of many expressions of love: drama, poetry, short stories, from Cuchulain to Yeats, Joyce, and Synge.

Plummer, Louise. *The Romantic Obsessions and Humiliations of Annie Sehlmeier*. New York: Delacorte, 1983.
Annie, a Dutch girl living in Utah, finds complexity is the name of the game as she falls for Tom Wooley.

Reynolds, Anne. *Sailboat Summer*. New York: New American Library, 1983.
A girl must decide between two boys, one a basketball hero, the other her cousin's best friend.

Rock, Gail. *Addie and the King of Hearts*. New York: Bantam, 1976.
Thirteen-year-old Addie's crush on her teacher causes her to discover real love elsewhere.

Ruby, Lois. *Two Truths in My Pocket*. New York: Fawcett Juniper, 1982.
Six stories of friends, families, and the different levels of love, from interracial dating to crushes on teachers, told with great humor and affection.

Stone, Irving. *Love is Eternal—A Novel About Mary Todd and Abraham Lincoln*. New York: Doubleday, 1954.
"Love is eternal"—young Abe Lincoln inscribed this on Mary's wedding ring. This is the story of their lives together.

Ungerer, Tomi. *The Beast of Monsieur Racine*. London: Puffin Books, 1975.
Two children bring joy and happiness into the life of retired tax collector Mr. Racine by dressing up as a cuddly beast and devouring his crop of pears.

Weinberg, Larry. *The Cry of the Seals*. New York: Bantam, 1984.
   Seventeen-year-old Cory tries to stop the slaughter of baby seals off Thunder Island and raises the hackles of those whose living is made this way, including a young seal hunter she comes to love.

Zindel, Paul. *The Girl Who Wanted a Boy*. New York: Bantam, 1982.
   Against opposition, 15-year-old brainy Sibella falls for the local loser.

————. *The Pigman*. New York: Harper and Row, 1968.
   A teenage boy and girl find new meanings in life when they play a lasting trick on an old man.

————. *The Pigman's Legacy*. New York: Harper and Row, 1980.
   John and Lorraine, still haunted by the memory of Mr. Pignati, take a big step toward maturity.

Plays for Valentine's Day

Charlesworth, John, and Tony Brown. *Tom Sawyer*. London: Heinemann Educational Books, 1987.
   An hour-and-a-half-long production, based upon Mark Twain's classic novel, with over 22 speaking roles, includes major highlights from the original story.

Dee, Peter. *Voices from the High School*. New York: Samuel French Inc., 1973.
   One of the best ensemble theatre pieces for teenagers available, *Voices* spans the gamut of emotions in a tale of growing up. For Valentine's Day there is an especially poignant monologue about those other girls who used to get all the cards back in third grade.

Hammerstein, Oscar, and Jerome Kern. *Show Boat*. London: Chappell's, 1987.
   Based on Edna Ferber's novel, this musical drama includes the famous song, "Old Man River."

Shakespeare, William. *Romeo and Juliet*. London: Macmillan, 1989.

The quintessential love story of all time, this drama still inspires young lovers four-hundred years after it was written.

Solshenitzyn, Alexander. *The Love-Girl and the Innocent*. New York: Bantam, 1969.

Set in a Stalinist labor camp, this four-act play concerns a new prisoner and his love affair with a girl in the compound.

Chapter 6
Grin and Bear It:
A Festival of Teddy Bears

From the beginning of the 20th century, Teddy Bears have shared children's lives across the world, accompanying them into adulthood, and sharing special places of honor. Teddy Bears are as much a part of western international culture as Christmas, television, and bedtime stories. This festival, then, sings the praises of Teddy Bears, those symbols of innocence, trust, and childhood wonder, through reading and storytelling, drama, music, and a Teddy Bears' Picnic.

No one really knows when the first Teddy saw the light of day, although German polio victim Margaret Steiff probably made the first one, sewing from her wheelchair, and exhibiting it at the insistence of her nephew at the Leipzig Fair of 1903. There it was spotted by a buyer from the New York toy firm of George Borgfeldt. Sensing that this little bear was eminently salesworthy, he ordered 3,000 copies, thus beginning the Steiff bear empire that still produces stuffed animals of the highest quality.

At the same time, the Ideal Toy Corporation, also of New York, began making bears. By 1908, sales of over one million Teddies were reported, and now, at the close of the century that saw their birth, the friendly bears seem more popular and more varied than ever, with their own myths, legends, and sub-culture of magazines, fan-clubs, and specialty shops. But why are they called "Teddy" Bears?

Just as no one knows who *really* made the first toy bear, opinion is divided over the origins of the name "Teddy." Some British experts believe they are named after the Prince of Wales, later King Edward VII, who highly admired a bear on a visit to the London Zoo in Regent's Park, thus giving the newspapers a chance to link the Prince's nickname, Teddy, with the bear. Most people, however, think that Teddy Bears were inspired by America's 26th President, Teddy Roosevelt. While in Mississippi to settle a boundary dispute between that state and Louisiana, the President, a great hunting man, refused to shoot a bear. Some legends say it was a little cub tied to a tree, others that it was a full-grown black bear being chased by hounds. On November 16, 1902, the *Washington Post* printed a cartoon by Clifford K. Berryman showing President Roosevelt and the lucky bear. Because the story and the cartoon proved so popular, Berryman adopted the bear as his logo, and it appeared on all his later work. Another cartoonist, Seymour Eaton, created "The Roosevelt Bears," named Teddy B. and Teddy G., for newspaper syndication, further stirring the popular image of cuddly bears and a humane President.

For this festival, Teddy Bears should be everywhere, sitting on bookshelves, lolling about on pillows and carpets, sitting in the librarian's and teacher's chairs, and posing endearingly on bulletin boards and posters. Children can be encouraged to share their Teddies during story hours through creative reading projects. Teenagers might permit their favorite bears to be put on display (carefully labeled to avoid mixups or loss), and adults could possibly be persuaded to exhibit their childhood bears, some of which might be quite valuable.

Leading up to the Teddy Bears' Picnic there will be a portrayal of Goldilocks' invasion of the Three Bears' house, perusal of some fine bear literature, and craft periods in which to make several kinds of bears. This festival will be a popular one, and an event which photographers will thoroughly enjoy.

Display: A Jumping Bear

A large jumping jack Teddy Bear is the focal point. Made of durable corrugated cardboard and string, he will be sturdy enough to dance for a long time when passersby pull his string. Instructions for making the jumping jack follow under "Art Projects." The jumping teddy can hang from a plain background, with the title of the festival beneath his feet or held on a sign in his hand (that moves every time his string is pulled), or you can create a forest silhouette from construction paper, including a picnic basket and a good book.

Teddy Bears, popular creatures that they are, feature in advertisements, department store display windows, books, and television shows. Capitalize on Teddy Bears' popularity by adapting famous bears for your display. Along with or instead of a jumping jack, put a multitude of Teddies, cut from magazines and newspapers and toy catalogs, on a field of green for a picnic of reading. Or enlarge a Teddy from a children's book to be the star of the

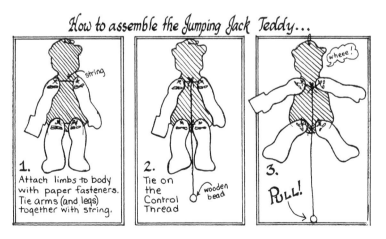

Figure 45

Jumping Teddy

- • small holes for thread or string.
- ⊕ larger holes for fasteners.

Figure 46

show. If the display area has a table, shelf, or floor in front, arrange a few stuffed Teddy Bears along it with some good books, a picnic basket, and a couple of jars of honey.

Art Projects

Jumping Jack Teddy

To Make a Large Teddy for Display

What You Need:

Corrugated Cardboard
Pencil
Craft Knife
Tempera or Acrylic Paint and brushes
Photocopy Machine to Enlarge Design (Figure 46)
Strong string
Sharp pointed tool (large needle, ice pick, awl, or cheap ballpoint
    pen)
Large paper fasteners, or Four Buttons and Flexible Wire
Masking tape
Wooden Bead or Empty Spool of Thread

What to Do:

Basic procedures for making a large bear for display are the same as those for making individual bears. To enlarge the original design (Figure 46) to your desired size, trace the five components onto graph paper. Then make a larger grid, and thereon draw the torso, two arms and two legs proportionately larger. Cut these out, and trace around them on the cardboard. Alternatively, enlarge the design on a photocopier to the size required. Cut out the five parts with a craft knife. Use a sharp pointed implement to pierce the holes for the string (indicated by a dot) and for the paper fasteners (indicated by a crossed circle).

Paint the bear before assembly. Keep the paint fairly dry. If the paint is too wet, the cardboard will warp when it dries. The color? It's up to you. Mix brown and yellows to achieve a golden bear.

Use black and white to make a panda, or use single colors to make an Eastern black bear or a polar bear. If you prefer not to have a dressed bear, omit the cap, waistcoat and tie, or create another costume from scratch. Wait until the paint is thoroughly dry before assembly. (Optional: to finish off the bear, paint the back one solid color. This may also help counteract any tendency for the cardboard to warp.)

Pierce the small holes first, one in each arm and leg, and five in the torso, as indicated in Figure 45. Then pierce the holes for the paper fasteners, one in each limb, four on the torso.

Put the large paper fasteners through the indicated holes on the torso. Turn the torso back side up on the work surface. Place the arms and legs in position, painted side down, on the back of the torso, and secure them *loosely* with the paper fasteners. If large paper fasteners are unavailable, use flexible wire instead. Thread the wire through a large button to keep it from slipping through the hole in the cardboard. Run both ends of the wire through the front of the hole and through the hole in the arm or leg, and secure *loosely* by splaying open and taping in place. (If there are no buttons large enough to thread wire through, make buttons from leftover cardboard.)

Thread the arms together with string from small dot to small dot. The string should go straight across when the arms hang down at the bear's side. Tie a knot at either end. To make sure the string won't pull through, tie the knot through a small button. Repeat this procedure with the legs. Then tie the Control String, first to the center of the arm strings, then to the center of the leg strings. Finally, tie a wooden bead or empty spool of thread to the bottom.

To display the bear, thread a piece of string through the hole at the top of the cap, and tie it with a secure knot. Hang the bear, pull down on the Control String, and he will dance. Let go, and the bear relaxes.

To Make Individual Jumping Teddies

What You Need:

Stiff artroom card or cereal boxes
Scissors
Pencils

Crayons, Felt tip pens, color pencils
Photocopy Machine to reproduce original design (Figure 46)
Stick glue or PVA glue
1/2″ paper fasteners (4 per jumping jack)
String or cotton thread
Needle
Wooden bead (optional)

What to Do:

This craft project is fun to do with students of any age. For younger children, the adults may want to prepare the torso and limbs beforehand, providing each student with a pre-cut package ready to color and assemble. For older students, the real enjoyment comes in making the jumping teddies from scratch. Creative students may want to alter the shape of the bear, giving it a fatter tummy or straighter or more angular arms and legs. Encourage students to design their own bear clothing, from shoes to T-shirts to baseball caps. And what can the bear hold in his hand? Anything from a cookie to a baseball to nothing at all.

Either (a) photocopy Figure 46 and glue it to stiff card, having first colored it with acrylic or tempera paints, crayons, pencils, felt-tips, or oil pastels; or (b) ask students to design their own, using the illustration as a guide only; or (c) trace over the photocopy onto carbon paper and stiff card. With either plan, pierce holes with a needle or paper punch at the indicated points, and cut out the torso, arms, and legs. Attach limbs *loosely* to the body with paper fasteners. To ensure freedom of movement, make sure the fasteners are not very tight. Test to see if the fasteners are too tight by jiggling the bear in one hand. If the limbs dance freely, proceed to the next step. If they don't, loosen the paper fasteners a little and try again.

Using a large needle and thread, string the limbs together from small dot to small dot. The thread should go straight across when the limbs hang down at the bear's side. Tie a knot in either end. Tie a Control Thread to the middle of both limb strings. Tie a wooden bead to the bottom. Pull down and the bar will dance.

A jumping Teddy Bear can also be made of plywood. To protect the working parts and string, you will need to make two torsos, joining them with wood screws from which will hang the arms and legs. Follow manufacturer's directions for use of electric jig saw and drill.

Flattened aluminum pie plates also make good jumping Teddy Bears. Besides being durable and easy to cut with ordinary scissors, aluminum pie plates can also be embossed with facial features, clothing, shoes, watches, and fur. To trace the limbs and torso onto a pie plate, first flatten the plate. You may need to unpick some of the crimping along the edge, or cut the edge with scissors, before rolling it out flat with a rolling pin. To emboss the cut-out shapes, place the pie plate on a thick layer of newspapers to allow the pencil point to make indentations.

To color aluminum, use acrylics or tempera into which PVA has been mixed. Some of the paint will rub off with use, giving an antique look to this kind of jumping jack.

A Pop-Up Paper Teddy Greeting Card

What You Need:

Rectangular sheet of sturdy artroom paper, or heavy grade paper
Photocopy of Figure 47
Pencils and erasers
Scissors
Coloring media: crayons, felt-tips, colored pencils
Ruler
Thread
Compass
Photocopier

What to Do:

The secret of making this Pop-Up Teddy lies in the folding of the correctly proportioned cut-out drawing. Enlarge the drawing (Figure 47) to the desired size on a photocopier, making certain that the enlargement fits inside the artroom paper, or use the drawing as it is. Cut around the outside lines to reveal the bear silhouette and the box on which it sits. Students may use the cut-out as a template around which to trace, or as a model for their own freehand drawings. Folds should be completed prior to decoration with felt tip pens, pencils, or crayons.

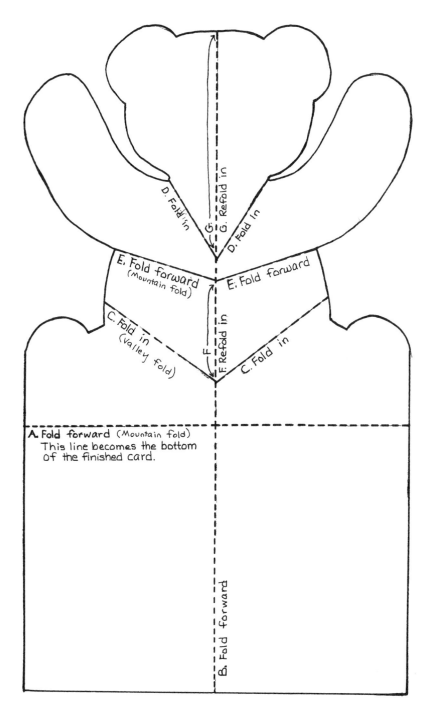

Figure 47

There are seven folds to be completed. Each fold, marked from A to B, should be done in alphabetical order, slowly. Each is marked *fold forward* or *fold in*. *Fold forward* means fold the paper away from you: a mountain fold. *Fold in* means fold the paper toward you: a valley fold. First, fold forward along Line A. The resulting fold forms the bottom of the finished card. Then fold forward along Line B, dissecting the bear in half.

The next two folds are slightly more difficult. Working from the lined side of the card, pick up the drawing so that the outside of fold C is grasped between the thumb and middle finger, the forefinger resting on top. Pinch *in* slightly. Then crease Fold C *in* all the way to the center. Repeat on the other side. You may start with either the left or right sides of this fold. Repeat this procedure with the right and left folds marked D.

Fold E is similar. Grasp the fold between the thumb and forefinger and pinch together, placing the middle finger beneath the crease. Then fold line E forward all the way to the center. When one side of Line E is folded, do the other.

The two remaining folds are the most complicated. Both lines F and G are *refolds*. Having folded line B forward to divide the card in half vertically, you now have to reverse that fold at F and G. The forward fold has to become an inward fold. Work slowly and patiently.

Now close card slowly, watching carefully to see that the folds bend in on each other correctly. When the card is shut, lay it on the work surface and crease the vertical fold again by running a ruler along the edge. Open and close the card a few times to make certain that it pops up well.

Using felt tips (or crayons) draw the features on the bear: eyes, a smile beneath a shiny nose, and perhaps some clothing—shoes and socks, jogging shorts, a T-shirt. Then invent a design for the front of the card, including a verse, such as:

| Beware! A Bear! | | Ready? Steady! |
| Open With Care! | or | Here Comes Teddy! |

The pop-up teddy bear card can be used to invite people to events during the festival. To avoid writing messages on the bear, make a balloon, a heart, or a basket shape from paper to hang around the bear's neck with a piece of thread. Cut out the preferred shape and write the message on it. Then tie the shape loosely around the bear's neck, having pierced two holes through which the string or ribbon is threaded. This prevents the cut-out shape from twisting.

Creative Reading With Teddy Bears

Books about bears form the core of the festival. With younger children, search through the library for books that have teddy bear connections as well as books about bears, hibernation, forests and wilderness habitats, and related subjects. For some students, this can be an opportunity to study the card catalog and the library's shelving system. For all students, it will provide time to browse and to dip into some very interesting materials. Students may help pull books from the collection to create a special display on a table or beneath the Jumping Jack Teddy.

Teachers and librarians can help students choose books to read creatively, first for personal enjoyment, then for sharing with peers as a festival event. This is a good opportunity for middle and high school students to read aloud to fellow students in the elementary grades. Cooperation among classroom teachers, drama teachers, and the librarian can help students learn a few reading aloud techniques, such as:

i. "Posture." Story-tellers usually like to sit on the floor with their listeners, or on a low chair with listeners gathered around. Story-tellers and readers should sit upright, and maintain eye-contact with their audience from time to time.

ii. "How to hold the book." If it is a picture book, learn the story so well that you only need to glance at it occasionally. Hold the book steadily, with illustrations facing the audience. Turn the pages as you tell the story. Where appropriate, rotate the book so that all the audience can see it.

If the book is primarily a story, and not a picture book, the reader may want to show the audience the title page or an occasional illustration. The reader should hold the book so that it doesn't hide his or her face from the audience, and the reader should know the story well enough to maintain occasional eye-contact with listeners.

Create a Festival Ambience

PAPER FRIEZES cut from accordion folds will add zip to walls, desks, and bulletin boards. Use them to frame doors and windows.

ART STUDENTS can use coloring media to add individual bear I.D. Cut bear friezes from gift wrap, newspapers, or grocery bags.

Cut slits with Scissors or craft knife

STAND-UP BEARS
cut from cardboard or stiff card enliven shelves, floors, desks, or window sills. The bears' hands hold signs or books.

cut out two arms and legs

join limbs and torso at slits

MOBILE BEARS IN BOXES

Remove tops from small cardboard boxes. Cover boxes with colorful paper. Suspend from ceilings with string or hang from windows, coatracks, doorways or clothes lines. Cut out paper bears to ride inside.

Use sides of boxes to advertize bear books or festival events.

BEAR IN MIND A BOOK for the WEEKEND

EARNING THEIR KEEP! Put real Teddies to work to promote books.

Daily 2 pm FREE BEAR COOKIES!

Hang several bears-in-boxes together to make a lively mobile!

Figure 48

iii. "How to tell/read the story." Readers and story-tellers may want to bring a teddy bear with them to share the chair or floor cushion. The teddy bear may be given words to speak, or the reader's friends may use their teddy bears as puppets to illustrate the story from time to time. Many students have natural dramatic aptitude and timing that enables them to read stories dynamically to an interested audience. Others will need some coaching on how to choose key words for emphasis, how to modulate their voice or accent for different moods and characters in the book, and how to use facial expressions and hand gestures.

iv. "Follow-up." Sometimes it is appropriate for readers to ask for questions from the audience at the end of the story, or to tell why they chose to read the book. Teachers may suggest ways of making concluding remarks or gestures (such as closing the book and bowing the head, or pausing for a few seconds and saying simply, "the end" or "and that's the end of [*title of book*]."

Students of all ages can read informally to their classmates or to a small group or just to a friend. They can share their books aloud with other classes, or they can take their teddy bears and their stories to retirement homes, children's hospitals, or to a neighboring school or day-care center. Students or teachers can select the best readers from their class to read aloud at special story-telling sessions during the festival in front of larger audiences. The librarian or drama teacher could offer short *story-telling workshops* or *dramatic reading workshops* to classes just prior to the festival.

A BAKER'S DOZEN: Excellent Bear Books for Reading Aloud

Berenstein, Stan and Jan. *The Bears' Holiday*. New York: Collins, 1969.
    For beginning readers, this story of bears on vacation makes an ideal play script because of its clear layout.

Bonners, Susan. *Panda*. London: Scholastic Press, 1981.
    As attractive as a story book, this documentary of the life of a panda and her cub is beautifully illustrated in Chinese style by the author.

du Bois, William Pène. *Bear Circus*. New York: Viking, 1971.
    Set among the gum trees of Australia, this illustrated story of koalas and kangaroos for young readers shows what happens when creative bears find a surprise parcel of circus paraphernalia.

Gretz, Susanna. *The Bears Who Went to the Seaside*. London: Ernest Benn, 1979.

Five lively teddies and a dalmation play by the seaside where they swim, fish, build sand castles, light campfires, and put up a tent. Several children may improvise together with this story, which is also ideal for one reader to tell aloud.

————. *Teddybears 1 to 10*. London: Ernest Benn, 1969.

Create a lively counting game with this whimsically illustrated picture book in which teddies take a bath in order to get ready for supper.

————. *Teddybears and the Cold Cure*. London: Ernest Benn, 1984.

William the teddy has a cold so his four teddy bear friends try all sorts of novel remedies, none of which work.

Kennedy, Jimmy. *The Teddy Bears' Picnic*. Illustrated by Alexandra Day. La Jolla, CA: Green Tiger Press, 1983.

The story of the great picnic down in the woods, with the song included on a record in the back cover. The illustrations provide lively ideas for a festival picnic, complete with decorations and games.

McPhail, David. *The Bear's Toothache*. London: Andre Deutsch, 1975.

With wonderful illustrations and interesting text, this warm story of an imaginative young boy who helps rid a huge bear of the toothache, and without his father ever finding out, will entertain festival audiences with its gentle humor.

Minarik, Else Holmelund. *A Kiss for Little Bear*. Tadworth, England: World's Work, 1969.

Pictures by Maurice Sendak work hand-in-hand with the author's gentle story of Little Bear who sends his granny a picture he drew. Granny, in thanks, sends Little Bear a kiss, and it takes a long time to get there.

Murphy, Hill. *Peace at Last*. New York: Macmillan, 1980.

Father Bear tries in vain to escape the loud snoring of his sleeping neighbors. This story provides plenty of opportunity for sound effects. The storyteller can appoint different members of the audience to snore at the right time in the narrative.

Waddell, Martin. *Can't You Sleep, Little Bear?* Illustrated by Barbara Firth. London: Walker Books, 1988.

This is a gentle, evocative, heart-warming picture story of a parent bear who lovingly cares for a cub, even though the youngster would rather play than hibernate. The story flows beautifully, and the double-page color illustrations are visual triumphs.

Winter, Paula. *The Bear and the Fly*. New York: Crown, 1976.

The clever fly comes in the window as the bear family sits down to supper. Chaos ensues as dad unsuccessfully pursues the fly with a swatter. This small picture book provides opportunities for buzzing fly sound effects, for use of a fly swatter to illustrate the action, and for plenty of audience laughter.

Yeoman, John. *The Bears' Water Picnic*. New York: Macmillan, 1970.

A bear, a pig, a hen, a squirrel, and a hedgehog float away on a raft into a pool full of curious frogs for an adventuresome picnic. This story is excellent for classrooms with lots of animal puppets on hand.

Creative Writing

1. For younger students, create a mood for poetry writing by allowing the Teddy Bears to join the children at their work areas. Ask them to write a poem or verse about themselves and their Teddy Bear. Some teachers don't like to give too many suggestions or titles for fear of structuring creativity too highly. Others may want to suggest themes, such as Bedtime, Shopping with Teddy, Traveling with Teddy, or Eating with Teddy.

2. Ask middle and high school students to write a short story about themes such as: (a) a camping trip in which they and their friends meet a bear in the forest; (b) owning a pet bear that frightens away an enemy; (c) overcoming their best friend's ridicule when he or she finds out they still sleep with their Teddy Bear.

3. Divide students into teams of two or three. Give them thirty minutes to come up with a bear story that begins with these words: "The picnic basket rolled down the side of the hill to the stream in the valley." Before the groups begin making their stories, lead a group discussion to find some possible plots. These and other questions will start the creative process. Why did the basket roll away—was it pushed, did it fall from a wagon, did the bear family drop it, did the little boy kick it by accident when the big bear appeared in the clearing? What color was the basket and what did it contain? How high was the hill? Was there a bridge over the stream? Was the valley in a city park or in the wilderness?

One way to divide the students into teams is to ask for a show of hands. How many want to make their story about teddy bears? How many want to write about real bears? How many want to make the bear a hero? How many want to make the bear a villain? Put like-minded students on the same teams. Other teams can be created alphabetically, numerically, or by drawing names from a hat.

Each team has to start with the given words, create a problem to be solved, and give a resolution. The stories may be presented orally, notecards having been written to aid the team in keeping to the story-line. They may be acted out, with team members functioning as narrators and actors; notecards may, once again, be required. The stories may be spoken into a tape-recorder, or they may be written on paper.

Later, the stories can be illustrated, either by the team, or by others. Cooperation with the art teacher could lead to the stories being given to art students as themes for individual or group drawing projects. Refer to chapter 8, "Out of the Frame: A Festival of Art," for further illustration ideas.

4. Tell the story of Smokey Bear, the rescued cub who became America's symbol of forest fire prevention. For leaflets and other information, write to: Smokey Bear State Park, Capitan, New Mexico 88316.

Write an account of the young cub's life before and after the fire. This can be realistic, anthropomorphic, poetic, or in cartoon style.

Guest Speakers

1. A *zoo keeper* who works with bears can talk about their habits, foods, and daily requirements.

2. A *National Parks Gamewarden* may be an authority on bears, especially in the Great Smokies or Yellowstone, Yosemite, or other wilderness areas.

3. Invite a local *craftsperson* to demonstrate how to make a stuffed teddy bear.

Foods to Make

To celebrate a Teddy Bears' Teaparty or to round off the Teddy Bears' Picnic, make an Apple Cake with Honey Icing, Honey Muffins, or Gingerbread Bears. If recipes are to be prepared as part of a festival demonstration, several young hands can help chop apples, beat eggs, grease baking sheets and cream the various ingredients.

Apple Cake with Honey Icing

(Recipe makes one cake, enough for about 15 slices)

What You Need:

1-1/2 cups vegetable oil	1/2 tsp salt
1/4 cup flour	1 cup chopped nuts
2 cups sugar	1 tsp vanilla
3 eggs	4 apples
2-3/4 cups flour	1 tube cake pan
1-1/2 tsp soda	

Set oven at 300 degrees F (150 degrees C). Grease and flour a tube cake pan.

Mix the oil and sugar well. Add the eggs, and beat thoroughly. Sift together 2-3/4 cups flour with soda and salt. Add this slowly to the oil mixture, beating thoroughly to blend well.

Mix the remaining flour with the chopped nuts, and stir into the batter, along with the vanilla. Pour into the cake pan, and bake for about 80–90 minutes. Test for doneness by inserting a toothpick, which should come out "clean."

Allow the cake to cool thoroughly before inverting onto a plate.

Honey-Vanilla Icing

1-1/2 cups unsalted butter, room temperature
1/2 cup honey, slightly warmed
1 Tbsp vanilla essence

Cream together the butter and honey, beating well until fluffy. Add the vanilla, and blend thoroughly. Spread the icing over the apple cake.

Honey Muffins

(Recipe makes 12)

What You Need:

3 Tbsp softened butter	1-1/3 cup sifted flour
2 Tbsp sugar	1 tsp baking powder
1 Tbsp clear warm honey	1/2 tsp salt
1/2 tsp vanilla essence	4 Tbsp milk
2 eggs	12 tsp orange marmalade
1 muffin Pan	

Heat the oven to 375 degrees F (190 degrees C). Grease muffin pan.
Cream together the butter and sugar. Add the honey, and blend well. Beat the eggs until frothy. Add the eggs and vanilla to the butter-honey mixture.
Sift together the flour, baking powder, and salt, and add gradually to the batter, alternating with milk. Stir thoroughly after each addition. Beat the batter until it is smooth.
Fill each muffin cup 2/3 full. Drop a tsp of marmalade onto the top of each muffin, and bake for twenty minutes.

Gingerbread Bears

What You Need:

2 cups all-purpose flour	6 Tbsp soft brown sugar
1 tsp baking soda	4 Tbsp clear, warm honey
2 tsps ground ginger	1 egg
4 Tbsp soft butter or margarine	raisins or chocolate drops
cookie trays	

Make bear-shaped templates from paper.

Heat oven to 375 degrees F (190 degrees C). Grease cookie trays.

Sift together flour, soda, and ginger into a bowl. Rub the butter into the dry ingredients until it reaches the consistency of corn-meal. Stir in the sugar, warmed honey, and egg. Stir the mixture until it is smooth. Turn onto a floured surface, and knead for one minute.

Roll out the dough to about 1/4-inch thick. Cut around the templates with a very sharp knife, placing them as close together as possible to avoid waste. Lift bears onto the cookie sheet with a spatula. Make the eyes and noses with raisins or chocolate drops. Bake for 10–15 minutes or until golden brown. Cool slightly before removing carefully to a wire rack.

Honey Crunch Cookies

(Makes about 90 cookies)

What You Need:

1 cup soft butter or margarine	2 cups all purpose flour
1 cup sugar	1 tsp baking soda
1 tsp salt	1 tsp ground cinnamon
1/4 cup clear, warm honey	1 tsp ground ginger
2 eggs	3 cups quick-cook oats, un
1/2 cup commercial sour cream	cooked
cookie trays	1 cup dates, chopped

(Optional: chocolate chips, raisins, chopped nuts)

Heat oven to 375 degrees F (190 degrees C). Grease cookie sheets.

Cream the warmed butter, and add the sugar and warmed honey, beating until fluffy. Beat the eggs, and whip them into the butter-honey mixture, blending well. Whisk in the sour cream, and mix thoroughly.

Sift the dry ingredients into another bowl. Slowly add to the creamed mixture, stirring thoroughly all the while. When this is smooth, stir in the uncooked oats and dates. (If desired, add chocolate chips, raisins, or nuts in combination or separately. To accommodate all tastes, divide the dough into four parts. Keep one part plain, and add single ingredients to the other three parts.)

Drop by teaspoonfuls onto the cookie sheets, leaving a two-inch gap between. Bake for 10–12 minutes. Cool on cookie sheets for about five minutes before removing to wire racks or wooden board.

Activities for Teddy Bear Day

1. Organize a Teddy Bear Day when everybody brings in a teddy bear to carry to classes, to eat lunch with, and to bring to festival activities, such as storytelling. Alternatively, prepare space to receive the Teddies when school opens so they can sit proudly and prominently all day in one safe location.

Hand out name tags prior to Teddy Bear Day to lessen chances of bears becoming permanently separated from their owners.

2. Read as many stories about bears and Teddy Bears as possible during the Festival. Ask classroom teachers to share bear books with their students. Read bear poems and stories in the library. Show a movie based on *Gentle Ben,* or locate a wildlife video about bears in a national park.

3. Visit a Zoo or Park to see live bears. Help focus children's attention by assigning chores beforehand: (a) research various species of bear to determine average height and weight, length of life, and native habitat; (b) find a poem, book or song that mentions a bear; (c) bring along a sketchpad to use when we spend twenty minutes (at least) drawing a bear.

4. Find the "Beary Best Biscuits" by organizing a cooking contest. Limit the entries to foods made with honey, a noted bears' treat. Ask for cookies, breads, salad dressings, cakes, sauces, hams, or vegetables—anything using honey.

Ask all entrants to provide a clearly written recipe (which may be printed in the festival booklet at the end of the celebrations) and a prepared sample of the food. Ask for volunteers, too, to demonstrate making their recipe during the festival.

Appoint judges to taste the foods. Award prizes by ages and by food category. Auction the foods afterwards for charity, to buy a Teddy Bear for the library, or for new library books.

5. Round off the Festival with a *Teddy Bears' Picnic*. Try to include the entire student body and their Teddy Bears, or at least an entire class, to make this culinary event as stupendous as possible.

What to do:

a. Find a location, preferably in a wooded park, with plenty of room for running around and games, out of the way of the picnic area. If possible, reserve the area far in advance. The picnic can take place in the school cafeteria, in a classroom or gymnasium, or in the library, but outdoors—even if only on the school campus—is best.

b. Organize the food. Send letters home in advance, asking that children bring a picnic lunch for themselves that should include just enough to keep them from getting hungry—but no dessert: there will be festival cakes and cookies in abundance. (If the picnic is not to replace a regular lunch, ask for a small snack only.)
     Ask for parent help in preparing some of the sweet items listed above. Make enough cake and cookies so that everybody has at least one piece.

c. Arrange transportation to and from the picnic, which may mean a walk across campus, a bus-ride, or a car-pool.

d. Play some games: Pin the Tail on the Bear; Relay Races and Volley Ball (divide into Bear Teams—Grizzlies vs. Polar Bears, Pandas vs. Black Bears); Find the Bear (Hide and Seek, in which "it" has to find the hidden bears); Loudest Roar (who can give the loudest and most convincing bear roar). Improvise some bear stories, from Davy Crockett to Gentle Ben. Sing "The Teddy Bears' Picnic."

e. Spread blankets on the ground, eat at picnic tables, or sit directly on the grass. Gather together the Teddy Bears. And eat! Serve honey cake or gingerbear cookies after the dinner theatre presentation.

f. Put on a play. With a drama group, rehearse "Goldilocks and the Three Bears" beforehand, and present it as a special entertainment between the sandwiches and the cake.

g. Dress up in a big bear costume from a theatre costume rental shop. Walk through the picnic grounds, waving and generally being amiable.

Festival Publications

In addition to a bibliography of materials in your school about bears and Teddies, including craft books, art books, slides, tapes, natural history and fiction, publish a cookbook from the recipes entered in the competition. Ask student journalists to write short articles, too, about the festival activities: reviews of the play performance, anecdotes about storytelling, a feature about the food competition. Include line drawings of bears. Publish some of the best bear stories written during the festival.

As a handout prior to and during the festival, publish the bibliography beforehand. Then publish the recipes and stories afterwards.

Songs to Sing

Singing is a fine accompaniment to picnics, a lively companion to storytelling, and an essential ingredient of musical drama. Sing this song about a bear in search of a good book anytime during the festival, either as part of "Goldilocks and the Three Bears" or as a theme-song for the entire event. Encourage students to invent new verses for this tune and for other well-known folksong melodies.

The Bear Went Over the Mountain

1. The Bear Went Over the Mountain,
   The Bear Went Over the Mountain,
   The Bear Went Over the Mountain
   To see what he could read.

2. He went into the library.
   "A likely source," said he.

3. He found a book about honey.
   "I think I shall proceed!"

4. The bear came home from the mountain
   With lots of books to read.

The Bear Went Over the Mountain

Words: Alan Heath

Traditional European folk melody, Arr. A. H.

1.Oh, the bear went o-ver the moun-tain, the bear went o-ver the moun-tain,

May be played as piano introduction to verse #1

The bear went o-ver the moun—tain to see what he could read! To

see what he could read——! To see what he could read——!

The bear went o-ver the moun-tain, the bear went o—ver the moun-tain,

The bear went o-ver the moun—tain to see what he could read!

Jimmy Kennedy's *The Teddy Bears' Picnic* has passed into world culture since it first appeared in the 1930s. Sheet music and recordings are readily available, so making it the festival theme song will be easy. Music teachers can help children learn the tune. Drama teachers can help them put actions to the words. Some story-telling events can begin or conclude with everyone singing the song.

Not as well known is Arnold Sundgaard's *Douglas Mountain,* with music by Alec Wilder and illustrated by Maurice Sendak. Essentially a lullaby, it is based on the winter snows bringing hibernation to the bears. A livelier tune in the same collection is *Infant Innocence,* by A. E. Housman, about a child and a grizzly. They appear in *Lullabies and Night Songs,* edited by William Engvick, with music by Alec Wilder and illustrations by Maurice Sendak.

A Play to Perform
Goldilocks and the Three Bears

This version of the Goldilocks story is suitable for lower school students to rehearse and perform for themselves, or for middle and high school students to perform as children's theatre. The play also makes a good reader's theatre project, performed in conjunction with excerpts from J. C. Harris's *Uncle Remus Stories* of Brer Bear and his friends. Performance time is just under twenty minutes.

The play may be performed without any props at all, or with minimal set and props: tables, chairs, books, and pillows on the floor for beds. Costumes should be indicative only. Bears may be indicated by taping paper ears to hair-bands or hair-clips. A bearish nose may be applied with make-up, or you may be able to buy a plastic one from a toy store or theatrical supply house. The policeman needs only a badge and a portable telephone or walkie-talkie.

Cast of Characters

Goldilocks
Her mother, Ursula
Her father, Bruin
A Police Officer

Porridge, the Baby Bear
Mother Bearinbaum
Father Bearinbaum

Non-speaking roles may be given to an ice-cream seller, strollers in the park, forest trees, or an accompanying police officer. Another speaking role could be given to a Narrator who would read the Setting at the beginning of each scene.

Scene One
(At home with Goldilocks and her parents)

> *As the play opens, Goldilocks is picking at her porridge disgustedly, while her parents are eating. Her mother is a fussy woman, and her dad is something of a "yes, dear" man.*

GOLDILOCKS: Oh, mother, do I *have* to eat my porridge? I hate porridge!

URSULA: Don't you want to grow up to be a big strong girl? Eat, Goldilocks, eat!

GOLDILOCKS: Dad? Do I *have* to?

BRUIN: You heard your mother, Goldilocks. Eat! Eat!

GOLDILOCKS: When I grow up I'm *never* going to make *my* kids eat porridge! In fact—I'm never going to *make* porridge.

URSULA: Eat up, dear, and we'll go for a nice walk in the park. She can play on the swings, can't she, dad?

BRUIN: Yes, of course! Would you pass the pepper, please, dear?

GOLDILOCKS: But I don't *like* porridge! And I don't *want* to go to the park. I want to watch T.V.!

URSULA: Here's the pepper, Bruin. Not too much! It'll make you sneeze.

BRUIN: I know, dear. (*He sprinkles pepper liberally as he speaks.*) Remember last week when . . .

URSULA: Careful, Bruin! You're going to . . .

GOLDILOCKS: Ah-CHOO!

BRUIN: Ahh . . . ahh . . . ahh-choooo!

URSULA: AH-CHOO! (*All three sneeze dramatically for a short time.*)

URSULA: (*Getting up.*) Come on! Let's go to the park *now*! I told you to be careful with that pepper, Bruin.

BRUIN:	I know you did, Ursula, dearest. I just got carried away.
GOLDILOCKS:	Ah-choooo!
URSULA:	Look, you've made poor Goldilocks sneeze all over her nice porridge.
GOLDILOCKS:	Ahhhh-CHOOO!
BRUIN:	(*Getting up.*) There, there, Goldilocks, come on. We'll get a nice ice-cream in the park.
GOLDILOCKS:	But you said I . . .
URSULA:	Come on, we're off to the park! Quality time, just for *you,* young lady. (*Mama and Papa exit. Goldilocks remains until she says her line to audience.*)
GOLDILOCKS:	Oh, goodie! Now I don't have to eat this yucky porridge. I was just faking that sneezing. It fools them every time.
URSULA:	(*Offstage.*) Come on, Goldilocks! Let's go! (*Goldilocks leaves spiritedly.*)

Scene Two
(At the Bearinbaum house, they, too, are eating supper)

PORRIDGE:	Oh, mother, do I *have* to eat my porridge? I *hate* porridge.
MOTHER:	Don't you want to grow up to be big and fierce like your father, sweetheart?
FATHER:	(*Strikes a he-bear muscle pose*) Grrrrr!
PORRIDGE:	Papa, do I *have* to eat my porridge?
FATHER:	Well, son, it *is* a bit hot. Perhaps we ought to go for a nice walk in the woods. When we get back, the porridge will be nice and cool. (*To mother.*) What do you think, dear?
MOTHER:	Personally, I *like* hot porridge. (*She savors a spoonful.*) Mmmmmmm. It's excellent! Have some more! Eat!
PORRIDGE:	But ma . . .
FATHER:	It's a beautiful day in the neighborhood, dear. Come on. Let's go for a walk. We'll eat later. And we can stop by the library on our way back and get some nice books to read tonight.

MOTHER:	Oh, very well. I'll get my sun bonnet.
PORRIDGE:	Whoopeee!
	(*The bears leave hand in hand, skipping, and singing "The Bear Went Over the Mountain".*)

Scene Three
(Goldilocks' parents are in the park. But where is Goldilocks?)

URSULA:	(*Calling*) Goldilocks! Where *are* you?
BRUIN:	Goldilocks! Come here this instant!
URSULA:	GO-O-OLDIE! Come here, sweetie!
BRUIN:	(*To his wife*) If you hadn't *insisted* she eat that porridge she'd not have run away, Ursula.
URSULA:	Me? Insisted? Why, you practically forced it down that dear child's throat!
BRUIN:	Me? Forced? Who promised her an ice-cream cone? (*A police officer strolls up.*)
URSULA:	Ice cream cone? Ice cream cone?
OFFICER:	Having a problem, folks? It's much too nice a day for a quarrel. Or disturbing the peace!
URSULA:	Oh, officer, it's our little girl . . .
BRUIN:	Goldilocks . . .
URSULA:	She's—she's— run away!
BRUIN:	Well, maybe not run away exactly. We came out for a walk in the park, and when we went to get an ice cream cone, she . . .
URSULA:	Left! Disappeared! Gone! And all because I made her eat her porridge!
OFFICER:	Porridge? Yuck! I hate porridge!

Scene Four
(Goldilocks sees the Bearinbaum house and enters.)

GOLDILOCKS:	Ah-hah! What have we here? A house! I'll just knock and see if I can get a drink of water. (*She knocks and waits. No response. She knocks again. She pushes door open and leans in.*) Yoo-hoo! Helloooo? Anybody home? (*pause, listen*) I'll just go in and help myself!

(*She tiptoes inside.*)

I only want a glass of water so I'll . . .

(*She sees the meal on the table.*)

Ah-hah! What have we *here*, eh? Soup? Cereal? Cake?

(*She looks closely at porridge.*)

Oh, no! It's—porridge! What's happening to me! I can't get away from this stuff!

(*She sniffs a bowl.*)

Well, I am kinda hungry. Maybe I'll just try it. (*She sips mama Bearinbaum's bowl.*)

Yowee! Too hot! Ow! (*Fans mouth, dances about! Then she tries papa Bearinbaum's bowl.*)

I'll just try this one. Brrr! It's too cold. Yuckeee! (*Her teeth chatter. She then tries Baby Porridge Bearinbaum's bowl.*)

Hmmmmm . . . not bad! Not bad at all!

(*She eats it all. Stretches comfortably. Looks around the house.*)

That was delicious! I wish *my* mother could make porridge like *that*! I wonder who lives here? (*She walks around, looking.*)

Oooooo! Nice chairs! Just right for watching some TV! I wonder which one . . .

(*She sits in mama bear's chair.*)

Ouch! Too hard! (*Moves to papa's chair.*)

Yuckoh! Too soft! (*Moves to baby's chair.*)

Ahhhhh! Just right! (*She settles comfortably and with exaggerated laziness, then suddenly falls out of the chair to indicate its "collapse"*)

Oh, shucky darn! Stupid chair! They just don't make 'em like they used to. (*She gets up, looks around some more, and finds three books.*)

Wow!! Books! I wonder what they are!

(*She tries to pick up a large book.*)

Gosh! Too heavy! I can't even—mph!—lift it!

(*She tries second book.*)

Hah! I knew it! I read this book two years go! (*She picks up a tiny book.*)

Now *this* is more like it! I could really get into a book like this! (*She reads aloud.*)

"Once upon a time there were three bears and a little girl named Goldilocks." Hey! That's me! "And the bears lived in a little house in the woods." Say, this is a neat book! Why don't I just make myself comfy and settle down for a little while. (*She moves to beds.*)

A-hah! A bed! I *love* to read in bed! (*She jumps onto first bed and bounces.*)

No way, José! This bed is too hard! (*She moves to next bed.*)

Let me outa here! This bed is too soft! (*She moves to tiniest bed.*)

Well, now. I could get used to this! (*She snuggles comfortably.*)

Yeah, this is the life. A good meal, a nice book, a comfortable bed . . . (*big yawn, stretch*)

I could . . . (*yawn*) take a nap. I'll just curl up . . . and (*she mumbles the following softly as she goes to sleep*) read the rest . . . of this book . . .

Scene Five
(Goldilocks' parents are in the park with the Officer. He is speaking into his portable unit.)

OFFICER: All points bulletin, chief! The girl was last seen heading away from the ice-cream wagon in the park.

URSULA: Tell them to find her!

BRUIN: Now, Ursula. They'll find her. Don't fret.

OFFICER: Roger. Over and Out. Ten-four. Sayonara, Rubber Duckie. So-long. (*He speaks now to parents.*) She was spotted over on Bearwood Road fifteen minutes ago. Come on, folks, let's see if we can find her.

URSULA:	Oh, thank you, officer! Lead the way! (*They all leave purposefully, the officer in front.*)

Scene Six
(The bears, each carrying a book, come home to find their uninvited visitor asleep. They are singing final words of "The Bear Came Over the Mountain.")

FATHER:	Now wasn't that a fine walk?
PORRIDGE:	And I got a great book at the library!
MOTHER:	I'm starved! Let's eat.
FATHER:	What's this! (*They all approach tables; look astonished, puzzled.*) Someone's been eating my porridge!
MOTHER:	Someone's been eating *my* porridge!
PORRIDGE:	Someone's been eating *my* porridge —
ALL 3 BEARS:	And they've eaten it all up!
MOTHER:	Dear oh dear oh dear! (*Mother and Father Bear devise some gestures and body movements to accompany these phrases, which become their "theme tune" as they discover what Goldilocks has done.*)
FATHER:	My oh my oh my!
PORRIDGE:	I want my porridge! I want my porridge!
MOTHER:	Let's just sit down and think this through. (*She moves to the chairs.*)
FATHER:	Look! Someone's been sitting in my chair!
MOTHER:	And someone's been sitting in *my* chair!
PORRIDGE:	*Some*one's been sitting in my chair —
ALL 3 BEARS:	And they've broken it to pieces!
MOTHER:	Dear oh dear oh dear!
FATHER:	My oh my oh my!
PORRIDGE:	I want my chair! I want my chair! Somebody broke my chair!
MOTHER:	Let's just gather up our books and . . .
FATHER:	Somebody tried to lift my book!
MOTHER:	Somebody tried, and *did* lift my book!
PORRIDGE:	Somebody lifted my book —

ALL 3 BEARS:	And took it clear away!
MOTHER:	(*Sniffing*) I think I smell a rat!
FATHER:	(*Sniffing*) I think I smell a fish!
MOTHER:	Let's see if we can find some tracks!
FATHER:	Look! There!
PORRIDGE:	Tracks leading to . . . to the bedroom! (*They tip-toe to the bedroom.*)
MOTHER:	Wouldn't you know it! Somebody's been messing up my bed! Whatever next! And I just washed that bedspread! Now look at it! I'll never get it clean!
FATHER:	Somebody's been in *my* bed!
PORRIDGE:	Hey! Look! There *is* somebody in my bed right now!
MOTHER:	Dear oh dear oh dear!
FATHER:	My oh my oh my! (*Their knees quake; they huddle up in fear, except for little bear who approaches Goldilocks bravely.*)
PORRIDGE:	Hey, buster! Scram! Get outa my bed or I'll . . .
GOLDILOCKS:	(*Sitting up quickly.*) Oh my! Bears! Don't I know you from somewhere?
PORRIDGE:	Get outa my bed! And give me my book!
GOLDILOCKS:	That's it! The book! You're the family in the book I was reading when I fell asleep. And I'm the girl who . . .
MOTHER:	So you've been reading my diary, have you, young lady! Just wait till I get my hands on you! (*Reaches for Goldilocks.*)
GOLDILOCKS:	(*Running out of house.*) Sorry, lady! I've got an appointment at the dentist's! I've gotta see a man about a dog. Gotta run! Sorry I can't stay for dinner!
FATHER:	Well! Did you ever . . .
PORRIDGE:	At least I got my book back!
MOTHER:	But now we've got to clean up this house! Look at this mess! This place is a wreck! Not to mention our food being eaten! (*She surveys the house.*) All right, you two! Get to work!

Scene Seven

(Back at Goldilocks' house, the family is sitting with the officer, who is eating porridge.)

GOLDILOCKS:	And that's when I got up and ran away! And there you were!
URSULA:	Honestly, Goldilocks. If you expect us to believe such a cockamamie story I just don't know where we went wrong. Bears, indeed! Huh! Porridge! Huh!
OFFICER:	By the way, *this* porridge is excellent!
BRUIN:	Could use some pepper, though.
URSULA:	Not on your life! Here, gimme that pepper before you spill it again.
GOLDILOCKS:	Well, that's what happened. And anyway, I don't care if you *don't* believe me.
OFFICER:	We believe you, little girl.
BRUIN:	Just eat your porridge, Goldilocks.
GOLDILOCKS:	But I just ate. Back at the Bears' house and I really . . .
URSULA:	That's it, young lady! You're grounded! Got that? Grounded.
GOLDILOCKS:	But . . .
BRUIN:	Go to your room this minute.
URSULA:	March!
BRUIN:	And not another word about bears! Nonsense! I just don't know what the younger generation is coming to! (*Doorbell rings, or there is a loud knock at the door, during this; it is the Bearinbaum family.*) Get to your room. Shall I see who it is, dear?
URSULA:	Isn't that usually what happens when the doorbell rings (*or* when someone knocks on the door)?
BRUIN:	I mean, shall I or shall you answer it?
OFFICER:	Never mind. Enjoy your porridge. You've had a hard day. I'll get it. (*He goes to the door and opens it.*) Yeeeessssss? (*His mouth opens in astonishment; he freezes and remains frozen until the play is over.*)

MOTHER BEAR:	Is this the home of a girl called Goldilocks?
PORRIDGE:	She ate my supper all up!
FATHER BEAR:	Shh, son. We'll overlook that.
MOTHER BEAR:	Well, who could blame her? My porridge *is* rather good. And it *was* sitting there on the table. Rather temptingly.
FATHER BEAR:	But about that broken chair. I reckon she ought to pay for that. So if you don't mind . . . so we just thought . . .
URSULA:	Who is it, officer?
BRUIN:	Tell them to come in and have some porridge.
PORRIDGE:	Did you say "porridge?" (*He rushes in.*)
URSULA:	Why, it's a . . .
BRUIN:	BEAR! Goldilocks was right! (*Other two bears come in.*)
FATHER BEAR:	Now about that broken chair. (*Ursula and Bruin and Officer faint onto floor. Bears look at them and at each other and shrug, as if to say, "stupid people!" Bears sit down to eat porridge. If there is a curtain, bears continue to eat as curtain falls. Otherwise, bears freeze for three beats. Then all rise from floor and seats, Goldilocks comes out to join them, and any non-speaking characters come on, for a bow.*)

Sources of Inspiration: Books About Bears

Bears and Other Carnivores. New York: Time Life, 1976.
From the writings of authors such as William Faulkner, Mark Twain, Ernest Seton and John Muir come anecdotes and observations about bears, illustrated with photographs.

Berenstein, Stanley. *The Bears' Nature Guide: Almost Everything Small Bears and Kids Need to Know About . . .* New York: Random House, 1975.
Papa Bear introduces the Little Bears to the wonders of nature.

Cook, Susannah. *A Closer Look at Bears and Pandas.* London: Hamish Hamilton, 1976.
This is a small book with lots of photographs of bears and pan-

das, accompanied by a lively text that describes their lives and natural habitats.

George, Jean Craighead. *The Moon of the Bears*. New York: Crowell, 1967.
George describes the seasonal cycle of mating and birth of a black bear in the Smoky Mountains of Tennessee.

Hill, Anthony. *The Giant Panda Book*. New York: Golden Press, 1974.
This beautifully illustrated book helps young readers become experts on where pandas live, what they eat, and how they survive in zoos.

Johnson, Fred. *The Big Bears*. Washington, D.C.: Wildlife Federation, 1973.
Take a close look at polar bears and grizzlies in this book of photographs and textual descriptions of the biggest bears on earth.

Mason, George F. *The Bear Family*. New York: William Morrow, 1960.
All about the life and habitat of bears, what they eat, where they like to live, and what happens when a bear hibernates.

For Teddy Bear Lovers

Bialosky, Peggy and Alan. *The Teddy Bear Catalog*. New York: Workman Publishing Company, 1983.
An extensive history of the teddy bear, this book is well illustrated with photographs of antique specimens as well as examples of teddies throughout the 1990s.

Engvick, William, ed. *Lullabies and Night Songs*. New York: Harper and Row, 1965.
With illustrations by Maurice Sendak and music by Alec Wilder, this book contains piano scores and words to nearly fifty poems, including two specifically about bears.

Kennedy, Jimmy. *The Teddy Bear's Picnic*. La Jolla: Green Tiger Press, 1983.
This picture book is based on the famous song, and includes a phonograph record inside the back cover.

Menton, Ted. *The Teddy Bear Lovers Catalogue*. London: Ebury Press, 1983.

Menton, an avid teddy bear collector, presents 150 pages of teddy bear stories, photos, puzzles, instructions on making a teddy bear at home, and lists of shops that sell bears.

The Teddy Bear Book. Milwaukee: Country Handcrafts, 1986.

A bear necessity for those seeking patterns to make teddy bears at home, this book contains ten designs with full instructions, along with a full-color photograph of each bear.

Bears in Fiction and Picture Books

Ainsworth, Ruth. *The Bear Who Liked Hugging People, and Other Stories*. New York: Crane Russak, 1976.

Here are thirteen stories about bears and other animals, witches, and clowns, designed to be read aloud.

Barrett, John. *The Bear Who Slept Through Christmas*. New York: Ideals Publications, 1980.

Blessed with an inquiring mind, Ted Edward Bear, a student at Grizzly University, forgoes hibernating one year to see what this thing called Christmas is all about.

Berenstein, Stanley. *The Berenstein Bears and the Missing Dinosaur Bone*. New York: Beginner Books, 1980.

The Little Bear Detectives and their hound dog Snuff set out to discover who stole the bone from a dinosaur skeleton.

Bond, Michael. *A Bear Called Paddington*. London: Collins, 1968.

Upon his arrival at London's Paddington Station from South America, a young teddy bear has to make his way in a strange environment.

———. *Paddington Takes the Air*. London: Collins, 1974.

This is one of the series of Paddington's adventures. Here he dances a wild rumba, and gets glued to his partner's back with his sticky marmalade sandwich.

Brenner, Barbara. *A Killing Season*. New York: Dell, 1981.

Brenner's story of a young girl and her life in rural Pennsylvania is based on the factual account of a black bear and its habitat.

Calhoun, Mary. *The Night the Monster Came*. New York: Morrow, 1982.
Unable to ignore frightening television shows, Andy is convinced that Bigfoot is lurking around the house.

Du Bois, William Pène. *Bear Circus*. New York: Viking, 1971.
Enjoy all the fun of the big top with a performing bear family in this picture book story.

Flory, Jane. *The Bear on the Doorstep*. New York: Houghton Mifflin, 1980.
A generous rabbit family adopts a baby bear left on their doorstep in this picture book.

Forester, Victoria. *Bears and Theirs*. New York: Atheneum, 1982.
The many uses of the word "bear" and its homonyms—bar-bear-ions, Bear-thoven, bear necessities—provide laughs and chuckles for bear enthusiasts.

Getz, William. *Sam Patch—Ballad of a Jumping Man*. New York: Franklin Watts, 1986.
This mature story of love and adventure is told by Bruin, the bear who accompanied a pioneer American's search for the meaning of life in jumping over waterfalls in the 1820s.

Grimm, Jacob. *The Bear and the Kingbird, a Tale from the Brothers Grimm*. New York: Farrar, Straus & Giroux, 1979.
Bear provokes war between winged creatures and quadrupeds, but Kingbird alights on a strategy to avoid battle.

Haas, Dorothy. *The Bears Upstairs*. New York: Dell, 1978.
Wendy is surprised to learn that the new couple upstairs, Otto and Ursula Ma'am, are talking bears.

Milne, A. A. *Winnie-the-Pooh*. London: Methuen and Company, 1967.
Winnie-the-Pooh is a teddy bear who, with Piglet, Eeyore, Rabbit, Owl, Kanga, Roo, and Christopher Robin, has adventures in the Bee Tree, the 100-acre wood, and the gloomy place. Classic illustrations by E. H. Shepard create the atmosphere beloved by

generations of readers since the book was published in the early part of the 20th century.

Morey, Walt. *Gentle Ben*. New York: Avon, 1965.
A perenial favorite Alaskan story about a bear who was anything but fierce.

Olsen, Jack. *Night of the Grizzlies*. New York: Putnam, 1969.
Read about the circumstances surrounding the only tragedy caused by grizzles in an American national park.

Wells, Rosemary. *Peabody*. New York: Dial, 1983.
Toy bear Peabody finds himself abandoned on the shelf after Annie gets a new doll.

Winter, Paula. *The Bear and the Fly*. New York: Crown, 1976.
A bear tries to catch a fly with disastrous results in this picture book.

Worthington, Phoebe. *Teddy Bear Postman*. London: Frederick Warne, 1981.
A colorful picture book which proves that teddy bears can do anything a human being can, and possibly better.

Chapter 7
A Festival of the Imagination: Puppets and Literature

One of the most famous characters in the western world is a puppet, a little jointed wooden doll who became, through the virtue of his maker and his own fidelity, a live human being. Pinocchio, created by an Italian educator in 1883, is known by every school child through one or more of the many adaptations of the original book. In India, a legend tells of two beautiful jointed dolls, so beautiful, in fact, that Lord Shiva and the Goddess Parvita entered them, causing them to dance. The toymaker was delighted, but when the gods departed, and the dolls fell lifeless to the table, the distraught craftsman attached strings to their limbs. To recreate the spirited dance, the old toymaker invented marionettes. Anthropologists have found that in many primitive cultures puppets were used in religious or shamanistic rites in which spirits were believed to inhabit the little figures. And in medieval Europe, religious plays were performed in the streets, using live actors and puppets to portray events in the lives of Biblical characters and the saints, and from this time comes the origin of marionette, meaning "little Mary."

Because puppets became a great popular entertainment, medieval and renaissance puppeteers gradually replaced their religious characters with worldly ones. Cross pollination of ideas between traveling actors and puppeteers helped create international favorites: in France, Polichinelle and Guignol; in Italy, Pulcinella; in Spain, Pulichinela; in Russia, Petruskha; and in England, Punch and Judy — the same puppets, but dressed in local costume and animated in local legends and theatrical traditions.

Puppets have never lost their popularity. In the Austrian city of Salzburg, a marionette theatre performs opera to packed houses of adults. In London, the Little Angel Marionette Theatre is booked weeks ahead by parties of school children. At the University of Connecticut, Storrs, there is the U.S. National Puppet Institute for the promotion of research and development in puppetry. Puppets appear on children's television shows, in movies, and in local performances in schools and public libraries. Today, glove puppets are available in toy stores, drug stores, and many other places a parent, teacher, or child is likely to shop. Ranging in price from a few dollars upwards, these puppets are excellent value. Representing animals, storybook characters or film heroes, these toys are not only good to look at, nestled at rest on a shelf; they also release the creative imagination of a child as they "live" and move through manipulation.

Educators have long known the many values of puppets in school. Many, in fact, acknowledge puppetry as a language in the sense that they communicate ideas and feelings just as words do. Some children will communicate well through art, poetry, speech making, or music; others will communicate naturally and effectively through puppetry. Puppetry promotes verbal development. It has been used successfully in teaching foreign languages or English as a second language. The *making* of puppets offers vast scope for arts and crafts. Through puppet manipulation, youngsters can learn mathematical concepts of relationship, time, and space; proportion, weight, height; sight-lines, precision scale drawings, viewing angles.

Through *decentering,* or removing the egocentric view of the world to appreciate another's viewpoint, children can begin to make mature moral judgments with puppets. By "walking in someone else's shoes" through puppet play, youngsters learn to see the several sides to arguments and viewpoints; Cinderella's ugly sisters, comic though they are, may be seen to have feelings, too, when one considers that *they* can't charm the handsome prince because they are unattractive. Through play with puppets, either individually or in small groups, children enter the roles of other people: adults, peers, parents, siblings, or teachers. Through play with puppets they enlarge their scope for empathy and understanding of human nature.

Puppets are ideal for use in drama, music, and movement. In order to sustain audience interest, a puppet must *move*. Whether glove puppet, marionette, shadow puppet, or simple finger puppet, its language is variety and quality of movement. Puppets can dance to music in performance, or privately when a child is alone with a cassette player.

Special needs of children can be met through puppets. A physically impaired child can often participate fully in producing a puppet show, boosting self-confidence and sense of belonging. Academically limited youngsters can sense achievement through participation in a puppet show. Part of the power of puppets comes from the theatre itself, which hides the puppeteer, letting the little figures take all the glory.

Finally, and basically, regardless of the lessons they can teach or inspirations they can provide, puppets are fun. Whether they are kept in a box in the corner of the classroom for playtime, used curricularly for dramatizations and rehearsed performances, or professionally for guided sessions in personal development, puppets are fun to make, fun to be with, and fun to watch. A Festival of the Imagination celebrates how wonderful they really are.

Display

1. Set up a puppet theatre, and paint the name of the festival on the front. Set up a few glove puppets on puppet stands on the stage, and arrange a variety of books on the floor nearby.

2. For a wall display, simulate a shadow play. On a white background, mount black silhouettes of puppets. Encourage the children to come up with ideas for characters, and let them design and make the display. With them, select books to put on a table beneath the artwork.

3. To accompany the display, duplicate instruction sheets for making a simple puppet, such as the jumping jack teddy bear (page 227), or one of the puppets which follow. Place the sheets in a "Take One"

Create a Festive Ambience

Crown a Carousel of Dancing Puppets

Make Dancing Storybook Puppets from card. Refer to Teddy Bear chapter for methods.

Make a crown from card. Draw a pointed design on stiff card. Staple two lengths together to make a bigger carousel. Cover with shiny wrapping paper. Bend into a circle and staple together. Tie three lengths of string at equal intervals onto the side of the crown. Tie the three ends together. Tie them, at the knot, to one long string to hang from the ceiling.

Suspend dancing characters at equal intervals from the crown. Hang the carousel from the ceiling or doorway.

Improvise! Encourage puppet play improvization by placing cardboard box theatres in classrooms & library.

Fill a child's wagon or a colorfully decorated wooden crate or cardboard box with books and glove puppets.

Figure 51

box. Include a bibliography of books about puppetry, folklore, drama, short stories, picture books, or other imagination movers.

Speakers? No!

A speech? No, no! Put on a puppet show! Tap the local grapevine to find a professional puppet troupe in your area, and arrange for them to perform at school, or take the students to them. Subscribe to *The Puppetry Journal,* official magazine of The Puppeteers of America, which lists educational programs, regional and local events, performers, and advisory services. The Puppeteers of America is a non-profit organization with members across the nation and in many foreign countries. Write to them:

> The Puppeteers of America
> Executive Director: Nancy L. Staub
> 2311 Connecticut Avenue
> Apartment 501
> Washington, DC 20008
> Telephone (202) 265-6564

For teachers, conduct a puppetry workshop before the festival. Plan ahead and gather together the necessary materials. Ask colleagues to share their knowledge of puppet making, and spend an afternoon elbow deep in papier mâché, felt, cardboard, or plaster of Paris with interested faculty members. Organize a team to build puppet theatres — from refrigerator boxes, plywood, or old sheets. Invite parent volunteers to help sew glove-puppet bodies. Ask the drama teacher, an English teacher, or another colleague to write a short puppet play. Encourage cross-curricular puppetry—build puppets in art class; in geography, use puppets to teach how other cultures raise crops; dramatize learning through puppets. Most schools offer in-service days to their teaching staff; take advantage of a ready-made slot, and fit into it.

For students, demonstrate some simple puppet building techniques that don't result in a messy aftermath. Puppets can be made from paper plates, cardboard, old socks, and other improbable improvisationals, instructions for which follow.

Making Puppets

1. Make some "creepy crawly" puppets from a piece of card, using anything from the back of a cereal box to artists' board (Figure 52). Before students make theirs, find a good story to read

The Creepy Crawly
needs two human fingers
to take a tabletop stroll.

Figure 52

aloud to them, one which you really enjoy, that could benefit from dramatization with these simple puppets. Make puppet characters yourself, and let them tell the tale.

Give each puppet maker a piece of card about 5 x 7 inches. If necessary, provide a template for artists to trace. This puppet uses two forefingers of a student's hand for either its hands or feet. The holes should be large enough to give the fingers a loose fit. The rest of the puppet is drawn onto the card and cut out.

Talking Tubes

Figure 53

2. A talking puppet can be made from a cardboard tube and a stick (Figure 53). If you are using a long tube from kitchen foil or paper towels, draw the eyes and lips on one end. Then carefully cut the tube apart along a straight line drawn between the lips all around the tube. Tape the stick or dowel inside the back of the top part of the head. To make the puppet talk, hold the bottom part of the face in one hand, and move the stick up and down with the other. If you are using short cardboard tubes (from toilet paper), use two to make one talking face.

Paint the tubes with tempera or acrylics, applied with just a tiny amount of water to keep the cardboard from coming apart. Decorate the puppet with yarn hair and beard, feather head-dresses, fake fur, and scraps of felt or cloth. Make a set of paper teeth to glue behind the lips.

Egg carton Dragon

Figure 54

3. Turn two cardboard egg cartons into a dragon (Figure 54). First, glue the top and bottom of each carton shut, and put a heavy book on top until the glue is dry and fast. Then with an artist's knife, cut off the last two egg cups from each carton to provide a place for your fingers and thumb.

Glue one set of cups onto the top carton to make dragon eyes. The remaining cups become teeth.

Paint the dragon in mysterious colors. Paint scales, stripes, warts, or spots. Give him a fine set of eyebrows by glueing yarn or fake fur to the top of the eyeballs. Provide a goatee by glueing string, yarn, or fake fur to the chin. Make horns by glueing a crescent of cardboard to the top piece behind the eyeballs.

Turn the dragon into a bear by painting it brown or black; a crocodile by painting it green; a vampire by painting it greenish white with black lips and bloodshot eyes.

4. Ask parents to donate odd socks. Turn a sock into a puppet by asking a child to pull it onto one hand (Figure 55). Push the toe of the sock well down into the palm to make a mouth. The puppet is ready in its simplest form.

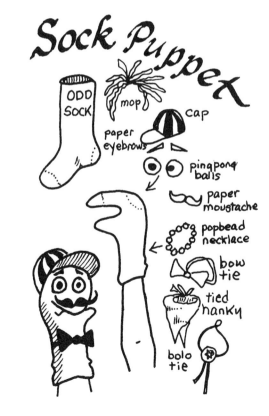

Figure 55

Make eyes by sewing on buttons or by glueing on cut-out felt pieces. Pingpong balls make comic eyes, too. Insert a small, short dowel into the bottom of a ball. With felt tip or enamel paint draw on the pupil. Hold the other end of the dowel between fingers when playing with the sock puppet. Make a tongue, moustache, eyebrows, or hair from felt and yarn. Glue them onto the sock.

Sock puppets work well on feet, too! An inventive performer can work four sock puppets, one on each hand and foot. A stocking cap could bring the number to five.

Figure 56

5. Children can turn their hands into puppets with makeup (Figure 56). Paint lips along the inside edge of thumb and forefinger, and make the mouth move by twiddling the thumb.

Figure 57

6. Turn old gloves into puppets. Make a spider or crab by glueing or sewing eyes onto the back of a glove (Figure 57) and letting it walk across a table. Make a Medusa by putting the eyes in the palm of the glove. Keep a box of old gloves in the library or classroom for puppet improvisation during quiet reading or activity time.

Make Puppet Stands

Puppets can be stored in drawers or boxes, but they make attractive displays and they certainly look inviting to children when they are arranged on shelves, upright on a stand.

1. Fill small plastic jars with sand, and secure the lid. Or use soft drink cans, sealing the top with plastic wrap. Slip glove puppets over them.

2. Drill a hole in the middle of a short plank of wood. Insert a dowel. Pop on a puppet.

3. Hammer a row of nails or picture hooks onto the wall. Sew

a loop onto the back of each puppet's shirt collar and hang them as wall ornaments.

4. Find a tree limb with several branches large enough to support puppets. Put the tree into an umbrella stand, a plant pot, or hang it from the ceiling with fishing line. Suspend puppets, either from loops (like Christmas ornaments), or by slipping them over upright twigs. Turn puppetry into puppet-tree!

Build a Puppet Theatre

For public performances at school, a simple theatre will suffice. Some productions need no theatre at all. Like ventriloquists' dummies, a puppet can be held in the lap, making it fully a partner in story-telling. There are several puppet theatres, however, that are easy to make, and help set the proper ambience for young puppeteers and audiences (Figure 58).

1. Use a *Door Frame*. Attach a sheet or curtain across the door frame high enough to cover the seated or kneeling puppeteers' heads. For extra strength, hang the sheet or curtain from a curtain rod. If the fabric is lightweight, adhesive tape might suffice. Young glove puppeteers tend to rest their hands on the top of the "stage," even if it has no width, so thumb tacks could be the best solution.

2. Perform from a ground floor *Window Sill*. The puppeteers can sit or kneel inside or outside, with the audience seated on the other side. If a backdrop is desired, throw a sheet or curtain over a portable rail for hanging clothes, or over a length of wood suspended from two step ladders.

3. Drape a sheet over a *Table* to hide the puppeteers, and use that as a stage. The advantage of this theatre is that it can hold several props as well as scenery items, such as flower pots with small shrubs and plants, doll's houses, and toy cars.

To make a permanent table theatre from a wooden table, cut out a performing hole, or trap door, from the middle of the surface through which students can manipulate the puppets. Instead of covering the table with a sheet, make a skirt to cover the sides of

Puppet Theatres

Hang a sheet across a doorway between performers and audience.

Puppeteers perform on one side of ground floor window while audience sits on other side

Saw a hole in a wooden tabletop. Hang a sheet around table to conceal puppeteers. Make a proscenium arch from a cardboard box for the top of the table.

A refrigerator box makes a great theatre! Cut out a back door for puppeteers. Cut out a proscenium. Hang a backdrop curtain from a broom handle.

A Plywood Theatre

Three sheets of plywood make a sturdy, long-lasting theatre. Cut out an arch. Attach hinges. Paint. To hang a curtain, put a broom handle over the folded side panels. Keep the handle in place with a cradle — 2 nails driven in upright on each side of the broom.

Figure 58

the table; attach an old sheet with thumb tacks. This table theatre can make use of a *Cardboard Box Proscenium Arch*. Find a suitable box at a grocery store, preferably one that is taller than it is wide. From one of the tall sides, cut an archway.

Trace the performing hole onto the bottom of the box, and cut it out with a sharp artist's knife.

Paint the box creatively. Look at examples of model theatres or photographs of European opera houses to find an extravagant design. Paint the interior one color.

To secure the box to the table, attach Velcro to the bottom corners and to the table.

4. Make a floor-length theatre from a *Refrigerator Box* (Figure 58). Cut out an opening above children's head height when seated. Cut out a door opening in the back. Cut out two circular holes near the top of the box so that a broom handle can be inserted parallel to the stage opening to provide a curtain backdrop.

Paint the box creatively, using latex paints. Tempera paints can be used to add decorative touches cheaply.

5. A *Portable Wooden Theatre* can be made from three pieces of plywood, four hinges, and optional decorative wooden molding, shutters, or stage.

Determine the height and width you require, and order the wood accordingly. Use an electric jigsaw to simplify the cutting of the proscenium. Two- or three-ply sheets may benefit from being nailed to a simple wooden framework for added stability. This will also reduce the chances of warping. Heavier plywoods should not require a frame.

Attach the side pieces with hinges so that when not in use the theatre may be folded flat. Backstage, screw in cup hooks for holding puppets, props, or scripts.

Puppet Activities

Quiet Improvisation

During this festival, puppets need to be freely available in classrooms, drama or movement areas, and in libraries for play, improvisation, and practice. Besides the puppets which children make during workshops, there ought to be a collection of glove puppets on hand which can be used, either with an adult's permission, or as part of a free activity box. Set aside special times each day leading up to the festival for imaginative play with puppets.

To make the puppets even more special, cover their storage box with bright paper and give it a title, such as "The Festival Box." Sew string loops onto the backs of the puppets so they can hang on the wall. Use projects from other festivals (such as the Tennessee log house, pp. 57ff., or the Shaker oval box, pp. 113–116) in conjunction with puppets. Make a fake TV from a cardboard box by cutting out an open "screen" on the front. Display the puppets there. Cut a hole in the bottom of the box, too, so puppeteers can make their own television specials.

Storytelling

To stimulate creative puppetry, adult storytellers can choose tales which lend themselves to dramatization with puppets. Choice of stories is, of course, up to the teller. They should be stories which the teller particularly enjoys, and which have been rehearsed before public telling, so that the puppet doesn't get in the way.

Some storytellers like to introduce the puppets before the telling begins, and hand the puppets to willing members of the audience, seated closely at the teller's feet. This gives the adult a chance to explain a little about how to handle a puppet carefully as well as telling something about how the puppet was made or where it came from. The teller may ask the listeners with the puppets to manipulate them while the story is told, or he may ask for them back so that he can use them himself.

Following the telling, it is good to ask the listeners to dramatize the story again, using the glove puppets, assuming character voices, and narrating. If the storyline gets lost, the adult can step in to help. Alternatively, instead of trying to recall the original tale, young puppeteers can invent another episode.

Following the story, and if there are enough puppets to go around the group, students can divide into Theatrical Teams or Puppet Partnerships to plan a play. The leader may want to suggest a theme, such as "Checking Out a Book," or "Too Much Homework!" or "The Three Little Pigs." Give the students five minutes to plan, improvise, and get into their characters. Then ask them to perform in the puppet theatre.

Some Literary Sources

The following books provide plenty of room for creative puppetry. In all cases, the stories contain lively, animated characters that youngsters love to impersonate in play, and in some cases the illustrations will inspire puppet theatre designers to make colorful backdrops.

In using these and other books for puppet shows, the stories may be presented verbatim by dividing the words into narrative and dialogue for several puppeteers. Alternatively, they may be rewritten, turning all the narrative into dialogue. Finally, they may be totally rewritten for performance, especially when long stories need to be condensed.

Ainsworth, Ruth. *Three Bags Full*. London: Heinemann, 1975.
Intended for adults working with children, this book is a lighthearted collection of activities, stories, riddles, and jokes that are ideal for enlivening puppetry.

Chase, Richard. *The Jack Tales*. Boston: Houghton Mifflin, 1971.
Eighteen Southern Appalachian tales provide roles for tricksters, singers, kings, and narrators. The interesting use of repeating rhymes and charms (such as "Tie, strop, tie; break, strop, break" in "Jack and the Bull") can involve audience participation.

Courlander, Harold, and George Herzog. *The Cowtail Switch*. New York: Holt, Rinehart, and Winston, 1966.
These West African stories give great scope for a variable number of human and animal puppets.

Feuerlicht, Roberta. *The Legends of Paul Bunyan*. Illustrated by Kurt Werth. New York: Collier, 1966.
Tall tales from the American forests provide adventuresome settings for puppet adaptations.

Harris, Joel Chandler. *The Favorite Uncle Remus*. Cambridge, Mass.: The Riverside Press, 1948.
Adapt animal characters to puppets available in the classroom;

i.e., Brer Fox can become Brer Dog: Brer Bear can be Sis Cat. Make or adapt existing puppets to fit the original stories.

Kehret, Peg. *Encore! More Winning Monologs for Young Actors.* Colorado Springs: Meriwether Publications, 1988.
Sixty-three "honest-to-life" monologs for teenage boys and girls bring out the humor and pathos of growing up. They are good starting points for puppet productions for older youngsters, and for creative script writing ideas.

Kipling, Rudyard. *The Jungle Book.* London: Macmillan, 1975.
These classic fables are thrilling stories, with a host of animal characters to animate with puppets.

Oxenbury, Helen. *The Helen Oxenbury Nursery Story Book.* New York: Alfred A. Knopf, 1985.
Ten tales, including Little Red Riding Hood, Henny Penny, and Goldilocks, are fun and easy to adapt into puppet shows. Look at the illustrations for ideas on simple props and backdrops.

Prokofiev, Sergei. *Peter and the Wolf.* Translated by Maria Carlson. New York: Viking, 1982.
The Russian-inspired illustrations by Charles Mikolaycak will inspire set designers for a puppet show about a young hero who saves his friends. Here the wolf does not die, but goes to live in a zoo.

Rice, Eve. *Once in a Wood: Ten Tales from Aesop.* New York: Green Willow Books, 1979.
This beginning reader offers simple, exciting retellings of sly, antic tales with lively animals.

Sarnoff, Jane, and Reynold Ruffins. *Take Warning: A Book of Superstition.* New York: Charles Scribner's Sons, 1978.
This entertaining alphabetical listing of superstitions could form the basis for a creative class puppet show called "Luck," "Dreams," or "Walking Under Ladders."

Sendak, Maurice. *Where The Wild Things Are.* New York: Harper and Row, 1963.

The tale of mischievous Max who, being sent to bed without any supper, meets various monsters in an exciting series of adventures, makes for an excellent puppet adaptation, perhaps using the commercially available Wild Things dolls.

Tolkien, J. R. R. *The Father Christmas Letters*. London: George Allen and Unwin, Ltd., 1976.

Warm-hearted letters that could be adapted for reading by a genial Santa puppet and a variety of helpers. Children in the classroom can write letters to fit in with Father Christmas' answers. Tolkien's colorful illustrations provide outstanding ideas for theatre backdrops.

White, E. B. *Charlotte's Web*. New York: Harper and Row, 1980.

This beloved story of a farm girl and the pig she loves offers several human characters as well as numerous animals for a puppet show.

Let the Students Choose

No matter how many lists of good books appear, some personal favorites will inevitably be omitted. Therefore, instead of directing the students' choice of literature for adaptation into a puppet play, divide them into interest groups (Animals, Outdoor Adventure, Christmas Holiday, and so forth) to select their own books. Or hold a round table discussion with an entire class to come up with a variety of titles. Write the choices on the board, and ask students to vote on one, two, or three titles to dramatize. Following this, students can divide into troupes to work on dramatizing the book of their choice.

Integrate Puppets into the Curriculum

Either as a required assignment or for extra credit in language arts or social studies, ask students to write scenes in the lives of historical characters currently being studied. Since these scenes are not likely to be humorous, such an assignment will give students a chance to work with puppets in a documentary manner that is entertaining without being comic. Depending upon the characters and the situation, the scenes may indeed by very serious.

Examples:

Topic	Write and perform a short play about:
1. Studying ancient Greece	Persephone, Zeus, Hercules, or another set of gods.
2. Studying ancient Egypt	a particular pharoah; Moses; an event in the lives of the gods.
3. Studying Native Americans	the coming of Europeans; Hiawatha; a famous leader, such as Crazy Horse.
4. Studying westward expansion	wagon train expeditions; frontier villages; prairie farming.

In primary level math, students can teach what they know about addition or subtraction through puppets. Suggest simple scenarios in which one puppet goes shopping. How many apples will she buy? How much money will she need? Does she have enough money left over to buy a candy bar? In health units, puppets can portray medical professionals who bring patients relief from colds and injury. Puppets can describe what it feels like to be ill or to feel healthy because of nutritious eating, exercise, and a proper balance of sports, study, and relaxation.

During health classes, students can discuss the nature of puppets: they are operated by a puppeteer. Without a puppeteer, they have no life of their own. Can people be like puppets? When is it good to be controlled by another person? What is the difference between obeying rules and being a human puppet?

Creative Writing

Following improvisations of puppet plays, ask students to write down what they have done in script form. Make this easier for those who have difficulty in writing, by giving them a tape recorder to use during the improvisations.

Form small teams with the assigned task of producing a completed play script. Each script must have:

1. A title
2. A list of characters
3. A synopsis of the story
4. Stage directions to help future puppeteers (optional)
5. Correct format—not written in paragraphs, but in script style, with name of character in capital letters on the left margin, followed by a colon. A standard indentation follows that, followed by the lines to be spoken.
6. Multiple copies of the script should be provided, either by computer printer, photocopy, or ditto sheets.

Each team is then responsible for performing the script, using existing puppets or ones which they make, in a puppet theatre of their choice.

For additional fun, swap scripts among teams, and ask them to perform a play written by a different group.

The Main Event: An Evening of Puppets

While the festival includes much preparatory work, build the main event around a series of puppet shows. Classes can divide into production crews, with each student responsible for different chores: building or repainting the puppet theatre, making or refurbishing a puppet, finding or writing a script, manipulating the puppets, finding or making sound effects and music, printing a program, making posters, or painting scenery—with as much or as little help from adults as required. During the festival, schedule as many puppet shows as possible.

When each participating class has refined and polished its puppet show through rehearsals and performances during school, present them all at a special Parents Night to showcase the students' achievements. Puppet shows can be scheduled to occur simultaneously in different rooms, followed by a refreshment break. Performances can be repeated at intervals so that audiences can see two or three plays during the evening, culminating with one big show for everybody in the library or other assembly point. An evening might be arranged something like this:

6:45	Assemble in Library. Welcome from Principal. Students from each production team speak briefly about their plays.
7:00	Performance Period One: Members of the audience go to one of several puppet plays on offer.
7:20	Refreshments. Cake, cookies, fruit juices, and coffee in the dining area. Audience and performers come in when plays finish.
7:40	Performance Period Two: Members of the audience choose another play to watch.
8:00	Performance Period Three: All members of the audience return to Library (or go to large assembly room) to watch one longer puppet play.

A similar daytime agenda can enable students to enjoy each other's puppet shows. Schedule performances every half hour in the library, or invite audiences to go from room to room.

When students have dramatized a book, their source of inspiration should be on display in the performance area. Alternatively, the library could display all the source books in a central location, and the librarian could call attention to them during the opening remarks. Students' relevant drawings and written work should also be on show.

To scale down the puppet presentations, schedule a puppet show as a preliminary event for a bigger school drama production. Coordinate with the drama director to set up a puppet play in a classroom, foyer, or theatre as the audience for the main production assembles.

EDIBLE TREATS: Puppet Cookies

Making puppets you can eat is a fun festival project, providing creative fun through designing puppet templates, mixing the ingredients, cutting out the puppets, and assembling them into "dancing figures" when they are finished.

Templates should be fairly simple, with soft curvilinear edges, rather like the Jumping Teddy on pages 225–230. Puppet cookies can be clowns, animals, or human beings, each with separate arms and legs, and a single-piece head and torso. Students can even paint features on their edible puppets with a culinary version of Renaissance egg tempera.

Teachers and librarians will want to practice this recipe at home first in order to make samples to bring to school.

What You Need:

3/4 cup softened butter or margarine
1/2 cup sugar
1 beaten egg
2 tsps grated lemon (or lime) zest (rind)
1 Tbsp freshly squeezed lemon (or lime) juice
1/3 cup crystallized (candied) ginger
1 pinch ground cinnamon
3-1/2 cups all-purpose flour
1 tsp baking powder
1/4 tsp salt

Egg Yolk Paint:
1 egg yolk
1/4 tsp water
Paste food coloring (assorted colors)

Mixing bowls and spoons
Electric hand-held mixer
Lightly floured rolling surface
Rolling pin
Greased cookie sheets
Saucers or small cups (to hold food color mixtures)
Small paintbrushes
Small ribbons (to tie cookie puppet together)

What You Do:

Finely chop the crystallized ginger into small fragments.

Beat the butter or margarine until it is creamy. Gradually add sugar, beating until mixture is fluffy. Stir in the egg, zest, juice, and finely chopped ginger.

Mix flour, baking powder, and salt. Add to butter mixture, blending well. Divide the dough in half, cover, and chill for about an hour in the refrigerator.

Mix the paint: combine the egg and water, and mix thoroughly. Divide the mixture into as many small cups or saucers as you have paste food colors. Create dark or light color tints by varying the amount of color you add to each saucer. Cover until ready to use. If the mixtures dry out, add a few drops of water and stir.

Preheat oven to 425 degrees F, 220 C.

Roll one half of the dough on a lightly floured surface until it is about 1/8 inch (3 cm) thick. Place templates on dough and cut around them with a sharp knife. With a spatula, place the cut-outs two inches (4 cm) apart on a greased cookie sheet. With a drinking straw, cut out holes in each shape (for the ribbon to be added after cookies are cooled).

With small paint brush, paint appropriate designs on the shapes: facial features, bow ties, buttons, vests, shoes, trousers, shirts, hair.

Bake for 6 to 8 minutes, or until they are golden brown. Remove to wire racks, and cool.

Repeat with next batch of dough.

When cookies are thoroughly cool, assemble shapes into puppets and tie together with small ribbons, just as arms and legs were attached to the jumping Teddies with paper fasteners.

The Duchess Comes to Tea
A Play for Seven Puppets and One Human Being

This comic play, in the folktale tradition yet tinged with modern humor, is set in Freddie's house. He invites the Duchess for a light snack. She misinterprets his intentions and falls starry-eyed in love. Meanwhile, Freddie is accused of stealing a pie from the store. Maybe the mail man can help Freddie out of both these tricky situations.

The Duchess Comes to Tea was prepared through improvisations with third and fourth graders at the American School in London, and written in its final form by Alan Heath. Improvisations began with reading several of Beatrix Potter's tales with dramatic puppetry, and went on to include rewatching some of the old Muppet TV series on video, and finished with a visit to Shakespeare's *A Midsummer Night's Dream*. From many sources, then, comes *The Duchess*.

The Characters

Master of Ceremonies—a human being, dressed colorfully and with an impressive voice. The M.C. stands beside the puppet theatre, and when not required may sit in a chair near the stage. One of the M.C.'s valuable functions is picking up any props that fall from the puppets' hands onto the floor and out of their reach.

Freddie—the hero, who may be an animal or human puppet. He was originally a fox puppet; omit or change references to foxes in the script if your Freddie is something else.

Savoy—Freddie's butler, who should speak with a very reserved, educated accent.

The Duchess—a fine lady, whom no one loves romantically. In the first performance of this play, she was a beautiful rabbit.

Melinda Louise—the Duchess' maid, a smart cookie.

The Postman—an excellent message carrier.

The Shopkeeper—an old-fashioned sort of guy.

Sludge—the clerk in the Shopkeeper's store.

Props Required

A letter from Freddie
A letter from the Duchess
An overcooked pie (modeling clay or papier mâché)
A succulent pie
A cardboard sword

Scene One: In Freddie's Study

	The puppet stage is empty. The Master of Cer- *emonies walks in. He or she may have the lines* *written down on a scroll of paper, to add to the* *effect. As the M.C. says the opening remarks,* *the puppets may pop up for a bow.*
M.C.:	Ladies and gentlemen, welcome to our play! The action occurs in the following way— Our Hero, Sir Freddie Fox, Esquire, Honored gentleman of the shire, Is about to have an afternoon tea party— Cakes, sandwiches, milk; you know, a hearty Feast of good things to eat. His guest? A lady so very neat! She is a Duchess in fact. So now, let's let the actors start to act!
FREDDIE:	(Reading letter which he has in his hand) "Dear Duchess"—or should I say *Dearest* Duchess? . . . What do you think, Savoy?
SAVOY:	Well, sir, I should not put in "Dearest." She will think you are in love with her.
FREDDIE:	What! That will never do! I'll just leave it the way it is, then. Shall I continue to read, Savoy?
SAVOY:	If it makes you happy, sir, by all means. Do carry on.
FREDDIE:	Now where was I . . . oh, yes! "Dear Duchess, Will you come to tea with me today? Come early, my dear Duchess, and we will have something so very nice that you will just flip. I am baking it in a pie-dish. You have never tasted anything so good. And you can eat it all yourself! I, myself, shall eat muffins. Sin cerely yours, Freddie Fox." Now that sounds like a good letter to me! I'll just phone the postman and ask him to deliver it.
SAVOY:	Shall I take it to the post office, sir?
FREDDIE:	Well, if you don't mind . . .
POSTMAN:	(Popping up most suddenly) You rang?

FREDDIE:	Gosh! That was quick!
POSTMAN:	We always aim to please, sir.
	Through thick and through thin,
	I am always in
	The mood to deliver letters.
	May I take yours?
FREDDIE:	Yes, this is for the Duchess!
	So be quick!
	(All puppets leave immediately. The Postman pops back up, letter in hand to begin the next scene.)

Scene Two: At the Duchess' Palace

POSTMAN:	*(Moving back and forth across the stage)* Now where is that Duchess? Her palace must be around here someplace. (Optional Scenery effect: Hold up sign on which is written Soggy Swamp Palace. This may be placed on stage by M.C. or held up by crew backstage.)
POSTMAN:	Ah! Here it is. SOGGY SWAMP PALACE, home of the Duchess of Soggy Swamp. I shall just rap politely on the door.
	(Sound effect backstage: knock three times. Or rig up doorbell chimes.)
MELINDA LOU:	*(Yells from backstage loudly)* Yeah, who is it? What do you want this time of the morning?
POSTMAN:	'Tis I, the postman, with a letter for you.
MELINDA:	*(Pops up quickly)* A letter for ME?
	Oh, my goodness gracious! Let me have it!
	(She grabs letter from postman.)
MELINDA:	Oh, you silly mail man! This is for the Duchess, not for me!
POSTMAN:	Well, aren't you the Duchess?
MELINDA:	Oh, everybody says I'm far prettier than the Duchess, and of course that is very true. But no, alas, I am a mere maid.
POSTMAN:	Then give me back that letter.
	It's private!

MELINDA:	No, no. Just trust me, my dear man. I'll give the Duchess the letter myself. *(Turns and yells backstage, as if Duchess were downstairs)* Your grace! There is a man here for you!
DUCHESS:	*(Below stage)* A MAN? For ME? I'll be right there! *(She pops up.)*
POSTMAN:	*(Bowing.)* Hello, Your Highness. I have a letter for you.
DUCHESS:	But I never get any mail! Give it to me, quickly. Now! Do you understand?
POSTMAN:	Here it is, your worship.
DUCHESS:	Gosh, how exciting! A letter for me?
MELINDA:	Shall I read it to you, Your Excellence? You know how tired your eyes are!
DUCHESS:	Nonsense, you stupid girl! Get down from here this instant. *(Melinda bows and leaves.)*
DUCHESS:	Good help is SO hard to find these days. Now let me read . . . *(Postman transfers letter to Duchess. M.C. may need to help.)*
DUCHESS:	"Dear Duchess, will you come to tea with me today . . ." Oh, hooray! I haven't been out of the palace for so long! *(Postman starts to leave.)* No, no! Postman, don't leave! Hold on a second! I'll send a reply. *(Duchess leaves, returning immediately with her letter to Freddie.)* Here, take this letter to that dear Fox, and assure him that I shall come to tea with him! *(Duchess exits; postman bows to her. Then he walks back and forth across stage to indicate journey back to Freddie's house. Remove sign for Soggy Swamp Palace.)*

Scene Three: Freddie's House

POSTMAN:	*(Sound effect: three knocks backstage as postman knocks at Freddie's house)* Hellooooooo, down there! Freddie!

	Here's the reply from the Duchess!
FREDDIE:	*(Popping up)* Thank you, my good man! Here, let me read it! "My dear Freddie, I will be at your house at three o'clock, so be sure to have the eats ready by then. I prefer very hot tea in china cups. I can't wait to sink my teeth into one of your scrummy cakes. Yours with love and kisses, The Duchess." Gosh, I hadn't counted on giving her any cakes!
SAVOY:	*(Popping up quickly)* Shall I go and tell her Duchessness that you won't be supplying any cakes?
FREDDIE:	Oh, no, that would never do! I'll just let her *think* she'll get cakes. But, Postman, go and tell her that I *am* giving her a special pie, and she will love it more than anything she has ever sunk her fangs into.
POSTMAN:	Through fire, and rain, and ice and snow, I carry the mail. Just watch me go! *(Freddie and Savoy leave. Postman walks animatedly back and forth across stage to indicate journey.)*
POSTMAN:	A mail man could certainly get tired quickly around here. Thank goodness I'm in good shape! I jog every morning. Lift weights every night. Eat health foods three times a day. *(Sign for Soggy Swamp Palace appears.)* Ah, here we are at the palace. Hellooooo, down there, Your Highness. I have a message from the Fox. About the tea.
MELINDA:	*(Pops up quickly)* You naughty man, you must *never* yell at Her Eminence that way! It's very rude.
DUCHESS:	*(Pops up)* Never mind, Melinda Louise. I'm always happy to have visitors, especially ones as handsome as this postman. Just look at those muscles.
POSTMAN:	Er, your Grace, I have a message.

DUCHESS:	Another letter? For me?
POSTMAN:	Well, sort of. Only this letter isn't written down. Freddie Fox says to tell you that he isn't giving you any cake.
DUCHESS:	*(faint sigh)* Ohhh!
POSTMAN:	Only pie.
MELINDA:	Pie?
POSTMAN:	Special pie for the Duchess alone.
DUCHESS:	Oh, well. That will have to do, then. But, you don't suppose it's made of rabbit, do you? I can't stand RABBIT. Especially after that awful fox caught my cousin Benjamin Bunny and turned him into a casserole!
POSTMAN:	Don't know, your Grace. I only wish *I* had an invitation to tea. *(Starts to leave)*
DUCHESS:	Oh, Melinda Louise! How exciting! Only I do hope it isn't rabbit pie!
MELINDA:	Maybe he's making a mushroom pie.
DUCHESS:	Or a potato pie. I just love vegetables. They make my skin so soft. But I must get dressed now. You know, powder my nose, adjust my crown, and so forth. I just mustn't be late. *(Duchess and Melinda make their exit. Remove Palace Sign.)*
M.C.:	Meanwhile, back in the home of Freddie Fox, disaster is just around the corner!

Scene Four: Freddie's house

FREDDIE:	Oh dear, oh dear, oh dear. I've burned my pie in the oven!
SAVOY:	*(Comes up holding blackened pie.)* The crust is rather well done, sir.
FREDDIE:	Oh, dear! It was the Duchess' favorite pie, too —RABBIT! Just caught it myself yesterday.
SAVOY:	*(Leaves, taking pie with him.)* Sorry, sir.
FREDDIE:	What shall I do? I guess I'll just have to go to the store and buy some cakes, and pretend that everything is ok. *(He leaves, and as he does, he says:)* Oh dear, oh dear.

Scene Five: The Grocery Store

	The Shopkeeper, Mr. Grocer, comes on stage carrying the good pie. To set the scene, prepare a sign *(optional)* with appropriate words, such as "Mr. Grocer's Store. Special today, Rabbit Pie."
SHOPKEEPER:	Oh, it is *so* pleasant here in my store! I have everything that anybody could want! Too bad I haven't any customers! But what's this! Somebody's coming!!
FREDDIE:	Hello, Mr. Grocer! Do you have any delicious pies? The Duchess is coming to tea, and I must have the very best!
SHOPKEEPER:	Do I have pies! Do *I* have *pies*? My boy, just look at this! The very juiciest Rabbit Pie!
FREDDIE:	Perfect! How much is it?
SHOPKEEPER:	Five grockels! Take it or leave it.
FREDDIE:	Isn't that a bit expensive? I had something cheaper in mind.
SHOPKEEPER:	Well, I do have some mushroom pancakes. They're ten demi-grockels each. And — wait a minute! I'll call my assistant. SLUDGE, come up here this instant!
FREDDIE:	What are those things over there in the counter?
SHOPKEEPER:	Fried toad-stools. Delicious. And they come with my special sauce.
FREDDIE:	What's in the sauce?
SHOPKEEPER:	Toe Jam. Now where is that assistant? SLUDGE, GET UP HERE!
SLUDGE:	*(Comes up slowly; he sounds sleepy.)* Did you call me?
SHOPKEEPER:	Go and find something nice for Sir Freddie. At once, do you hear me?
SLUDGE:	What sort of something nice?
FREDDIE:	Something fit to serve the Duchess. She is coming to tea with me.
SLUDGE:	What, that old bean bag?

SHOPKEEPER: *(Slaps Sludge.)* Why, you naughty boy! Go and wash your mouth out. But first, you must apologize to Freddie!

FREDDIE: No, no, that isn't necessary. I'll just take the Rabbit Pie, even though your price is very steep.

SHOPKEEPER: *(handing Freddie the pie)* You won't regret it, Freddie Fox. Enjoy!

FREDDIE: *(Grabs pie and leaves quickly)* Thanks!

SHOPKEEPER: Hey, come back! Where's my money? Sludge, after him! He's stolen the pie!
(Mr. Grocer leaves; Sludge stays up.)

SLUDGE: What's all the rush? It was only a pie. But now that we're here, I think I'll recite a poem that I learned in school. Do you mind?
(M.C. starts to interrupt, but Sludge clears his throat loudly, and begins to recite. If your Freddie is not a fox, you'll need to change some of the words to fit.)
Foxes are a dirty breed that look a lot like dogs.
Never trust them with a pie.
They're worse than thieving hogs.
They'll come into a grocery store,
And run away with pies.
It takes a man—a man like me!
To cut them down to size!
(Sludge takes a big bow and leaves.)

M.C.: Sorry about that intrusion, folks.
It wasn't a very good poem, and we certainly don't want you to think it was part of our show. Any dogs and foxes, not to mention swine, in the audience, please accept our apologies. Let's go back, and see how Freddie is getting on back at his house.

Scene Six: Freddie's House

FREDDIE: Ah, how nice to be home, and in time to get rid of my burnt pie. The Duchess will be here in no time.

	(Sound effect: loud knock at the door.)
DUCHESS:	*(Popping up)* Hello there, dear Freddie. I hope you don't mind. I just let myself in.
FREDDIE:	*(bowing)* Oh, Your Grace! I am so happy that you could come to tea! I have the most delicious pie!
DUCHESS:	I can't wait to sink my teeth into it, dear. I only hope it isn't rabbit.
FREDDIE:	Rabbit?
DUCHESS:	It *isn't* rabbit, is it?
FREDDIE:	*(Leans far over stage to talk to audience or M.C.)* Oh no! She doesn't like RABBIT! What am I going to do? *(Sound effect: Loud knocking and banging backstage.)*
SHOPKEEPER:	*(Backstage, yelling)* Freddie Fox, Freddie Fox! Come here at once! You've stolen my pie!
FREDDIE:	Rats! That nasty grocer has followed me home!
DUCHESS:	Did I hear correctly? You've *stolen* a pie?
FREDDIE:	No, no, your Serene Majesty! He said that, uh, that he sells *swollen* pies. You know, fat pies. That's it, fat pies. And his pies *are* very fat, I must say, heh, heh, heh.
SHOPKEEPER:	*(Popping up)* Freddie Fox, give me my money, or I'll box your ears!
FREDDIE:	Whatever do you mean?
SHOPKEEPER:	On guard, you thief! *(Starts to pounce on Freddie.)*
FREDDIE:	Savoy, bring me my sword at once!
DUCHESS:	Oh, you lovely men! Always fighting! Isn't it romantic!?
SAVOY:	*(Bringing up cardboard sword)* Here you are, sir.
FREDDIE:	All right, Grocer! Beware the fury of an angered Fox!
DUCHESS:	Boys, boys! Stop this at once!
SHOPKEEPER:	That Fox stole my pie, and it's here. I can smell it *(loud sniffs as he searches for it)*.
DUCHESS:	But, surely—
SHOPKEEPER:	*(Bowing low.)* Hello, your Duchessness. Sorry to disturb the tea party, but I must warn you. I will not rest until that pie is paid for!

DUCHESS: Oh, never mind about that! Just add the pie to my account.

SHOPKEEPER: But you don't have an account.

DUCHESS: Then I'll start one. I'll pay for it later. But only, Freddie Fox, if—

FREDDIE: Yes, your sublime highness?

DUCHESS: Only if you'll—marry me!!

FREDDIE: What! Marry you? A tea party is one thing, but marriage is another. Never! I'd sooner marry a fence-post! *(He runs off.)*

DUCHESS: Oh, well. Just thought I'd try. But now that we two are alone *(she moves close to the grocer),* let's have tea by ourselves. Isn't it romantic?

SHOPKEEPER: But are you still going to pay for my pie?

DUCHESS: Of course.

SHOPKEEPER: OK, then, let's eat! *(They both go beneath stage, where loud munching and gobbling sounds are heard.)*

DUCHESS: *(Pops up)* Oh, horrors! This is RABBIT pie! I hate rabbit pie!

SHOPKEEPER: *(Pops up)* But I *like* rabbit pie! Let's eat!

DUCHESS: Well . . . only if you'll marry me.

SHOPKEEPER: What! Marry you! Rabbit pie is one thing, but marriage is another! Marry you?
Not on your nelly. Goodbye! (exits)

DUCHESS: Oh, dear. And just when things were going so well, too.
(Sound effect: loud knocking at door.)

DUCHESS: Where is that Savoy? Surely *he* can open the door! *(Knocking again.)*
All right, I'm coming, I'm coming! Who is it?

POSTMAN: *(Popping up.)* Only the mail man again. But this time no letters. I'm just hanging around outside, I mean, I'm just passing by, and thought you could spare a bit of that pie.

DUCHESS: Oh, my darling man, of course! Do come in! I was just about to get married. I mean, er, I was just about to eat. So help yourself to the pie. It's down there in the kitchen.
(Postman exits. Makes lots of gurgling, slurping, munching sounds.)

DUCHESS:	He certainly is making a pig of himself.
POSTMAN:	*(Pops up)* Yum, was that good or what?
DUCHESS:	You mean you ate the whole thing?
POSTMAN:	No, no. Only the crust and the filling.
DUCHESS:	That *was* the whole thing, you dummy!
POSTMAN:	Oh, no, your Grace. I didn't eat the plate.
DUCHESS:	Well, I forgive you. If, that is . . .
POSTMAN:	Yesss?
DUCHESS:	If you'll . . . marry me.
POSTMAN:	What! Marry you? Pie is one thing, but marriage is another! I'd rather deliver letters in a howling blizzard! Goodbye! *(Quick exit)*
DUCHESS:	How sad I am! Will no one marry me? After all, I *am* rather beautiful. What's wrong with me? Why won't somebody marry me?
SAVOY:	Roses are red, violets are blue. You have a big mouth, So nobody wants to marry you. Also, marriage ain't everything.
DUCHESS:	If there is anyone in the audience who would like to come to tea with me after the show, and wouldn't mind potato pie, I shall be at home. Come by, have a bit of food, and we can discuss marriage. *(She leaves)*
SAVOY:	That's all, folks. *(exit)*
M.C.:	But not quite all. The moral of this tale is plain to see. Whenever you invite someone to tea Never serve them rabbit pie.
ALL:	Why? *(All characters appear on stage)*
M.C.:	Like the Duchess, they may not like it. They may prefer some sausage, or a little bit Of gravy poured over rice. Come to think of it, They may want a cube of ice. But moral number two is more important still. When your guests have eaten their fill Of cakes and pies of fresh strawberries—
GROCER:	Never ask them if they want to marry.
MELINDA:	Marriage is one sure way to kill a party dead.

FREDDIE: Many prefer to remain single instead.
ALL: At least for a while.
M.C.:   Now the play is over,
                     And you may clap your hands.
                     Applause is sweeter to us actors
                     Than the sound of brass bands.
                     (M.C. and puppets bow. M.C. steps to one side, extending hand to acknowledge puppets and elicit more applause from audience. M.C. leaves, puppets withdraw.)

Sources of Inspiration

Puppets

Allan, Ray. *Gottle o' Geer!* London: Pagoda Books, 1987.
    Here are the tricks of ventriloquism, including how to talk without moving your lips, how to make a talking doll, and how to make several types of puppet.

Allport, Alan J. *Model Theaters and How to Make Them.* New York: Charles Scribner's Sons, 1978.
    Written by a British paper sculptor and former Royal Air Force officer, this book captures the magic of theater through clear-cut instructions and illustrations for making miniature paper models. He uses *The Merchant of Venice, Romeo and Juliet,* and *A Midsummer Night's Dream* to illustrate construction of stage scenery and rod puppets.

Amery, Heather. *The Know-How Make and Do Encyclopedia.* London: Usborne, 1972.
    This crafty book tells how to make games, working models from paper and wood, and, best of all, puppets.

Bainbridge, Cecil. *Hand Puppets.* London: Museum Press, 1968.
    Using the patterns shown here, teachers and students can devise their own puppet characters.

Byrom, Michael. *Punch in the Italian Puppet Theatre.* London: Centaur, 1983.
    This very readable history of Italian puppetry includes several

practical play scripts that bring the traditional Punch/Pulcinello to life.

Currell, David. *The Complete Book of Puppet Theatre.* London: A. and C. Black, 1985.
This encyclopedic book includes a superb history of puppets and puppet-craft, chapters on puppets in schools and special education, puppet design, control, and manipulation, organization techniques for putting on a puppet show, and interviews with master puppeteers.

————. *Learning With Puppets: Practical Guidelines for Primary and Middle Schools.* London: Ward Lock Educational, 1980.
Following a very helpful section on puppetry in education, Currell describes how to make puppets in schools.

Dean, Audrey Vincente. *Puppets That Are Different.* London: Faber and Faber, 1973.
Here are puppets with moving mouths (Sad Blue Hound Dog) and moving legs (Hoppy Rabbit), puppet toys (Kangaroo and Baby), and instructions for casting a folktale.

Fettig, Hansjurgen. *Hand and Rod Puppets: A Handbook of Technique.* Boston: Plays, 1973.
Find out how to construct and manipulate glove and mechanical puppets that mimic various human traits and postures in this very sophisticated book, best suited for adults with some basic knowledge of woodwork.

Green, M.C. *Space Age Puppets and Masks.* London: George Harrap, 1969.
Anyone who has ever wondered what to do with everyday odds and ends around the house will find an entertaining solution in this book which helps teachers and students create out-of-the-ordinary puppets.

Hawkesworth, Eric. *Puppet Shows to Make: How to Entertain with All Kinds of Puppets.* London: Faber and Faber, 1972.
Ideas for Punch and Judy portable puppet booths, finger puppet theatres, TV shadow puppets, rod puppets, and more puppet ex-

plorations make this detailed book an especially valuable asset to a teacher.

Henson Associates. *The Art of the Muppets: A Retrospective Look at Twenty-five Years of Muppet Magic*. New York: Bantam, 1980.
Take an enjoyable look at the many puppets made by Jim Henson and his staff since 1955, including, of course, Miss Piggy and Kermit the Frog.

Jackson, Sheila. *Simple Puppetry*. London: Studio Vista, 1969.
Line drawings and text show how to make a variety of simple puppets from cloth and wood.

Jagendorf, Moritz. *Puppets for Beginners*. Illus. by Jean Michener. Boston: Plays, 1952.
Patterns and instructions help children and their teachers make simple and advanced puppets and marionettes, construct stages, scenery, and props, and improvise and write plays.

Lasky, Kathryn. *Puppeteer*. Photos by Christopher G. Knight. New York: Macmillan, 1985.
Follow professional puppet maker Paul Davis's year in the creation of hand puppets for "Aladdin and His Wonderful Lamp," from research and script writing to costuming, scenery, and performances.

Lynch-Watson, Janet. *The Shadow Puppet Book*. New York: Sterling, 1980.
This exciting book gives idea after idea for making shadow puppets and theatres, along with plays and music and songs to sing, with complete patterns, plans and text.

Moloney, Joan. *Making Puppets and Puppet Theatres*. New York: Fell, 1974.
After describing how to make traditional and modern puppets, Moloney shows how to construct a theatre and a stage.

Morton, Brenda. *Sleeve Puppets*. Illus. by Juliet Renny. London: Faber and Faber, 1978.
Mischievous or mournful, appealing or appalling, sleeve pup-

pets from Big Bad Bertie to Cock-a-Doodle-Do can be made from the easy-to-follow instructions here.

Paluden, Lis. *Playing with Puppets*. London: Mills and Boon, 1974.
Ideal for schools, this fully illustrated book shows how to make and use finger puppets, hand puppets, glove puppets, animal puppets, rod puppets, dancing puppets, and scenery to go with them.

Payne, G. C. *Fun with Paper Modeling*. Harmondsworth, England: Penguin, 1966.
Make puppets, other toys, and games.

Philpott. A. R. *Let's Make Puppets: Starting Points*. London: Evans Brothers, 1972.
Make puppets from scraps of paper and cloth, sponges, buttons and paper clips with this entertaining, easy to follow, color illustrated book.

Philpott. Violet. *The Know-How Book of Puppets*. London: Usborne, 1975.
Like all the "Know-How" series, this one is particularly rich in easy-to-follow illustrations that invite the reader to participate fully in making and utilizing puppets.

Ross, Laura. *Finger Puppets! Easy to Make, Fun To Use*. Kingswood, Surrey, England: World's Work, 1973.
Nine play scripts, from Chicken Licken to the Pied Piper, plus names for all the fingers, *plus* ways to turn them into puppets make this a great rainy day or schoolroom activity book.

———. *Hand Puppets: How to Make and Use them*. Kingswood, Surrey, England: World's Work, 1973.
Patterns, lists of materials, and clear instructions help help teachers and children make their own puppets from papier mâché and cloth, after which they can perform Rumpelstiltskin, Punch and Judy, and A Visit from Outer Space, the scripts of which are included.

Slade, Richard. *You Can Make a String Puppet*. Boston: Plays, 1972.
This well-illustrated book shows how to make professional quality marionettes, and lists all necessary materials to take one from planning stages to final stringing.

Tichenor, Tom. *Folk Plays for Puppets You Can Make*. Nashville: Abingdon, 1959.

Famous Nashville puppeteer (who began his career at the age of 14 at the Nashville Public Library), Tichenor gives easy-to-follow instructions for making puppets, stages, and scenery, followed by scripts for five simple plays, including The Three Billy Goats Gruff, The City Mouse and the Country Mouse, and The Little Red Hen.

Wright, John. *Rod, Shadow and Glove Puppets from the Little Angel Theatre*. London: Robert Hale, 1986.

This practical handbook reveals the secrets of puppet design and construction with diagrams, photos of modeling, casting, woodcarving, sewing, and lighting at London's foremost puppet theatre.

Puppets (of Several Types) in Fiction

Chaffee, Allen. *Pinocchio*. Illus. by Lois Lenski. New York: Random House, 1946.

Based upon the novel-length Collodi story, this reduction for young readers loses none of the excitement of adventure, and is, in fact, enhanced by Lenski's exquisite pastel illustrations.

Collodi, Carlo. *The Adventures of Pinocchio*. New York: Lancer, 1968.

This "Magnum Easy Eye" large-type version makes the story easy on young eyes while giving the complete text in an anonymous translation from the Italian.

————. *Pinocchio—The Tale of a Puppet*. New York: E. P. Dutton, 1957.

This translation by M. A. Murray brings the familiar tale of the famous puppet/boy to life in a 200-page novel.

Cutts, David. *Pinocchio Goes to School*. Mahwah, New Jersey: Troll Associates, 1983.

The puppet works hard in school because the fairy promises to reward his efforts with humanization.

————. *Pinocchio Meets the Cat and Fox*. Mahwah, New Jersey: Troll Associates, 1983.
On the way home, Pinocchio is tricked out of his money by the cunning Fox and the wily Cat.

Heinlein, Robert. *The Puppet Masters*. New York: New American Library, 1951.
Earthlings become puppets under the control of invading alien creatures with indestructible reproductive powers in this science fiction thriller.

MacLean, Alistair. *Puppet on a Chain*. London: Fontana, 1969.
This is a peacetime action thriller by the author of *Ice Station Zebra* and *The Guns of Navarone*.

Paterson, Katherine. *The Master Puppeteer*. New York: Crowell, 1975.
An apprentice puppeteer in 18th-century Japan discovers that his master is involved in corruption.

Puppet Plays

Colson, J. G. *Shakembones' Magic and Other Plays for Puppets*. London: A. and C. Black, 1988.
If for no other reason than the enchanting title, this handy book of puppet plays, based on folklore and other sources, ought to be available to young puppeteers.

Carlson, Bernice W. *Act It Out*. Nashville: Abingdon, 1956.
Invent characters, dress up, make strange faces, improvise, and use puppets to create situations of intrigue.

Emberley, Ed. *Punch and Judy*. Boston: Little, Brown, 1965.
Punch and Judy are among the oldest puppet characters in Britain, and their black comic buffoonery can still be enjoyed in every British town in parks, public squares, and seasides. This script is full of the original rambunctiousness, comic hen-pecking and violence, and quick repartee.

Izumo, Takeda. *Chusingura (The Treasury of Royal Retainers): A Puppet Play*. New York: Columbia University Press, 1971.
This is the most famous drama in all of Japan, written in 1748 as a puppet play, now better known in Kabuki theatre. A story of revenge, it is presented in a translation by Donald Keene.

Jones, Taffy. *Whistle Stop Puppet Plays*. Jefferson, NC: MacFarland, 1983.
Fifteen great little plays with sympathetic characters, instructions for making puppets and theatres to house them, illustrated with drawings and photographs of kids at play.

Mahlmann, Lewis. *Folk Tale Plays for Puppets: Thirteen Royalty-Free Plays for Hand Puppets, Rod Puppets, or Marionettes*. Boston: Plays, 1980.
Based on popular folk tales, these easy, short plays are perfect for children.

Ross, Laura. *Puppet Shows Using Poems and Stories*. London: Kay and Ward, 1970.
Ross, a former teacher and librarian, provides plays and traditional poems for all kinds of puppets, and for live silhouette mime behind a screen or sheet. She gives production notes for technique, action, and setting.

Are You a Puppet?

Dyer, Wayne. *Pulling Your Own Strings*. New York: Crowell, 1978.
Are you a puppet, or do you exercise control over your thoughts and actions? "Be assertive" is the message of this book.

Silberman, Melvin. *How to Discipline Without Feeling Guilty: Assert Relationships with Children*. New York: Hawthorn, 1980.
Are teachers puppet masters, or is there more to developing discipline: attitude, verbal skills, mimicry of adult behavior.

Townsend, John. *The Persuading Stick*. New York: Lothrop, Lee, and Shepard, 1987.

A quiet British girl uses a magic stick to improve her assertiveness in this young adult novel.

Wilson, Johniece Marshall. *Oh, Brother*. New York: Scholastic, 1988.
Alex's older brother steals his bike and generally bullies him around until the youngster learns to stand up for himself.

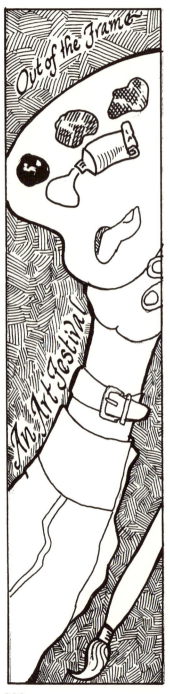

Chapter 8
Out of the Frame and Into Your Art:
A Festival of Art

Art is the common thread that runs through almost every aspect of human life; yet it is often taken for granted, for art has become part and parcel of existence. If it's in a frame, then it must be art, right? Wrong! We can't escape art. It's everywhere! We *eat* on artwork—an artist designed those plates. We *sleep* on artwork—someone made that bed. We *drive* artwork—someone's artistic dream called that car into existence. This festival takes art out of its frame, so to speak, calling attention to the things that make the world a more pleasant place: picture books, photography, wood carving, patchwork quilting, sculpture, embroidery, architecture—and, yes, paintings, too. Because of its obvious importance, art is easy to celebrate.

Pick up some of the threads of art and see where they lead: to an art gallery or museum? Schedule a class visit to see the works on display. Then learn about the artists through research in the library. To an artist's studio or workshop? Invite a local artist to speak or become the school's artist-in-residence for a day or a week. Do the threads of art lead to the home of a patchwork quilter, a potter, a flower arranger? Do they lead to the children's picture book collection in the elementary school library? If art were a sweater, it would be woven from many types of wool. A school art festival, therefore, can celebrate any aspect of the theme, concentrating on local availabilities, and emphasizing the student's own art through projects and displays.

In the activities which follow, we emphasize the creative aspects of art, (a) through library research into the lives of famous illustrators and artists; (b) through writing and illustration and binding of books at school on cross-disciplinary themes; (c) through simple print-making, paper mosaics, and cartooning; (d) through visiting artists and galleries; (d) through baking artistic cookies; (e) and through focusing art appreciation through essay writing. Many of the activities in other chapters, from reading to crafts projects, fit the art festival theme, too, so it is entirely appropriate to use them here.

A festival of art can be celebrated to coincide with the opening of a major exhibition in a big art gallery or museum; during the school's annual fine arts fair; on the commemoration of founder's day of a museum or gallery; on the completion of a school art department project; to honor an art teacher's show of work; or on an artist's birthday. Art fits in any time.

The Display: A Painter's Palette

A universally recognized symbol of art is the artist's hand-held palette. Create a striking display by cutting a greatly enlarged palette from cardboard (Figure 60).

What You Need

Cardboard boxes or panels
Pencil
Craft knife
Paints
Staples
Tape
PVA

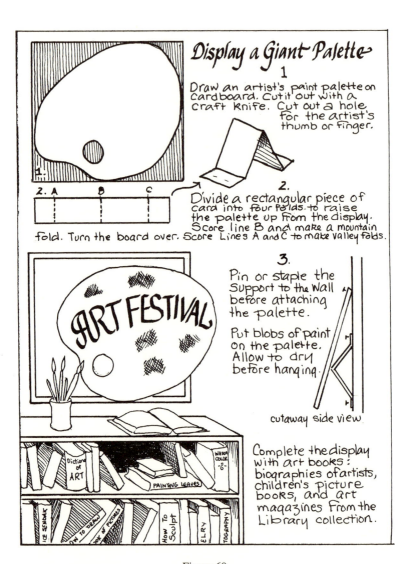

Display a Giant Palette

1

Draw an artist's paint palette on cardboard. Cut it out with a craft knife. Cut out a hole for the artist's thumb or finger.

2.

Divide a rectangular piece of card into four folds to raise the palette up from the display. Score line B and make a mountain fold. Turn the board over. Score Lines A and C to make valley folds.

2. A   B   C

3.

Pin or staple the support to the wall before attaching the palette.

Put blobs of paint on the palette. Allow to dry before hanging.

cutaway side view

ART FESTIVAL

Complete the display with art books: biographies of artists, children's picture books, and art magazines from the Library collection.

Dictionary of ART

WATER COLOR -8-

PAINTING LEAVES

ICE SENDAK

ON TO DRAW

OOK OF PICTURES

How To Sculpt

ELRY

TOGRAPHY

Figure 60

Draw the biggest paint *palette* possible on the cardboard available. The oval shape is basically a rounded-off rectangle with an indentation and finger hole at the bottom for the artist's hand. Cut out the design with a craft knife.

Cut out a cardboard *support* to make the palette jut out from the bulletin board. The support is a long rectangle, scored along right-angle lines at each end, and folded to make a V-shape.

To decorate the palette, apply large daubs of different colors of household latex or school tempera paints at intervals around the edge. If you prefer to paint the entire palette beforehand, choose a light color; white or tan. Or paint directly onto plain cardboard.

Display the palette on a bulletin board or directly on the wall. Line the area with a solid color paper. Hold the palette up to the wall, letting one edge jut out slightly. If the display is above eye level, put the cardboard support beneath the top of the palette. If the palette is more or less at eye level, put the cardboard support beneath either of the sides or beneath the bottom of the palette. Pin or staple to the wall at the desired location. Then attach the palette to the wall.

For stability, pierce two small holes through the palette on either side of the support, and tie the two together with strong thread.

The festival title can be painted directly onto the palette. Another variation: paint or print the title on a plain piece of paper. Make a paper frame for it, and position it on the bulletin board so that it is slightly obscured by the palette. Or cut out the letters and pin them to the background.

To emphasize particular types of art, such as Old Masters' paintings, pin two or three poster print reproductions onto the wall before putting up the palette. Pin about three inches from the top and bottom edges of the prints to create scroll effects. Cut out colorful dust jackets from children's picture books and treat them the same way. On smaller-scale bulletin boards meant to be examined close-up, pin postcard reproductions of art work, gallery style, on the board before putting up the palette.

To focus on a particular artist, such as Beatrix Potter, Andrew Wyeth, or Maurice Sendak, feature a commercially available print of one of the artist's pictures along with a suitable title, such as "Beatrix Potter: Artist and Farmer," or "Maurice Sendak, We Love You!" Near the display, of course, should be a collection of the artist's books.

Create an Artistic Ambience

Set up a STILL Life. Invite students to pose with it for 5 minutes without moving! Or to draw it. Give prizes to the Most Abstract, smallest, most colorful, most realistic, or funniest.

Puns make the art grow fonder! Give pats on the back to those who pun most ART-FULLY.

Be kind to doodle bugs!

Put up rolls of paper and invite students to doodle, draw cartoons, leave messages. Provide crayons, pens, pencils...

Organize a *Teachers' Art Show* in the Library to exhibit paintings, needlework, carving or other arts and crafts.

Plant old paint brushes! Watch them grow! Get old, exhausted brushes from the art room. Paint handles green. Dip brush end into primary colors and allow to dry. Display with paper cut-out leaves in vases and flower pots.

Happy Birthday To You!

Celebrate an artist's or author's birthday with a big Birthday Cake! Check Ann Commire's Something About the Author for a thorough choice!

Figure 61

Festival Art Activities

Inventive mimicry: an integrated art project

Every lower school library has a huge collection of picture books, beloved by pre-readers and students up to 8 or 9 years old. As youngsters grow in reading skill, they go on to other books, relegating picture books to childhood past. Occasionally they will recall an old favorite when a younger sibling discovers Dr. Seuss or Maurice Sendak, yet rarely will they take time to peruse them again. Through constant contact, teachers and librarians are among the few adults who continue to cherish and appreciate these books and their creators.

Integrate art fully into the school curriculum during the arts festival through a unit of study based on children's artists and illustrators, giving middle and high schoolers an opportunity to rediscover old friends while expanding their own creative talents. In cooperation with the art teacher, the festival coordinator can plan a unit based on particular children's artists, this time to appreciate the books for their artistic merit. Certain goals can be achieved by students and teachers alike, such as observing art for children to improve one's own line drawings or watercolors; studying children's books to see how certain artists use linoleum, woodblock or styrofoam printing techniques; or seeing how artists use different methods in making their work accessible and enjoyable. Children's picture books provide a ready-made art gallery to study. An old saying has it that mimicry is the sincerest compliment; and a proven successful form of mimicry for art students is the copying of works by great artists in order to learn technique. Read Vasari's biography of 15th-century whiz-kid Raphael of Urbino, who copied the unfinished Sistine Chapel paintings of art supremo Michelangelo Buonarroti—artists have always borrowed from one another.

Integrate this project into the mainstream curriculum by coordinating a literature unit with the language arts department, a writing project with social studies, or even a counting book project with mathematics. Subject integration of this type can not be done, of course, by one person, however dedicated. The festival coordinator must win friends and influence people in order to promote this union of art and other academic disciplines.

The final result of the integrated program should be an illustrated story. Students may choose to write and illustrate in the style of one artist, or they may want to write in the style of Beatrix Potter while producing illustrations in the style of Ezra Jack Keats. Requirements can vary. Some stories may need only one or two illustrations; others, such as an ABC or counting book, will need more. Students can work in teams or alone.

Here are some ideas for action. The festival coordinator presents the plan to stimulate creative writing and artwork. Each student is to create an illustrated work in *one* of his current courses, either for extra credit or as an integral part of the required learning. In English or foreign-language classes, students could write a short story or poem. The story can be based upon that of a particular author, perhaps, or an event, a mood, or other theme that fits in with the ongoing curriculum. In addition to writing the story, students can, with the librarian's help, study picture books to see how children's authors have treated that theme, verbally and in pictures.

In a social studies project, students could write a short piece of historical fiction or a factual account of an event. In mathematics, how about producing a counting book for kindergartners, or an illustrated guide to addition, division, or multiplication? In science, integrate art into the curriculum by offering opportunities to illustrate essays on natural history: hibernation, how an egg hatches, or why leaves fall in autumn.

During the festival, every student could be inspired to: (a) write a story or ABC book; (b) write a short historical biography or story; (c) prepare and write a counting book, or other mathematical book; (d) write and illustrate a scientific explanation of some natural phenomenon. If the school curriculum is too structured to contemplate this integration, the festival organizer can open up these creative opportunities in the form of a competition, an *extra*curricular activity for a selected group of volunteers.

How to proceed

Look at the different ways book illustrators create art: *drawing* with pencil, pen and ink, crayon, or pastels; *painting* with watercolor, tempera, acrylic or oil; *printmaking* with styrofoam, linoleum, or wood; *photography; collage* with torn paper, cut fabric, and found objects. Study children's books from each style or category. With the art teacher, gather as many books as possible so that students can study artistic styles at length, and be able to identify how an illustration was made. Then experiment with some ways to create art, such as Fruit Printing.

Fruit Printing: What You Need:

Hard fruits and vegetables
Sharp Knives
Paper
Paper towels
Water-based printing ink or tempera'
Saucers for the ink

Place a big bowl of hard fruits and vegetables in the library or classroom. Experiment with apples, pears, bell peppers, potatoes, mushrooms, carrots, and empty citrus-shells. Watery fruits like melons, strawberries, and peaches generally won't work.

Students select a fruit, and cut it neatly in half. Dry off any excess juices which may have exuded. Dip the cut side down into printing ink or tempera, and press gently onto paper. Use the fruit and vegetable printing blocks to decorate stationery, gift wrap, or notebook covers. When the prints have dried, turn them into people by drawing on arms, legs, and faces. Invent stories about the characters, such as "Miss Pepper's Hot Day" or "Why the Apple Family Fell Out of the Tree."

Create a frieze of fruit block prints on a long strip of butcher paper. Carve designs into potato and carrot segments to make characters. Experiment with different amounts of ink to see what effects can be achieved.

Mosaics: What You Need:

Pre-cut colored paper from the scrap box, cut into tiny squares
Sheets of colored paper
Scissors
Stick glue
Pencils

If fruit and vegetable printing seems too messy to undertake in the library or classroom, try creating paper mosaics. Before the students begin, pre-cut construction paper, gift wrap, newsprint, or any other paper in the scrap box, into tiny squares or geometric shapes. Then look at mosaic designs in books to see how artists create pictures from tiny elements of cloth or marble.

Next, each student should draw a simple outline design in pencil on a sheet of colored paper. The drawing should be fairly streamlined, with very little finicky detail. The object is to fill in the design with colored pieces of paper, cutting some pieces to fit when necessary. Maintain minimal space between pieces, just enough to let the background paper show through. When the mosaic is completed, mount it on a larger piece of colored paper to create a frame.

Experiment with creating a "crazy paving" paper frieze with a group of students, gluing areas of alternating hot and cool colors onto butcher paper. Divide into teams to make mosaic letters of the alphabet or numbers one to ten.

Cartooning: What You Need:

Comic books (ask kids to bring in their favorites)
Comic strips (such as *Far Side* calendars, or *Wizard of Id* from
  the newspaper)
Jokes (ask kids to share their favorites)
Rulers
Paper
Pencils
Fine-point black felt-tip pens

Comic books are as popular today as they were in the 1950s. Kids watch popular cartoon programs on television and in the cinema. And highly respected children's artists produce clean, crisp drawings in cartoon-style books. Maurice Sendak's *Some Swell Pup—Or Are You Sure You Want a Dog?* (London: Bodley Head, 1976), Ann Jonas' *Hoes and Peeks* (New York: Greenwillow, 1984) and Jan Pienkowski's *Homes* (London: Heineman, 1979) are three cartoon books that could provide examples of this form.

Cartooning is an art form which many students will find leads directly on from doodling. It is an art form that can provide a feeling of achievement and success almost immediately. Before drawing, allow time to look at and talk about cartoons. Look at cartoon strips in the newspaper. Discuss the humor of Gary Larson's *Far*

Side series, looking perhaps at one of his collected works, such as
The Far Side Gallery (New York: Andrews and McMeel, 1980).
As students share the cartoons they brought to school, discuss the
nature of humor. What is it that makes people laugh? Discuss favorite cartoons and comic characters and how they are drawn.

Words to Learn

Students should know the meanings of these words before they
begin to draw.

Cartoon
Frame
Strip
Thought Bubble
Voice Bubble
Continuity

During drawing time, help students choose a theme like "The
Day _____ Went Shopping at the Mall" or "What
_____ Learned in School." Or illustrate a favorite joke with
a cartoon, either in a single frame or in a longer strip series. To begin, students share their jokes or riddles: "Why did the chicken
cross the road?" "Knock! Knock! Who's There?" After the
laughs, talk about creating a funny character through costume, facial features, or paraphernalia such as handbags, large shoes, or
household tools. Discuss continuity of character. If the star of the
comic story has a bow tie on in the first frame, then the bow tie
should remain throughout the sequence of strips.

Integrate an informal spelling and vocabulary lesson into the art
project by checking the words in the cartoon voice and thought
bubbles. Add a bit of mathematics by refreshing younger students'
knowledge of measuring so that the cartoon frames are consistent.

Display the finished cartoons on a wall in the school lunch
room. Give the exhibition a catchy title: "Laugh While You Eat,"
"7th Grade Cartoon Capers," or "Gary Larson, Eat Your Heart
Out." Invite editors of the school paper to choose cartoons for
publication. Photocopy the entire collection. Bind them and sell
them cheaply to raise money for a charity or to buy cartoon books
for the school library.

Vincent Van Gogh-ing: What You Need:

Print of a Van Gogh painting, such as "The Sunflowers" or "The
    Siesta"
Tempera paints
Brushes
Felt-tips, crayons, colored pencils
Paper
Pencils

With students in grade six and up, study prints of Vincent Van
Gogh's paintings. Show slides of his work. Using your library or
art department collection, research his painting and his life. With
tempera, water, brushes and good quality paper, try to paint in Van
Gogh's swirling, flowing style. Capture a local scene or a still life
in the manner of Van Gogh, or copy one of his paintings from a
print or book. Ask students to bring in a photo of themselves or
their family, or of their house or pet, to copy in the Van Gogh technique. Illustrate one of the integrated art projects in the style of Van
Gogh. To keep artistic mess at a minimum, try this project using
felt-tips, crayons, or colored pencils on small pieces of art paper.

A Van Gogh Frottage: What You Need:

Crayons
Pencils
Paper
Textured items such as:
    evergreen tree twigs
    tree leaves
    coins
    string

The German artist Max Ernst introduced "frottage" into painting early in the twentieth century. Frottage is an easy method of
transferring existing relief patterns—coins, combs, engraved
wood or metal—onto paper. Place the paper over the object and
rub with crayon or pencil to reproduce the pattern. To make Van
Gogh-like trees, pick some small twigs (2–3 inches, 5–8 cm.) from
an evergreen, such as a cedar, yew or pine, and place them beneath
a sheet of paper. Create the image of the twigs by rubbing them

firmly with a crayon. Make a forest of trees by moving the twigs to new locations under the paper. Try placing short bits of string and twine beneath the paper, too. Rub with different colors to create effects of light and shade, autumn, or fantasy.

Raining Cats and Dogs! Impossible Art: What You Need:

Paper
Various art tools from pencils to rubber stamps

Talk about metaphors, similes, and idioms that have become common in daily speech, focusing on "raining cats and dogs." Ask students to spend ten minutes drawing that figure of speech. Using the theme, ask them to come up with other descriptions of a hard rain. Could it be raining Christmas trees or holly leaves, paintbrushes or watercolors? What other images could illustrate an unusual rainfall? Ask students to use any graphic tools, from pencils to crayons to rubber stamps, to draw a picture of repeating images falling as rain from the sky.

When the pictures are completed and displayed on a wall, encourage students to invent stories about their favorites. In small groups, students can improvise scenes about the day it rained encyclopedias or the night it poured popcorn. An overnight assignment can be to write a short story about one of the drawings.

Make an Artistic Animal Alphabet

Artists of all ages enjoy this project (Figure 62), and the charm of third graders' work rivals that of sophisticated adult designs.

What You Need:

Paper
Photocopied grid system made by the teacher
Pencils
Pens
Dry coloring materials

First, artists select the animal they wish to draw. They make several cartoon sketches, showing the anthropomorphic animal asleep, posing with a smile, eating, scratching, or exercising. The

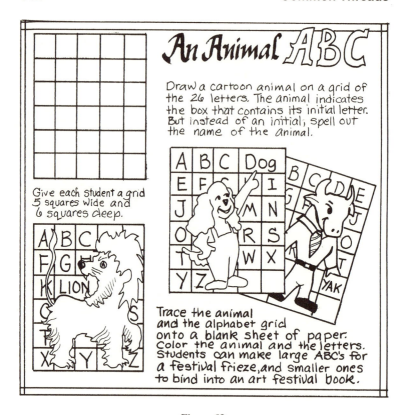

Figure 62

teacher can encourage greater expression, suggest alternative poses, and help younger artists develop caricature skills. The best designs are usually simple outlines with cartoon-style expressions.

Next, artists begin the layout for their alphabet, which may be the most difficult part for youngsters. Ideally, the letters should be in neat rows, of the same style and size, and relatively plain. Five letters across and six rows down is a good, workable format. *To save time, teachers may want to supply photocopies of a ready-made grid rather than use this activity as a lesson in linear measurement.* To make a grid, divide a sheet of paper into squares, five across and six down. Go over the lines in black ink, photocopy, and give each student one. Students begin the alphabet in the upper left corner, and work across. In working with this layout, students have to decide where their animal will appear: hanging from the top like a bird or monkey, or standing on the bottom like a horse or pig, or clinging to the side like a lizard or cat.

The cartoon animals should be drawn so that they point to the position of their initial in the alphabet. They can point with their ears, tails, hands, or feet. Replace the initial letter with the full spelling of the animal. That is, replace letter B with the word "bat," or letter F with the word "fish." Animals with short names (dog, lion, fox) fit easily into this system: their short number of letters doesn't disturb the flow of the alphabet. Animals with longer names (elephant, hippopotamus, giraffe) will have to be written in small letters in order to fit inside the grid. Alternatively, shift the alphabet around. There are four extra spaces in the grid system, so move the letters around to make room. When students trace their final copies onto a separate sheet of paper, the extra grid lines can be omitted.

Join the alphabet and the cartoon by placing both drawings on a light table or holding them up to a window. When the animal is in the right position, trace its outline over the alphabet grid. Then trace the design again onto blank paper. Go over the final copy with felt-tips and erase any pencils markings. Students may color in the animal and add special color details to the box with the animal's name.

Display the finished alphabet animals as a classroom frieze during the art festival. Adapt the project for use in conjunction with one of the book-making activities. Experiment with collective groups other than animals. Try fruits and vegetables, cities and countries, personal names, or names of artists and writers.

Bind a Book

Adults and students can work together or produce their own art books. These books provide artistic stimulation in several ways: in the making, in filling in the blank pages with art, and in simply enjoying the finished product long after it has been completed. Students can make traditional books, with hard covers made of cardboard, and shape books, cut to look like an animal or an object. For some, the act of making and owning a blank book will motivate literary and artistic creativity. For others, already created work may inspire the making of the book in which to keep it. Here are four different kinds of books to make.

Make a Traditional Book (Figure 63)

What You Need:

Corrugated cardboard or lightweight poster board
Child-proof paper cutter
Heavy-duty scissors
Craft knives
Mystic tape®
Masking tape

Figure 63

Blank sheets of typing paper or completed stories and artwork
Stapler
Pencil and ruler
Stick glue

To Make One Book

1. Cutting the Binding from Cardboard

Cut two pieces of cardboard for the front and back covers. For 8-1/2 by 11-inch standard typing paper, cut the board 9 by 11-1/2 inches. Older students may measure and cut by themselves, while younger students may be unable to do this without adult reassurance. To make the front cover open and close, draw a line in pencil one-half inch from one of the 11-inch sides. With heavy scissors or craft knife, cut off this strip.

Lay the half-inch strip next to the board from which it was taken, leaving a gap of about one-sixteenth inch. With masking tape, secure the half-inch strip to the piece of cardboard to make a hinge. Then carefully use Mystic tape to cover the gap, bearing in mind that Mystic tape can not be readjusted once it is put in place. Work slowly. Finally, lay the back cover on top of the hinged cover. The back cover will now be slightly smaller than the hinged cover. Make both covers the same size by trimming off any extra cardboard on the hinged piece.

This method works for books of any size. The only measurement that needs to remain the same is the half-inch (1 cm) strip and one-sixteenth inch (.2 cm) gap in the front cover hinge.

2. Assembling the Book

Place the back cover on the work surface. Put the blank or completed pages on top of the back cover, lining them up with the left side. Use stick glue to hold each piece in place, starting with the last sheet. Fill in with any number of pages, from three or four up to twenty-five. Place the front cover on top, with the hinged strip to the left, tape side down. Staple along the hinged strip, or secure with metal paper fasteners. To finish the book, cover the stapled hinge with a wide strip of Mystic cloth.

Reluctant writers can begin to fill their books with artwork from other festival projects, such as cartoons, fruit and vegetable prints, and mosaics. Older students can bind their original alphabet and counting books, their derivative art studies and sketches, or photographs.

Students can enhance the covers by gluing on giftwrap, collages of pictures and colored paper, or by writing on the title with felt-tip pens.

Make Shape Books (Figure 64)

Books don't have to be rectangular. Using the above method, students can make books shaped like shoes, animals, eggs, city-scapes, or cars. They can invent their own patterns, based upon the project at hand: a science assignment could be bound in a test-tube-shaped book; English homework could be bound in an inkwell- or word processor-shaped book; an art project could be bound in a paint palette shape. Start with the basic rectangular shaped book covers. Draw on the shape, making certain that it touches the hinge along the left side. Cut out the pages to match the shape of the covers. Proceed as above. The librarian or teacher might want to begin a list of shapes that pertain to various topics to help students get started. By writing this list on the overhead projector or chalkboard, the teacher can add new shape ideas during class discussion.

Students can make interesting ABC books to bind in appropriate shapes. Try playing this game before embarking on the shape book project. Begin by saying:

> My best friend Harry invited me on a picnic, so I got out my picnic basket and put in an apple.

Each student repeats the entire sentence in turn, but adds another item to put in the picnic basket, starting with the next letter of the alphabet. The next person could put in a *b*anana, the next a *c*an of beans, the next a *d*irty napkin, and so on. By the end of the game, the last person has to repeat all the items previously put in, in ABC order, besides adding his own. The game can be changed to include any number of items. Instead of a picnic, my best friend can invite students to go camping, to visit an art gallery, or to spend the summer in an exotic location.

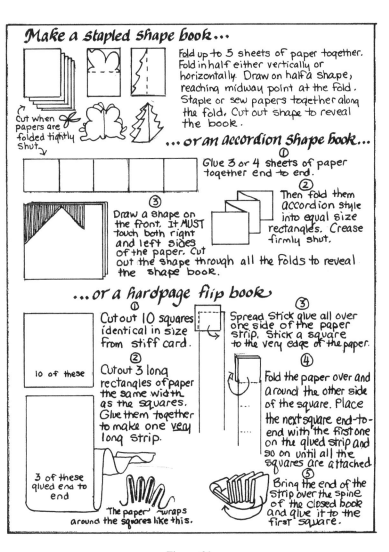

Make a stapled shape book...

Fold up to 5 sheets of paper together. Fold in half either vertically or horizontally. Draw on half a shape, reaching midway point at the fold. Staple or sew papers together along the fold. Cut out shape to reveal the book.

Cut when papers are folded tightly shut.

...or an accordion shape book...

① Glue 3 or 4 sheets of paper together end to end.

② Then fold them accordion style into equal size rectangles. Crease firmly shut.

③ Draw a shape on the front. It MUST touch both right and left sides of the paper. Cut out the shape through all the folds to reveal the shape book.

...or a hardpage flip book

① Cut out 10 squares identical in size from stiff card.

10 of these

② Cut out 3 long rectangles of paper the same width as the squares. Glue them together to make one very long strip.

3 of these glued end to end

The paper wraps around the squares like this.

③ Spread stick glue all over one side of the paper strip. Stick a square to the very edge of the paper.

④ Fold the paper over and around the other side of the square. Place the next square end-to-end with the first one on the glued strip and so on until all the squares are attached.

⑤ Bring the end of the strip over the spine of the closed book and glue it to the first square.

Figure 64

Turn the game into book form by asking students to make an appropriately shaped cover, such as a picnic basket, suitcase, picnic blanket, or drink can. Then fill the shape book with the twenty-six picnic items.

Soft-cover Shape Books

What You Need:

Typing paper or art room paper
Cereal box or lightweight poster paper
Glue
Tape
Staples or needle and thread
Scissors
Pencil

Type 1

Shape books can be made without hard covers. Assemble up to five pieces of paper (Figure 64). Fold them in half, and draw half a shape on the top piece, making certain that the whole meets at the fold. Cut out the shape. Open up the paper and staple or sew it together along the fold. Students can make a hard cover for this book out of a cereal box or from extremely light poster board. They need to trace the shape on the plain side of the cardboard, cut it out, fold it in half, and attach it to the pages at the stapling stage.

Type 2

Accordion-shape books are made from several pieces of paper glued or taped together, either end to end, or side to side. When the glue has dried, the sheets are folded evenly together to make an accordion. Draw the shape on the top sheet, making certain that a significant proportion of the drawing touches the folds on each side. Cut out the shape. To make covers, take two sheets of cardboard the same size as the accordion. Trace the chosen shape on the covers. Cut them out. Glue the top sheet to the inside front cover and bottom sheet to the inside back cover.

Make a Hardpage Flip Book

These unusual little books are ideal for counting, poetry, or alphabets. The pages are formed of long strips of paper folded over and glued to squares of cardboard (Figure 64). In this version, the pages become the actual binding that holds the book together.

What You Need:

Stiff poster board or cardboard
Paper
    white
    plain colored
    brown grocery bags
    gift wrap (non-shiny)
Stick glue or PVA
Pencils
Rulers
T-square
Scissors
Craft knives
Art room paper cutter

To make one book

Measure a 3-inch (8.5 cm) square on a piece of card. Make certain that it is perfectly square. Cut it out and use it as a template to make ten—or more—squares from cardboard or stiff card.

On paper of your choice, measure and mark a length that is the same width as the squares. Cut it out, and make two more identical lengths. Overlap them at the ends, and glue them together to make one long rectangle.

Spread glue all along one side of the paper rectangle. Attach the first cardboard square to the end of the paper, aligning it perfectly along the sides and end. Fold the paper around the other side of the cardboard so that it sticks to both sides. Then place the next cardboard square end-to-end with the first one on the glued paper. Fold the paper around it, and proceed to the next square until all are enclosed in the paper strip.

When you reach the last square, shut the book firmly, creasing down the inside folds well, and bring the end of the strip around the outside edge of the folded paper. Stick the paper to the square on the other side, and tuck it inside, overlapping it onto the sheet that is already there. Cut off the extra length. The pages have, in effect, now bound the book together. If you run out of paper at any stage, simply overlap another length onto the end of the rectangular strip, and continue binding.

Guest Speakers

Very few communities are devoid of artists. They may not be painters, of course. *Artists can be interior decorators, decoy duck carvers, or wrought iron workers.* Invite persons whose artwork would be interesting to a student group, asking them to speak about themselves, their work, and how they go about it. Prepare the students beforehand so they can have some interesting questions, from how much does the artwork cost to how long does it take to finish.

Contact a favorite *book illustrator* through his or her publisher. Ask if the illustrator would be willing to travel to your festival. If not,would he or she be available for telephone contact at a specified time during a school day? Write to a publisher for a list of illustrators who would be willing to visit your school.

A *local gallery owner* or *museum curator* might be able to describe the history of graphic art in your area, gearing the discussion to the age of the audience, perhaps showing slides, or bringing some examples of work. A pre-seminar conference between the festival facilitator and the curator could enable you to make a study sheet for the students to use during or prior to the lecture. Such a lecture is an ideal preamble to a gallery visit.

Art Trips

If there is no art gallery within easy driving distance, think about taking an overnight trip with an art class. If there is a museum or gallery nearby, prepare a study sheet for the students prior to the visit so that their time there will be educationally beneficial and non-disruptive to other visitors. Small children will enjoy finding animals and children in paintings—create a detective search or treasure hunt for them. Older students can exercise greater skill in analyzing styles, making comparisons, and reaching thoughtful conclusions. Consider written assignments based on the art gallery visit: essays on artistic styles; biographies of artists on display, using library reference materials; or a journalistic account of the trip for the school paper.

An artist's workspace is an ideal place to see how things are made. Take a trip to an artist's studio, to an arts and crafts gallery, or to a quilter's sewing room at home. Find out particularly how many students would be welcomed at any one time before arriving with several bus loads of ten-year-olds! Beforehand, decide with the artist the appropriate content of the visit: a demonstration of production methods, a talk, opportunities for students to try their hands, or simply perusal of samples of work.

Take a few students to an interesting local scenic view, building, park, or interior space. Sketchbooks and pencils in hand, spend an hour observing, seeing, watching shadows, looking for interesting perspectives. Take the sketches back to the festival where they can be displayed and used for studio work in the art room later.

If there is a publishing company nearby, arrange a tour of the plant so that students can see how an artist's work is turned into a book or magazine illustration. Follow-up with creative writing or cartooning projects that describe the printing process.

What Is Art? Creative Writing Projects

An Essay Competition

The Festival can show that art permeates every aspect of our lives. To give students practice in articulate, verbal self-expression, hold an Essay Contest in which writers:

a. describe the nature of art
b. determine the difference between beauty and ugliness
c. discuss the matter of personal taste
d. describe how art in its many forms makes life in the local community more pleasant
e. refer to ways poets, essayists, and novelists have written about art, artists, and the nature of beauty

Beforehand, discuss the project with language arts teachers to see if the essay can be worked into the current curriculum. Find out if English students can be directed toward biographies of artists and to essays on art by critics. Can the essay competition become a required assignment? Judge the competition in age categories. Invite writers to illustrate their work with drawings or photographs. Plan with the editors of the local paper to publicize the school's Art Festival by printing the winning essays.

A Short Story

Using the theme of art and artists, encourage students to write short stories, either through cooperation with language arts teachers or through a festival competition. The festival coordinator may wish to provide a theme with which every writer must work. A tried and true theme, such as the stereotypical starving artist living in a garret, can be given a new slant when the artist is a poor farmer's wife who suddenly finds that her quilts are worth thousands of dollars in the big city. Prior to the festival, discuss the short story competition with English classes to get ideas rolling.

Ask teachers to form a panel of judges to award prizes to the most creative stories. Offer the stories to a local paper for publication. Display all the entries in the library.

Artistic Taste Treats

A Baking Contest

A highlight of an arts festival should involve artistically presented food. This can take the form of a *Most Artistically Decorated Cake competition.* Students and teachers may enter their cakes at a specified time during the festival, preferably in the library, so that they can be on public display. A panel of judges determines winners in age categories (one for each grade, perhaps, and one winner among adult entries), based upon artistic appearance of the cake and taste. Each entry should be accompanied by the recipe on a plain sheet of paper. At the end of the festival, all the recipes could be published in a school Cake Book, the proceeds from sales going to provide cook books or art books for the library.

But what to do with the entries? Take photographs of the cakes for the library album or school yearbook. Invite the editor and photographers of the local paper to the judging event. Sell individual portions of cake after school or after lunch to raise money for new books. Take one or two cakes to a retirement home as a special treat. Put a cake in the teachers' lounge. Auction individual cakes to the highest bidder. Provide each classroom with one cake to be shared before the end of school.

Invite a professional patissier or cake decorator to talk to small groups about creating artistic food. Ask him or her to offer critical comments on the entries before the judges pronounce their decisions. Ask if the cake decorator would be willing to do an icing demonstration as a special festival event before or after the winners are announced.

Artistic Cookies

Before putting these ingredients together, give participants a piece of paper about three inches square. The assignment is to come up with an "artistic cookie" template. To make a symmetrical design, fold the paper in half, and draw half of a star, animal, or other shape, the middle of which must be on the fold. Cut through the folded paper, and unfold. To make any other design, just draw directly on the square of paper. Cookie designs must be simple, and should not contain cutouts. Eyes, daubs of color on artists' palettes, and other details, can be added later with chocolate drops, nuts, or raisins. Cookie eaters should be told that the more space their design takes up, the more cookie will result. When the designs are drawn and cut out, they should be identified with the name of the artist to help them claim their cookies when they come from the oven.

It will take about three hours to complete this cookie project, from designing the cookie shapes, to mixing the ingredients, to chilling in the refrigerator, to rolling and cutting, baking, cooling, and displaying for eating. Several teams can prepare cookie batter at once, thus making large quantities. Parent volunteers could also be encouraged to bake the recipe at home prior to festival time to ensure a good supply of seconds. This recipe makes 30–40 cookies.

2 cups molasses
1 tbsp ground ginger
1/4 tsp ground cinnamon
1 tbsp vinegar
1 tbsp baking powder
1/2 tsp salt
1/4 cup white sugar and 1/4 cup brown sugar, mixed
2 eggs beaten
8 cups plain flour

Bring molasses to a boil in a large pan. Remove from heat. Stir in spices, sugar mixture, salt, beaten eggs, and vinegar. Add soda and stir. Take care, for the soda causes a frothing action which could rise above the edge of a small pan unless it is stirred heartily. Add the flour one cup at a time, stirring well after each addition until all the ingredients are well blended.

Roll the batter into a ball. Wrap it in waxed paper and chill it in the refrigerator for about thirty minutes.

Preheat oven to 350 degrees F, 180 C.

Cut the dough into four parts. Roll out on a floured board or table to about 1/8-inch thick. Use the specially designed and cut-out templates by placing them one at a time near the edge of the rolled-out dough. Cut around them carefully with a sharp knife and lift them off the table with a spatula. To hang the cookies for display, pierce the top with a drinking straw. Insert a ribbon or embroidery thread after the cookie is baked. Place cookies on a baking sheet, two inches apart. Bake from eight to ten minutes. Cookies should be golden brown and firm. Let them cool on a flat surface.

Students may wish to decorate their cookies with icing to create faces or other features:

16 ounces confectioner's sugar
1 egg white
1 tbsp lemon juice
(optional: a few drops of food coloring)

Beat egg whites until soft and foamy. Gradually stir in the sugar, alternating with drops of lemon juice. Add food coloring if desired. Spread the icing on the cooled cookies. Use kitchen knives, forks, clean twigs, or art implements to make designs on the icing. Use chocolate sprinkles, chocolate shavings, and chocolate drops, candied fruit, raisins, nuts, or small amounts of powdered drinking chocolate to add further features. These cookies may be eaten the day they are made, but for those who can resist, they may be stored in air-tight containers for a few weeks.

Festival Publications

After the festival has finished, facilitators and cooperating teachers should look over the projects that have been generated, selecting some of the written work (recipes, short stories, journalistic reports of events and trips) and pen and ink drawings to publish as a school booklet. The librarian may wish to include select art bibliographies to encourage further reading. If facilities permit, photographs of events should also be included. Ideally, the publication will be given away to everyone who participated, and made available as a handout in the library, school reception area, and main offices. To raise money, the booklet (or newspaper or magazine) may be sold.

As a fund-raiser, print a school art calendar for the following academic year, using pen and ink drawings and photographs from the festival to illustrate each month. Or use the calendar as an opportunity for young artists to enshrine their work permanently by asking for further black and white drawings, perhaps for another art contest. With desktop publishing or the services of a local printer, produce and bind the calendar, and sell it for further festival funds, for charity, or for buying art supplies or books for the school. Publication expenses might be offset through sponsorship by local businesses. It never hurts to ask.

Sources of Inspiration

Books About Art

Alberti, Leon Battista. *On Painting*. John Spencer, trans. New Haven: Yale University Press, 1966.
This is the first modern analytical study of painting, a pioneer-

ing treatise on art first published in 1435 when the Middle Ages were breaking into the Renaissance.

Arnotsky, Jim. *Drawing from Nature*. New York: Lothrop, 1982.
Drawing from life is easier when following the simple instructions and illustrations in this book for all ages.

Bayer, Jonathon. *Reading Photographs: Understanding the Aesthetics of Photography*. New York Pantheon, 1977.
Bayer shows how spatial ambiguity, surrealism, symbols, light and time make modern photography a true art form.

Biskupic, Bozho. *Ivan Lackovitch*. Zagreb: Savod Hrvatske, 1985.
This large collection of imaginative line drawings of famous Croatian artist Ivan Lackovitch shows his skill with pen and ink in interpreting native scenes and events. The biographical and informational text is in both English and Serbo-Croat.

The Book of Art: A Pictorial Encyclopedia of Painting, Drawing, and Sculpture. 10 v. New York: Grolier, 1971.
A world pictorial survey that covers the origins and development of the fine arts in the West and Orient, this lengthy reference set provides excellent background detail for a student of art.

Brockie, Keith. *One Man's Island*. London: J. M. Dent, 1984.
One hundred and fifty paintings and drawings from the Isle of Man in the Scottish Firth of Forth illustrate a year in the life of a talented young artist who lived among the seas, terns, puffins and native flora in an isolated croft to gain artistic insight into the local ecology.

Brommer, Gerald F. *Drawing: Ideas, Materials, and Techniques*. London: Davis, 1972.
This guide offers the teacher a number of ideas for developing and encouraging student creativity.

Brown, Milton. *American Art: Painting, Sculpture, Architecture, Decorative Arts*. New York: Abrams, 1979.
This illustrated survey shows the development of art in the USA since colonial times.

Canaday, John. *What Is Art? An Introduction to Painting, Sculpture, and Architecture.* New York: J. Hochman, 1979.
This prolifically illustrated book examines techniques, composition, vision, and the nature of realism, expressionism and abstraction.

Cennini, Cennino d'Andrea. *The Craftsman's Handbook: Il Libro dell'Arte.* Daniel Thompson, trans. New York: Dover, 1961.
Written in 1390, this instruction manual tells how to grind pigments, size panels for paintings, apply gold leaf, and emulate heaven and earth in art. It also tells how to keep miniver tails from being moth-eaten.

Coe, Brian. *The Snapshot Photograph: The Rise of Popular Photography, 1888–1939.* London: Ash and Grant, 1977.
Coe gives a history of the family camera, with glimpses into photography albums, art galleries and dark rooms.

Condivi, Asconio. *The Life of Michelangelo Buonarroti.* George Bull, trans. New York: Oxford University Press, 1992.
Written in Michelangelo's lifetime by one of his students, this biography corrects many of the mistakes made by Giorgio Vasari in his contemporary account of the master's life. It appears with a collection of Michelangelo's poetry and letters.

Cott, Jonathan. *Forever Young.* New York: Random House, 1977.
Eight creative men and women talk about enthusiasm, wonder, and openness to experience as part of the artistic imagination.

Earnest, Adele. *The Art of the Decoy: American Bird Carvings,* rev. ed. Exton, PA: Schiffer Publications, 1982.
Line drawings and over 200 black and white and color photographs trace the history of carved wooden decoys from 1700 to the present.

Emberley, Edward. *Ed Emberley's Big Green Drawing Book.* Boston: Little, Brown and Co., 1979.
Emberley shows how to draw animals and machines in this book suitable for young people and adults.

Ferguson, George. *Signs and Symbols in Christian Art*. New York: Oxford University Press, 1961.
Reissued in paperback, this handy reference book explains the symbols used by medieval and Renaissance artists which frequently appear in contemporary architecture and sculpture.

Gardner, Howard. *Artful Scribbles—the Significance of Children's Drawings*. London: Basic Books, 1980.
Besides looking at the psychological aspects of children's artwork, this book also provides insight into what constitutes aesthetic values.

Handberg, Ejner. *Shop Drawings of Shaker Furniture and Woodenware,* 3 vols. Stockbridge, MA: Berkshire Traveller Press, 1977.
A skilled cabinet maker writes about and draws plans for nearly 100 Shaker items, from longcase clocks to washstands.

Henri, Robert. *The Art Spirit*. New York: Harper and Row, 1984.
First published in the 1920s, this collection of witticisms and artistic philosophy of the great American painter and teacher Robert Henri urges students to cultivate their talents.

Hilman, Anthony. *Carving Early American Weathervanes*. New York: Dover Press, 1986.
Follow the patterns and instructions for these 16 wooden animals to recreate 19th century naive weathervanes.

Holme, Bryan. *Enchanted World: The Magic of Pictures*. London: Oxford University Press, 1979.
This view of the fine arts concentrates on what artists choose to portray in their varied forms of expression, from painting to photographs.

Horwitz, Elinor Lander. *American Contemporary Folk Artists*. Philadelphia: Lippincott, 1975.
Pictures and descriptions introduce the work of 22 folk painters and sculptors.

Innes, Jocasta. *Paint Magic*. London: Frances Lincoln, 1985.
The decorator's complete illustrated guide to paint finishes leads the amateur artist through hundreds of styles and techniques

from marbling, antiquing, and vinegar painting to stencilling, stippling, combing, and gilding. Product sources are listed for both the US and UK.

Kandinsky, Wassily. *Concerning the Spiritual in Art*. M. T. Sadler, trans. New York: Dover, 1977.
This book is a pioneering, early 20th century work in the movement to free art from its traditional bonds of material reality into a spiritual abstraction.

Keithley, Moy. *Investigating Art: A Practical Guide for Young People*. London: Elek, 1976.
This is, simply, a book of art appreciation for young people.

Lanes, Selma. *The Art of Maurice Sendak*. Toronto: Bodley Head, 1980.
Sendak's life and art are explored in affectionate detail in this prolifically illustrated picture biography.

Larkin, David. *The Fantastic Kingdom*. London: Pan Books, 1974.
The collection of full-color illustrations from Victorian story books includes the work of Rackham, Dulac, Parrish and others.

Larkin, Oliver. *Art and Life in America,* rev. ed. New York: Holt, Rinehart, and Winston, 1960.
This panorama of various art forms shows how American artists have expressed themselves, and why.

Leonardo (da Vinci). *The Notebooks of Leonardo da Vinci*. Richter, Irma, ed. New York: Oxford University Press, 1990.
From Leonardo's notes and drawings emerges the picture of the true Renaissance man of genius.

Lipman, Jean. *American Primitive Painting*. New York: Dover, 1972.
Lipman exalts the unpretentious quality of 19th-century U.S. folk art.

Macauley, David. *Cathedral: The Story of its Construction*. New York: Houghton Mifflin, 1973.
Watch a gothic cathedral being built from start to finish in this book of finely drawn pen and ink illustrations.

Murray, Peter and Linda. *The Art of the Renaissance*. New York: Thames and Hudson, 1989.
For a readable survey of the art and the times that produced it, this Renaissance history is a must for school libraries.

Naylor, Rod. *Woodcarving Techniques*. London: Batsford Press, 1979.
Diagrams and text introduce the prospective carver to woods, techniques, tools, design, and furniture restoration.

Nicolaides, Kimon. *The Natural Way to Draw: A Working Plan*. New York: Houghton Mifflin, 1941.
This series of exercises assists the art student to develop his own creativity rather than imitating that of others.

Nochlin, Linda. *The Politics of Vision*. New York: Thames and Hudson, 1991.
A leading critic and historian of 19th-century art and society explores the interaction of art, society, ideas, and politics, from male domination and colonialism to Degas' anti-Semitism to Van Gogh, Corbet, and Pissarro.

Osborne, Harold, ed. *The Oxford Companion to Art*. Oxford: Clarendon Press, 1975.
Over 3000 entries cover worldwide human artistic endeavor through all time.

Roberts, Howard. *Fun with Sun Prints and Box Cameras: Creative Photography with and without a Camera*. New York: McKay, 1981.
This fascinating book offers creative potential to artists young and old.

Rubin, Cynthia E. *Southern Folk Art*. Birmingham Ala.: Oxmoor House, 1985.
From the Moravians of North Carolina, the Shakers of Kentucky, the Germans of Texas, and the French of Louisiana to the Africans throughout the region, the folk arts of the American South include basketry, pottery, native paintings, quilting, carving, and architecture.

Smith, Ray. *How to Draw and Paint What You See*. London: Kindersley, 1984.
This practical course in drawing covers everything from pencil sketches to large canvas oils, and includes chapters on materials, techniques, design, and creativity.

Townsend, William. *Canadian Art Today*. New York: Graphic Press, 1970.
Townsend reviews developments in the Canadian art scene, comparing it to work in the USA and Europe.

Vasari, Giorgio. *Lives of the Artists,* 2 vols. George Bull, trans. New York: Viking Penguin, 1987.
Vasari (1511–1574) was an artist known today not for his painting but for his intimate biographies of Donatello, Cimabue, Giotto, Michelangelo, and other great Renaissance sculptors and painters. This is the basis of any study of art history.

Warner, Marina. *Queen Victoria's Sketchbook*. London: Macmillan, 1979.
All her life, Queen Victoria painted, recording everything around her, from her "dear Highland hills" at Balmoral to the Solent and the Isle of Wight. This is a record of her life as an artist, during which she was tutored by Edward Lear.

Woodford, Susan. *Looking at Pictures*. New York: Cambridge University Press, 1983.
A way to art appreciation, its subtleties and drama, lies within the pages of this companion to art.

Art in Fiction

Arnow, Harriet. *The Dollmaker*. New York: Avon Books, 1972.
A story of human inhumanity, or a tale of human strength in the face of adversity, this powerful saga of Gertrude Nevel's move from the green hills of Kentucky to the grime of 1940s Detroit centers upon her native ability to carve beautiful objects in wood, bringing beauty into the lives of those she touches.

Baker, Betty. *Dupper*. New York: Greenwillow, 1976.
Can prairie dogs really paint pictures? In this book, yes, they can!

Bellair, R. L. *Double Take*. New York: Morrow, 1979.
An awkward young man learns to go beyond appearances through his skillful and somewhat deceptive use of photography.

Benson, E. F. *Mapp and Lucia*. London: Black Swan, 1986.
One of a series of humorous novels set in the mythic English town of Tilling, this story involves the society queen Lucia and her constant companion, the eccentric Georgie, both of whom like to dabble in watercolors and petit-point, much to the horror of Lucia's arch-rival, Elizabeth Mapp, who sees her own artistic work as above criticism.

Brenner, Barbara. *A Killing Season*. New York: Dell, 1981.
A factual, photographic account of a black bear's life is the basis for this novel about a young girl's search for identity in rural Pennsylvania.

Cohen, Miriam. *No Good in Art*. New York: Greenwillow, 1980.
Maybe his drawing isn't so bad after all—a young boy decides he can draw creatively despite no encouragement from his teacher.

Heller, Joseph. *Picture This*. New York: Putnam, 1988.
When Rembrandt paints Aristotle's ear, the man on the canvas can hear! When he paints the eye, Aristotle can see! Aristotle's reflections form the basis for this unusual novel.

Markham, Marion. *The Christmas Present Mystery*. New York: Houghton Mifflin, 1984.
A mysterious face in a photograph leads Mickey and Kate to search for a poltergeist.

Wilde, Oscar. *The Portrait of Dorian Gray*. London: Penguin, 1987.
A painting grows old while the subject does not in this classic tale of vanity and human mortality.

Chapter 9
Rolling Along: A River Festival

They just keep rolling, those rivers. Constantly moving, never the same, yet always flowing down to a distant sea, beckoning, calling, "Go with me! See what I can show you!" Along the banks of the Tigris and Euphrates Rivers in the Middle East, Biblical stories were enacted. Some say Eden was there. Along the great rivers of Africa, the Congo, the Nile, and the great, gray, greasy Limpopo beloved by Kipling, civilizations grew and prospered. In Europe, the Rhone, the Rhine, the Danube, the Thames; in Asia, the Ganges, the Yangtze, the Mekong; in South America, the Amazon; in North America, the Potomac, the James, the Colorado, the St. Lawrence, the Tennessee and Cumberland, the Ohio, the Missouri, and greatest of all, the Mississippi—led to commerce, political warfare and stability, and to the building of great cities. Rivers evoke a spirit of freedom, adventure, exploration, and relaxation.

What *Kind* of River Festival?

A river festival can feature a local stream, canal, or natural water-way, celebrating its role in history, recreation, or commerce. A river festival can promote increased geographical awareness, not only of one's own region but of selected areas across the world. During a river festival, students can meet literary giants, steam-boat pilots, crews from the Army Corps of Engineers, yachtsmen and houseboat owners, and artists who use water and boats as their themes in painting and model building. Students can visit mills along the fall line, dams and lakes, fisheries, and conservation pro-jects. They can spend some time learning about pollution, and can take part in a litter removal project. They can ride on the river, and become a part of its eternal magic.

On the other hand, the River Festival can simply be an avenue for promoting fun with books. Build a Book Barge in the library to make browsing an adventure. Put up a wall display that invites readers to sail away with a good book. Hang thematic mobiles, such as paper sailboats or fish, and organize a competition on river trivia to see how much students know.

The festival could, of course, focus on Mark Twain, Rivers of Africa, Steamboating, the Tennessee Valley Authority, Grist Mills in Pioneer Days, or River Pollution. Here the librarian and class-room teachers can work closely together in offering literary, sci-entific, and artistic activities. Further narrowing of the subject can be done by concentrating on river wildlife, river cities and indus-try, bridges and engineering, floods, or the water cycle. Look over the library collection for inspiration. Could you take an armchair journey along the rivers of China through the materials in your col-lection? If so, consider "Week Along the Yangtze" or the Yellow or Li Rivers to promote multicultural awareness. Instead of mak-ing a cardboard paddlewheeler, work with students to build a junk or a simple South China flatboat. The following suggestions for displays, speakers, and activities are general enough that they can be incorporated into most river themes. Some of them, such as building boats from milk cartons, are obviously for the very young; others are for middle and high schoolers. And, of course, there is reading. During the festival, librarians and teachers can use several promotional ideas, or gimmicks, to unite books and readers. Using some of the following ideas, the local festival-makers can build their own unique river week, adding local enthusiasm and expertise to create a valuable period of fun and learning.

River Displays

Capture the romance of the age of steam with a silhouette of a Mississippi paddle wheeler rolling down Old Muddy. For a more relaxing mood, encourage students to look for a good book with which to while away the hour by picturing a fishing boat moored at the edge of the river.

What You Need:

Construction paper, black, white, green, or other colors
Coloring media, watercolor or tempera
brushes
pencils
scissors and craft knife
staples or tacks

The Paddle Wheeler

Keep the design simple. The silhouettes can be made from black paper, and stapled or pinned to a plain white background, or to give it a hint of reality, cut the steamboat and riverbank from dark green paper. Use watercolors to paint a sunset (or sunrise) for the background. Choose a title to complement the nature of the local festival: "Rivers—Arteries of the Nation"; "The Mississippi—Tom Sawyer's Playground"; "Rolling on the River."

The Fishing Boat

An essentially humorous display features a "Book Boat" and a fisherman, but you can add a dog, a cat, aquatic animals, and plants to enrich the detail (Fig. 66). Try putting a cane fishing pole on the side of the display, its line attached to a dust jacket or lightweight paperback. Think of nautical titles for this display, such as "Sail Away with a Good Book" or "Reading Down the River," or "I'm Sold on Books—Hook, Line, and Sinker."

Figure 66

Build a Book Barge to Promote Reading

What You Need:

Cardboard boxes (from large household appliances)
Low table
Tempera paints, or leftover household latex paints
Brushes
Pencils
Craft knife
Masking tape
White glue
Hammer and nails, optional
Reference book (for pictures of river barges)

Depending upon the height of the table and the number of cardboard boxes available, the enthusiastic teacher or librarian can create a tugboat or a barge to display books or to use as a reading nook. This is a good project to make with students, too. Alternative designs are numerous, and various kinds of boats can be built. Here are two.

The Book Barge: Basically, this is made by surrounding an old coffee table with cardboard cut to resemble a barge. Instead of a coffee table, try building the barge around wooden crates turned bottom up.

1. Dismantle the cardboard box so that there is enough cardboard to go along both sides of the table. Draw the sides of the barge on the cardboard and cut out with a craft knife.

2. Draw the front of the barge on cardboard and cut out, making sure to include *tabs* for taping to the side pieces. Repeat to make the back of the barge.

3. To make a grander barge, stand a large cardboard box (of the type used to pack a refrigerator or washing machine) on its bottom. Draw on windows, and cut them out with the craft knife. Attach this to the rear of the coffee table to make the captain's quarters. Further embellishments include a smokestack (from rolled up cardboard or a cardboard tube from a carpet store), a roof (cut from a large cardboard box), and a ship's flag (made from paper or a large handerkerchief).

Note: Make the cardboard sides of the enlarged barge long enough to cover the captain's quarters.

4. To assemble, lean the sides and end pieces of the barge against the table. Apply glue to the tabs, and beginning at the front, attach the tabs to one of the side pieces, and tape securely. Repeat on the opposite side, and follow the same procedure at the rear.

If you have opted for the deluxe barge, glue and tape the sides to the upright captain's quarters box.

5. Paint and decorate. Spread newspapers over the floor, slipping them beneath the cardboard to avoid getting the floor messy. Choose a single bright color, and paint the entire ship.

Add highlights, such as stripes and outlines around the windows of the captain's quarters, with another color. Paint the name of the ship, *Book Barge,* in big letters on the front. Hang the flag or pennant from the smokestack.

6. Load the table with books and encourage readers to browse.

The Floating Book Nook: Ideally, you will be able to borrow a dinghy, clean it up a bit, and put it in the library or classroom. Put a few pillows inside it for comfort, and make it available for students' quiet reading. Failing that, make one from an old refrigerator box.

1. Turn the box on its side, and draw the curving top outline of a boat on both sides. Cut off the top with a craft knife.

Create a Festive Ambience

GIVE AWAY BLANK OUTLINE MAPS of the region, country, continent or world. Award those who best complete maps with river systems, lakes, and other features: cities, boundaries, industries, agriculture ...

FEATURE PRODUCTS of water-powered mills.

RIVER MILL
x x x
Stone Ground
FLOUR

MISS MARY'S STONE GROUND **CORN MEAL**

GRITS Stone Ground

Stone Ground

SOUTHERN GOODNESS

SET SAIL with paper model boats.

HANG MOBILES OF PAPER FISH from poles. Hang dust jackets and boats, too.

SHOWCASE DECOY DUCKS

STOCK A FISHTANK with local plants and animals: minnows, snails, and greenery. Use an aeration pump!

MAKE BULLRUSHES (cat-tails) from green paper to decorate doors, plate glass windows, bookshelf ends.

MAKE WAVES! Cut out wave borders for door- and window-frames, sides of desks, wainscot rails.

DRESS UP A DEPARTMENT STORE DUMMY AS A SAILOR, FISHERMAN, OR SHIP'S CAPTAIN!

BOOK BOAT TUGBOAT TALES FISHY FICTION RIVER RAFT of READING

LANGUAGE LAUGHS: ALLITERATE! Give awards to the best alliterations:

Figure 67

2. Turn the boat over, topside down, and draw the pointed prow on the front of the box. Cut it out with a craft knife.

3. Bring the two sides together so that they meet at the point of the prow. Glue and tape them together. Use large metal paper fasteners or industrial size staples for greater security, or pierce holes with an awl, and tie the pieces together.

4. Paint the boat a cheerful color. Add cushions to the interior, and invite readers to relax inside.

Other Display Ideas

Another display can feature a *children's mural of a river scene.* With adult direction (and perhaps construction of a "paint by number" design) students can use tempera, felt-tips, crayons, or water colors to show the life of a river from its source to its mouth, including some flora and fauna, industries, shipping, recreation, dams, lakes, waterfalls, and other natural features. This display could be the culmination of a geography or local history unit and a river festival could sum up six weeks' work with a period of stories, games, and art work.

To *focus on river pollution,* set up a display of discarded items, such as old rubber tires, plastic bottles, rusty machine parts, oil cans and other human detritus. Arrange the refuse on a table with some cat-tails and willow branches in front of an enlarged photograph of a river scene. Not intended to be a pretty sight, this display calls attention to human mismanagement and spoliation.

If the river theme concentrates on *leisure or fishing,* pull in a fiberglass boat, some fishing equipment, and a mounted fish or two. Put the boat in the school foyer or in the library. Add pertinent books to the atmospheric paraphernalia. Ask a local department store if you can borrow a mannequin to dress in fishing clothing to put inside or beside the boat. Offer free advertising to a fishing goods store if it will donate the clothing, rods and reels, nets, baskets, and other items; make a sign which says "This display brought to you by *The Cod Piece — The Fisherman's Friend.*" If the display is not in the library, make adequate signs so that would-be readers know where they can go to check out the books.

Organize several student and teacher teams to make river displays throughout the school, each display showing another variation on the theme, from Mark Twain to Rudyard Kipling to kayaking and sailing to fishing and barge-hauling. Rather than limiting the visual impact of the festival to the library or classroom, use as many display spaces as possible, attracting attention wherever students congregate. Finally, arrange with a shopping center or public building to donate space—a window or a wall—for some of the displays when the festival is over. This offers good publicity for the library and its overall role in local education.

Guest Speakers

Even if the river theme is confined to promoting recreational reading by the librarian, one way of drumming up enthusiasm is to feature a specialist during the festival. Brainstorm, therefore, with students and teachers to discover knowledgeable community resource persons: kayakers, white water enthusiasts, or small-boat sailors who can talk about their sport, show slides, or do a demonstration on site. Is there a river boat pilot, either on a recreational or industrial vessel, who could talk to a group about his or her work, and perhaps take students on a ride later? Perhaps there is an older member of the community who could talk and share pictures about former river traffic.

It shouldn't be too hard to locate a fishing enthusiast who would delight in talking about the joys of sitting on river banks or in row boats, rod and reel in hand, watching the river roll by. A fisherman (or fisherwoman) could demonstrate the refined arts of fly-casting, ice-fishing, baiting a hook, and fly-tying, and might even be persuaded to organize a river fishing contest.

Contact the U.S. Army Corps of Engineers (consult the yellow pages or get their number from the operator in Washington, D.C.) for a speaker about water conservation, flood control, the Tennessee Valley Authority dams and lakes, and electricity generation. Ask a water-mill owner to talk about grinding corn and flour. Pay a visit to a grist mill and watch the water wheel turn around, rotating the cogs and stone grinders inside.

Some Mark Twain Activities

Talk about rivers and who else but Mark Twain comes to mind? His all-American tales of Tom Sawyer, Huckleberry Finn, Injun

Joe, Aunt Polly, and Becky are synonymous with life on the Mississippi. A river festival can promote Twain's novels and collections of short stories. Librarians and teachers can select passages to read aloud to groups. They can also work with students to excerpt lines from *Tom Sawyer* and *Huckleberry Finn* to present a readers' threatre performance. There are several other activities, too, to base on the works of Samuel Clemens:

1. *Tom Sawyer's Fence Painting Contest.* This is not an activity to be done indoors! Participants must dress in old clothes. And it may be advisable to cover the grass or pavement around the fence with paint cloths or sheets of plastic.

How to do it: first, read and re-read the story of the fence. Ask students to improvise the scene in short drama skits. Aunt Polly wants her fence painted, and suggests that Tom do it. He, being a canny lad, uses a great advertising technique to get out of doing any of the work himself.

To hold the contest, there must be a wooden fence, ideally in a municipal park or a local farm. If there isn't one available, find a plot that needs one, and build it (a good project for a vocational arts class?). The fence can be made of pickets, planks, or rails. Secure permission to use the fence in the project, and call for volunteers to participate.

Each participant needs a brush and paint, nothing more. Within a given time period (from one to three minutes) the winner is the one who can cover the most fence thoroughly with paint. Or, the winner is the one who paints a given space in the shortest amount of time.

Additional points can be given for neatness, least amount of paint spilled, good coverage, and technique. Points can likewise be taken away for messiness, paint spilled, poor coverage, and sloppy technique. Judges will need to be appointed, and also a time-keeper.

The winner can be given a title (such as "Tom Sawyer—1998"), a shopping voucher from a book store, a certificate, a photograph in the local paper, a watercolor set, or other appropriate prizes.

A clean-up crew must be on hand as soon as the event is over to tidy up the area. A good rule to follow is that all participants have to finish painting the fence as soon as the contest is over—except for the winner.

2. *Build a model of a vintage Mississippi stern-wheeler* (Figure 68). This project uses cardboard to make a replica of a 19th-cen-

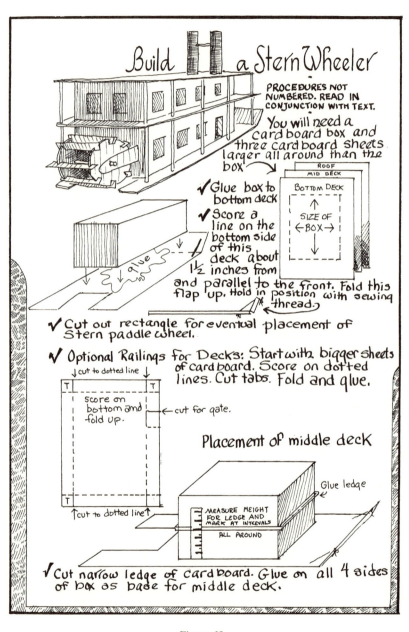

Build a Stern Wheeler

PROCEDURES NOT NUMBERED. READ IN CONJUNCTION WITH TEXT.

You will need a cardboard box and three cardboard sheets larger all around than the box

ROOF
MID DECK
BOTTOM DECK

↑
SIZE OF
← BOX →
↓

✓ Glue box to bottom deck

✓ Score a line on the bottom side of this deck about 1½ inches from and parallel to the front. Fold this flap up. Hold in position with sewing thread.

glue

✓ Cut out rectangle for eventual placement of stern paddle wheel.

✓ Optional Railings for Decks: Start with bigger sheets of cardboard. Score on dotted lines. Cut tabs. Fold and glue.

↓ cut to dotted line ↓

T   T

score on bottom and fold up.

← cut for gate.

T   T

↑ cut to dotted line ↑

Placement of middle deck

Glue ledge

MEASURE HEIGHT FOR LEDGE AND MARK AT INTERVALS
ALL AROUND

✓ Cut narrow ledge of cardboard. Glue on all 4 sides of box as base for middle deck.

Figure 68

√ Trace outline of box in center of middle deck. Cut out that space. Push deck onto box, level with ledge.

√ Make templates for doors and windows. Trace them at intervals on both decks. Cut out openings with art knife.

√ Cut out two circles for the wheel. Pierce the axis of each to receive the axle (a pencil or dowel). Cut slits at 12, 3, 6, and 9 o'clock; then cut a slit between each of them. ⬜ = paddle ⬯ = axle

Make paddles from pliable card, slightly longer than the distance between the wheels.

Tab

slits

Make two arms to hold the wheel. Cut two slits on rear wall of boat for the tabs.

pencil

√ Build smoke stacks from tubes. Cut holes in roof corresponding in size to tubes. Insert tubes and glue in place. Connect smoke stacks with a pencil or dowel.

Porch Posts: Fit dowels cut to size through middle deck.

Middle Deck
Punch holes for posts

Tie string from post to post for a guard rail →

Porch posts reach from roof to bottom.

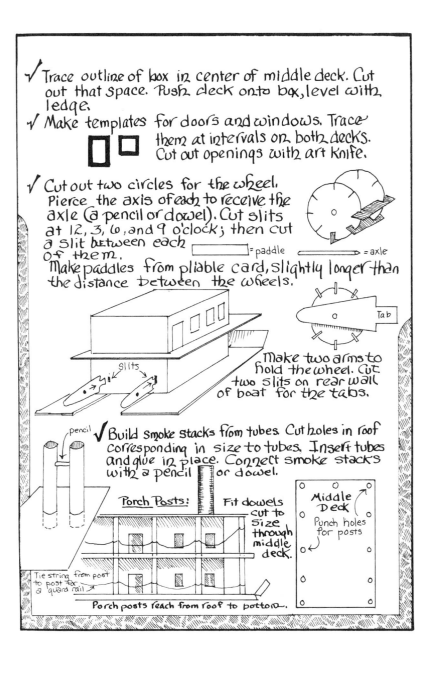

tury river boat. It is suitable for middle school age students and up, and is best achieved with careful measuring and cutting. Read through the diagrams and instructions thoroughly before embarking on the project.

What You Need:

1 sturdy medium-sized cardboard box (such as a photocopy paper box or a super-market box) with lid intact
3 sheets of cardboard larger than the top and bottom of the box (such as the sides of a major appliance carton)
2 cardboard tubes (from paper towels or foil)
2 additional sheets of cardboard (or sides of medium-sized boxes)
2 short wooden dowel rods (for wheel spoke and stack support)
6 to 8 wooden dowels (for "porch posts" on decks)
1 craft knife
1 compass
1 container white glue
1 roll of masking tape
1 pencil
1 measuring tool (tape or ruler)
Paint (tempera, poster paint or household latex paint)

What to Do:

1. The cardboard box will become the body of the steamboat, with windows and doors. To begin, place this box in the center of one of the three sheets of cardboard. Trace around the box to show where it will later be glued into position. This sheet will be the bottom deck. Label this cardboard "bottom deck." The other cardboard sheets will become the middle deck and the roof. All of them should be wider and longer than the box to form adequate porches around the four sides of the boat. Measure accurately so that the bottom deck is parallel to the sides of the cardboard box. Allow ample space (several inches) for the porch on each side. The front and rear decks and roof may be considerably longer.

Cut out the bottom deck, and use it as a template to trace around the other two sheets, and cut them out, too. The bottom rear deck needs a space cut out for the paddle wheel (steps 8 and 9). The size of this rectangular space will vary according to the size of the wheel and of the boat itself. It needs to be only large enough to permit the wheel to fit without touching the sides of the deck.

2. An optional variation in cutting the decks will give the steamboat a railing along each side (Figure 68). Before cutting out the two decks, draw parallel lines about two inches (more or less, depending upon the size of the boat) around the deck. This extra space will be made into a ship's rail. Cut out the decks along the outside line. Score along the *inside lines*. Cut away the four corners and bend the cardboard back. Tape the rail together.

The roof can also be cut in this way. It may be attached to the top of the box with the rail pointing up, or with the rail pointing down.

3. Measure the height of the cardboard box (Figure 68). Draw a line horizontally all around the four sides of the box slightly higher than halfway up. This line is where the middle deck will be placed. It also indicates the bottom of middle deck doors, which you can now draw in.

Save time and energy by drawing one door on a piece of paper, measuring it carefully to get it square. Then use this door as a template for all the others, and trace around it wherever you want a door—to saloons, cabins, and sleeping quarters. Line up all doors on the middle deck with the line you have drawn.

4. With the craft knife, cut out the doors (Figure 68). To make the doors open inward, score along one upright side on the outside of the box, and cut through the other side and the top and bottom. To make the door swing outward, score along one upright side on the inside of the box, and proceed as above. To make swinging saloon-type doors, make the doorway twice as wide as a single door. Score along both upright sides (inside or outside, but not both) and cut along the central upright and along both top and bottom. Cut away the top and bottom of the doors, leaving a middle portion to paint later as louvered saloon doors.

5. Make another template for windows, which should be spaced regularly around both decks, front, back and sides. For working shutters, follow the cutting procedure for saloon doors in step four above. For shutter-less windows, cut out the entire opening. To

simulate glass, tape and glue clear acetate to the insides of the window openings.

6. From the cardboard left over from the decks and roof cut a narrow strip to form a horizontal ledge around the box which you drew in step three. This ledge will support the middle deck, and prevent it from slipping down. Glue the ledge slightly lower than the bottoms of the doorways on the upper floor to enable outward opening doors to function. You can make the bottom of the ledge as ornate as you wish to simulate the Victorian ironwork with which many riverboats were decorated.

7. (An alternate method of preventing the middle deck from slipping is to cut the doorways to form brackets. Cut out the top and two sides, and score along the inside bottom of the door. Fold the door back to form supports for the middle deck.)

8. Make the paddle wheel by cutting two identical circles from cardboard, using the compass or tracing around a round object such as a saucer or plate. The paddle wheel should be only big enough to fit under the middle deck without touching it. In real steamboats, the wheel would obviously go below water level, but to enable the model to rest on a table, artistic license lets you cheat a little bit.

Using a straight edge, bisect both circles through the center, creating perfect quarters. Then divide the circles again, into eighths. If there is room, you can divide once more into sixteenths. Pierce the center of each circle, making a hole large enough for the spoke, which can be a length of dowel or a pencil. The spoke must be long enough to fit into the supporting arms on either side of the wheel.

Make slits 1/2 to 1 inch long from the outside of the wheel down each bisecting line. With the craft knife make the slits wide enough to receive the cardboard paddles.

The wheel should be about half as wide as the steamboat itself, so make the paddles accordingly. Cut enough paddles from cardboard to link the two circles together, with a slight overlap on each end. Cut two slits 1/2 inch or so deep on each paddle to insert into the slits on the wheels.

9. Attach the paddle wheel to the boat with two cardboard arms. Pierce the arms where the spoke of the wheel should be supported.

These holes will not need to be made until the wheel is moved into position. Attach the arms to the back of the boat by inserting them into slits in the box, cut slightly smaller than the arms. Stick the arms into the slits, and secure them in position with tape and glue.

10. Make smokestacks from two cardboard tubes. These go side by side at the top front of the roof. Trace their positions with pencil, and cut out holes in the roof (and top of the box beneath) only slightly smaller than the tubes. Insert the tubes into the holes, securing them with glue. Pierce the inner-facing sides of the smokestacks with a hole just large enough to receive a dowel or pencil. Insert the wooden piece further to support the smokestackes.

11. Decide where the deck should be supported with posts. There should be a dowel support at each corner, and depending upon the length of the boat, one, two or more posts at regular intervals along the deck. Measure carefully, and pierce holes in the middle deck to receive the dowels.
    Cut the dowels just as high as the cardboard box. The four corner dowels may be made taller than the box, and inserted through the roof to provide stability as well as opportunity for further decoration.

12. The order of assembly:
    a. Glue the bottom deck to the cardboard box.
    b. Glue the ledge to the box.
    c. Attach the paddle wheel supporting arms and the wheel itself.
    d. Place the middle deck onto the ledge.
    e. Glue the roof to the top of the box.
    f. Attach the supporting dowels as porch posts.
    g. Attach the smokestacks.

13. Paint the box white. Paint the smokestacks and roof black. Paint the floor of the two decks brown to simulate wood. Paint the doors, shutters, and window surrounds in *one* color of your choice. Paint the wheel and paddles red. Paint the supporting arms red or black. Paint the dowel supports black or white.

14. Make the steamboat come to life with a crew, passengers, and cargo make from household throwaways. Small aspirin canisters

or boxes can be painted to look like barrels and containers. Match-boxes can become crates. Wooden or plastic thread spools can be hogsheads or barrels. Larger boxes, such as ones surrounding shampoo bottles or toothpaste, can be adapted to make benches or cargo containers. Roll twine or strong cord into ship's rope to hang along the bottom rail.

Draw people on stiff card (unlined 3 × 5 notecards are ideal) and color them with felt-tips. Cut them out, and support them with a folded triangle of paper and place them on the decks.

Turn the vessel into a showboat by making a small sign announcing the name of the production, dates and times, and name of leading lady.

Decide on the name of the boat, and paint her name at prominent places.

Make flags and pennants to hang from her smokestacks. Attach a few pennants to a length of thread and suspend them between the smokestacks or drape them along one of the rails.

Build a gangplank from a rectangle of cardboard, painted to simulate wood planks. Cut a gap in the lower deck rail and lean the gangplank on it.

Simpler Vessels

Younger participants, for whom a replica steamboat may be too difficult to make, can construct other river vessels from milk cartons, turned on their sides, and cut to resemble a boat. Coated with a waterproof substance, these boats can float indefinitely, and once in water can be used for festival races, games or for bath-time fun at home.

To make a milk carton boat, turn the empty carton on its side, and imagine what kind of vessel it can make. A houseboat? Cut with sharp scissors, beginning at the unopened spout end, to reveal the hull. Leave a portion of the carton intact to represent the cabin. Cut out windows. Turn the milk carton into a steamboat by cutting away half to a third of the top side. Glue an empty cocoa box into the hull, and insert a smokestack made of rolled up white paper, inserted into a hole pierced by scissors, and rotated. Cut out doors and windows. A milk carton can become a barge by cutting away all the top side and filling it with a lightweight cargo, such as scrap paper wads or pine cones (make it something biodegradable if the barge is to be floated outdoors where there is potential for its escaping downstream).

To turn the milk carton into a sailing vessel, cut away the top half, and glue another cardboard box inside the hull. Pierce the top of the box with two holes big enough to hold masts: twigs from a tree or dowels. Cut two sails from stiff paper and make two holes on a line drawn down the exact vertical center. The holes should be a quarter of the distance from top to bottom. Push the sails over the masts, and insert the masts into the box. A slight breeze will cause this boat to skate across the water.

Projects and Discussions

Run a Relay Race

During the Fishermen's Festival in Boothbay Harbor, Maine, every Spring, one of the activities involves competitors dressing in oilskins and hip boots (which they have to change three times during the race), holding a codfish without dropping it, and running a lengthy relay. During your River Festival, organize a similar relay race between classes or interested individuals. Variations on the theme include using a real (dead) fish as a baton to pass from runner to runner; using a plastic fish as a baton; "running" on all fours (the crabwalk); running three-legged partnerships.

Name That River!

Encourage use of the library's reference collection with a written competition in which students have to name rivers from around the world by identifying buildings or natural features. Here are a few questions for starters.

1. Beside which river was the Eiffel Tower built?
2. Westminster Abbey stands near which river?
3. The St. Louis Arch is near which river?
4. What river divides Kentucky from Ohio?
5. Washington's National Airport is beside which river?
6. New York's Palisades face which river?

7. Which river tumbles over Angel Falls?
8. Near which river was Shakespeare born?
9. Name the river which turned Rotterdam into a wealthy port city.
10. Which river flows through the Golden Triangle of northern Thailand?
11. Which river is blocked by Old Hickory Dam?
12. Which river is spanned by the Charles Bridge?
13. Name five American states which share their names with a river.
14. Where would you be if you were on the River Styx?
15. Which river connects Belgrade and Vienna?

Students can come up with questions, too. In fact, having shown them a few question samples, let one class set the questions for another. Mr. Jones's homeroom answers the questions of Mrs. Smith's homeroom, while they answer the questions from Ms. Brown's homeroom. Winners could be the individuals or classes which finish correctly first. Prizes could be book tokens, movie tickets, a popcorn party, or an award ribbon.

How Did the River Affect Local Settlement?

Even communities that don't have a river nearby may have been settled originally by people who floated on flat-bottom boats from existing population centers to the frontier, continuing on foot or horseback. How did river transport affect your area? Encourage students to research early river transport and industry. How is the river used today? How has the river shaped our lives and how did it shape the lives of our ancestors?

National River Festivals

Across North America, many towns celebrate the life along their rivers with fishing festivals, grist mill festivals, and Tom Sawyer Days. Write to their organizers for information, and borrow their ideas for encouraging reading and activities in your school:

Johnny Cake Festival celebrates the role of the grist mill on the Queen's River in West Kingston, Rhode Island, every October with food, crafts, antique shows, and parades. Members of the Narragansett Indian tribe are honored as originators of the local Johnny Cake.

 *Contact: Kenyon Corn Meal,
    P.O. Box 221 Usquepaugh,
    West Kingston, Rhode Island 02901

Seafood Festival in Hempstead, New York, in early September features culinary treats, regattas, sand-sculpting, and music.

 *Contact: Department of Industry and Commerce
    350 Front Street
    Hempstead, New York 11550

Blowing Rock Trout Derby offers trophies and cash prizes to anglers who catch the largest trout in the official April opening of the fishing season.

 *Contact: Blowing Rock Parks and Recreation
    P.O. Box 47
    Blowing Rock, North Carolina 28605

Corn Island Storytelling Festival features September storytelling trips on a paddlewheeler down the Ohio River.

 *Contact: Corn Island Storytelling Festival
    133 Outer Loop
    Louisville, Kentucky 40214

Tom Sawyer Days draw events such as fence-painting, ice cream socials and Mississippi raft races from Mark Twain's book early in July.

 *Contact: Hannibal Tourism Commission
    P.O. Box 624
    Hannibal, Missouri 63401

Wheels, Wings and Water on the Mississippi River at St. Cloud, Minnesota, features canoe races, fishing for a specially tagged fish worth over $10,000 in prize money, water skiing, and river rafting.

 *Contact: Chamber of Commerce
    Box 487
    St. Cloud, Minnesota 56302

Aquatennial is Minneapolis' celebration of lakes and rivers in July. There are milk carton boat races, powerboat races, and parades.
    *Contact: Minneapolis Aquatennial Association
            Commodore Court
            702 Wayzata Boulevard
            Minneapolis, Minnesota 55403

Covered Bridge Festival recaptures 19th-century life through story-telling, craft demonstrations, spelling bees, and fiddling competitions. Bus tours take October visitors to visit seven historic wooden covered bridges over rivers and creeks in Madison County, Iowa.
    *Contact: Chamber of Commerce
            Box 55
            Winterset, Iowa 50273

Irrigation Festival celebrates the bringing of river water to barren lands east of the Olympic Mountains just before the turn of the century with historic exhibits, horse-shoe pitching, and horse races.
    *Contact: Chamber of Commerce
            P.O. Box 907
            Sequim, Washington 98392

Wooden Boat Festival in early September celebrates the nautical skills of the Pacific Northwest with regattas, demonstrations of sailmaking, planking and caulking, and displays of historic wooden boats.
    *Contact: Wooden Boat Foundation
            637 Water Street
            Port Townsend, Washington 98368

Klondike Days in Alberta features Saskatchewan River rafting, Gay '90s costume parades, and sourdough in its many forms.
    *Contact: Convention and Tourism Authority
            9797 Jasper Avenue
            Edmonton, Alberta, Canada T5J 1N9

River Reading

From the bibliography at the end of this chapter, or from river-related books in your school or library, organize special reading ses-

sions, some of them devoted to research on river ecology, maintenance, and wildlife and some devoted to reading for relaxation and
enjoyment. To coincide with a sixth-grade unit on ecology, for instance, offer books about riverside industrial development, and its
effect upon the terrain. As a special project in American history, offer to help with a demographic study of the Mississippi, showing the
different patterns of ethnic settlement from Minnesota to Louisiana.
Publish a bibliography of river books available in your school.

Play a selection of river songs, anything from "Old Man River"
to "Blue Danube" to "Rollin' on the River," during quiet reading
time, to introduce a booktalk, or to set the mood for a guest
speaker or arts and craft project.

Festival Food Treats

What would make an ideal picnic for a river journey? Sandwiches,
fruit, a chocolate bar? Milk, a soft drink, fruit juice? Plan thematic
picnics for different classes in the library during the river festival.
Students could bring their own packed lunches to eat around the
Book Barge, or they could provide a pot-luck treat. Teachers, librarians, parents and students could brainstorm to find the tastiest
foods (and the easiest to prepare). From a list of favorites (sandwiches, apples, bananas, potato chips, and so forth) students could
sign up for a particular category, then bring in enough of that item
to provide for three other people. Arrange the foods inside the
Book Barge, and students serve themselves buffet-style.

To emphasize the role of watermills in the early development of
the United States, teachers may want to peruse the library cookbook collection to find recipes that use stoneground wheat or corn.
Then as a cooking demonstration during the festival, or at home,
the adult could help students prepare a treat using ingredients
ground by a waterwheel. Try this recipe:

Stone Ground Round Cookies (Makes About 120 Cookies)

What You Need:

1 cup soft shortening
1 cup sugar
1 cup firmly packed brown sugar

2 cups stone-ground flour
2 Tbsps stone-ground cornmeal plus extra for rolling
1 tsp baking powder
1 tsp baking soda
1 tsp ground cinnamon
2 cups stone-ground oats (or quick-cooking oats, uncooked)
2 cups corn flakes
Eggs (1 egg per 2 cups of cookie dough)
Optional: chopped nuts, chocolate chips

Mixing bowls
Ungreased cookie sheets
Cooking spoons
Wire cooling rack

What You Do:

Preheat over to 375 degrees F, 190 degrees C, for 10 minutes
prior to baking.

Combine shortening and sugar in a large bowl. Combine all the
other ingredients, tossing with a large spoon to blend. Add the dry
ingredients to the sugar mixture and blend well.

Work with small amounts of dough at a time. Follow this procedure:

Combine 2 cups of the cookie dough and 1 egg in a bowl. (At
this stage you may add optional ingredients: 1/2 cup chopped nuts;
or 1/2 cup chocolate chips.)

Shape the dough into walnut-sized balls. Lightly roll them in a
small bowl of stone-ground corn meal. Place them 2 inches apart
on cookie sheets, and bake for 10 to 12 minutes. Remove to wire
rack to cool.

The dough can be stored in the refrigerator in a covered bowl if
you don't want to make all the cookies at once.

Sources of Inspiration: Books About Rivers

Arch, Gwyn. *Five Days on the River.* Exeter, England: Wheaton
Press, 1973.

David and Meg go on an exciting river trip on their dad's
cruiser, observing plants and animals, visiting towns and villages

along the way, and singing river songs, which are printed for young readers to try out for themselves.

Ault, Phil. *Whistles Round the Bend—Travel on America's Waterways*. New York: Dodd-Mead, 1982.
From the canoes of Native Americans to steamboats on lakes and rivers, this history examines past modes of transportation on America's waterways.

Bartlett, Margaret. *The Clear Brook*. London: A. and C. Black, 1971.
For beginning readers, this beautiful book shows what an ecologically clean stream looks like, what kinds of life it supports, and how young children may enjoy it. The illustrations by Aldren Watson are superb.

————. *Where the Brook Begins*. London: A. and C. Black, 1970.
With beautiful illustrations by Aldren Watson and a simple but exciting text, this book invites stream exploration from source to brook to river to sea during all seasons of the year.

Batchelor, John. *The Euphrates*. Denver: Wayland/Silver Burdett, 1981.
Travel through Turkey, Syria, Iraq, and Kuwait to see the life and culture of the people on the banks of this ancient river.

Blaustein, John. *The Hidden Canyon: A River Journey*. New York: Penguin, 1977.
Take a journey by wooden dory down the Colorado River with superb photographs and excerpts from John Wesley Powell's historical diary.

Bord, Janet, and Colin Bord. *Sacred Waters*. New York: Granada, 1985.
Water symbolized The Great Mother, the basis of all life, and has been universally used in rites of religious purification, healing, and renewal. The authors tell the story of holy wells, river ghosts, and water lore in Britain and Ireland, from pagan times to the present.

Brander, Bruce. *The River Nile*. Washington, D.C.: The National Geographic Society, 1983.

Maps, drawings, and photographs show the Egyptian landscape and the River Nile from its source in the heart of Africa to its Mediterranean delta.

Dabcovich, Lydia. *Follow the River*. New York: E.P. Dutton, 1980.

This picture book traces a river from its mountain spring source through woods, falls, fields, and towns until it pours into the sea, depicting all the creatures that live in and on it.

Darrell-Brown, Susan. *The Mississippi*. Denver: Wayland/Silver Burdett, 1979.

Although emphasizing the river's importance as a transport system, the book talks also of history, wildlife, ecology, and shore towns.

Goetz, Delia. *Great Rivers*. New York: Morrow, 1969.

This survey of some of the world's rivers examines in detail the flora and fauna found on the shores of the Potamac, and the importance of conservation.

Gregory, K. J. *The Yellow River*. Denver: Wayland/Silver Burdett, 1980.

The story of this great Chinese River involves agriculture, fishing, warfare, and political intrigue.

Havighurst, Walter. *River to the West: Three Centuries of the Ohio*. New York: Putnam, 1970.

From the days of native inhabitants to the present, the Ohio River has been an economic political, military, and cultural determinator.

Hills, C. A. R. *The Danube*. Denver:Wayland/Silver Burdett, 1979.

From Black Forest to Black Sea, the Danube is rich in wildlife, cultural attachments, music, and beauty.

————. *The Rhine*. Denver: Silver Burdett/Wayland, 1979.

Read about the legends, the great cities and castles, the pollution, and the scenery of this historic German waterway that spills into the North Sea.

Keating, Bern. *The Mighty Mississippi*. Washington, D.C.: National Geographic Society, 1971.
A superbly illustrated tour of the river from its source in Minnesota to its mouth in the Gulf of Mexico, the book traces the prehistoric origins of the Mississippi, and examines the lives of modern-day river-bank residents.

Lauber, Patricia. *The Congo, River into Central Africa*. Champaign, Illinois: Garrard, 1964.
The Congo is a mighty highway and source of abundant resources which the author describes in this book for young readers.

Lyte, Charles. *The Thames*. Denver: Wayland/Silver Burdett, 1980.
England's only major inland waterway is relatively small in world terms, but incredibly large in terms of history, art, and culture.

McCague, James. *Flatboat Days on Frontier Rivers*. Champaign, Ill.: Garrard, 1968.
The late 1700s on the Mississippi and Ohio Rivers were dangerous and exciting, and opened the waterways to western expansion.

McConnell, Rosemary. *The Amazon*. Denver: Wayland/Silver Burdett, 1979.
The inhabitants, flora and fauna of the mighty Amazon continue to intrigue, especially in light of present-day destruction of rain forest in the river basin.

Meltzer, Milton. *Mark Twain: A Writer's Life*. New York: Franklin Watts, 1985.
This story of Samuel Clemens' life tells of his boyhood in Missouri, his job as Mississippi steamboat captain, and his fame as a great writer.

Morrison, Sean, and Ira Freeman. *Water: Where It Comes from and Where It Goes*. New York: Random House, 1969.
This pop-up science book tells all about water in its many precipitative forms, from humidity to clouds to rain and snow, from storms to rivers to lakes.

Naden, Corrine J. *The First Book of Rivers*. New York: Franklin Watts, 1967.
Six chapters describe what a river is, how it changes the land, how mankind uses rivers, and talk about some large rivers of the world.

O'Neil, Paul. *The Rivermen*. New York: Time-Life Books, 1975.
A comprehensive, illustrated history of river traffic from colonial days to the 1880s emphasizes the golden age of steamboats from the 1830s to the 1870s.

Peterson, Ottis. *Junior Science Book of Water*. Champaign, Illinois: Garrard, 1966.
This analysis of water tells how it is formed and how it makes a continuing cycle from sky to earth, benefitting man, plant, and animal.

Rand McNally Encyclopedia of World Rivers. Chicago: Rand McNally, 1980.
This large book describes the courses of the world's most important rivers, bridges, and surrounding terrain.

Scarry, Huck. *Life on a Barge: A Sketch Book*. New York: Prentice-Hall, 1982.
This is a colorful record of the author's travels on a barge in various locations, from Amsterdam to the Erie Canal, with details of barges and the people who live and work on them.

Snoopy's Facts and Fun Book About Boats. Based on the Charles M. Schultz Characters. New York: Random House, 1979.
Snoopy tells kids about several kinds of boats, describing distinctive characteristics of supertankers, cargo ships, houseboats, motor boats and submarines.

Svend, Otto. *Children of the Yangtze River*. London: Pelham, 1982.
This picture story tells how Chinese people live with and benefit from the floods of the mighty Yangtze.

Twain, Mark. *Life on the Mississippi*. New York: Airmont, 1965.
Twain celebrates the golden age of steamboating just before the Civil War when "to get on the river" was the dream of every boy

along the Mississippi, and when "pilot was the grandest position of all."

Winks, Honor Leigh. *The St. Lawrence*. Denver: Wayland/Silver Burdett, 1980.
  The history and geography of the St. Lawrence river and the Canadian cities on its banks, show the importance of this huge, navigable seaway.

Winks, Robin. *The Colorado*. Denver: Wayland/Silver Burdett, 1980.
  This illustrated exploration of a river important in legend, geographical manipulation, and commerce tells how and why people settled along its banks.

Books About River Cities

Cable, Mary. *Lost New Orleans*. Boston: Houghton Mifflin, 1980.
  Old photographs and drawings recapture the beauty of homes, churches, theatres, and other New Orleans buildings that no longer exist.

Cincinnati: A Guide to the Queen City and Its Neighbors. New York: Somerset Publications, 1981.
  A reprint of the Federal Writers Project edition of 1943, this book also offers updated background and tourist information.

Crawford, Charles, ed. *Memphis Memories*. Knoxville: University of Tennessee Press, 1983.
  A small book of thirty-two historic postcard views of this Cotton City on the southwestern corner of Tennessee provides a historical glimpse of an aggressive Southern metropolitan area that grew up because of river trade.

Ebel, Suzanne, and Doreen Impney. *London's Riverside*. London: William Luscombe, 1975.
  From Hampton Court Palace in the west to Greenwich Palace in the east, this book takes the reader on an informative trip down the twenty-eight-mile London stretch of the Thames, giving details of historic events in castles, pubs, churches, streets, and riverside walkways.

Eglitis, Ilga. *Minneapolis Cityscape, An Artist's View*. Plymouth, Minnesota: MacIlo Publications, 1986.

This is an attractive paperback survey of the beauties of this northern Mississippi River town.

Huber, Leonard. *New Orleans: A Pictorial History*. New York: Crown, 1971.

Photographs and text reveal the life, past and present, of this historic and romantic southern river port.

Morgan, William. *Louisville: Architecture and Urban Environment*. Dublin, New Hampshire: Bauhan, 1979.

Morgan takes a close look at this northern Kentucky industrial city beside the Ohio River.

New Orleans City Guide: The Federal Writers Project Guide to 1930s New Orleans. New York: Pantheon, 1983.

This is still an authoritative guide to a dynamic city, which benefits from a recent revision to bring information up to date.

Troen, Selwyn K. *St. Louis*. New York: Wiener Publications, 1977.

A paperback look at the history, art galleries, river traffic, and things to see and do in this Missouri city; a perfect backpack companion on a tourist trip.

Vienna. Lausanne, Switzerland: Editions Berlitz, 1979.

The Danube, flowing through this legendary capital, has inspired music famous the world over. This guide-book shows why Vienna was established at this crossroads on the banks of a mighty river.

Rivers in fiction

Aaron, Chester. *An American Ghost*. Harmondsworth, Middlesex, England: Puffin Books, 1976.

Young pioneer Albie awakes one morning to find himself, a mountain lion and his house crashing downstream in a Mississippi flood that leads to the Gulf of Mexico.

Anderson, La Vere. *Abe Lincoln and the River Robbers.* Champaign, Illinois: Garrard, 1971.
On a flatboat down the Mississippi to New Orleans, Lincoln and Allen Gentry encounter storms, shifting currents, and river pirates.

Botkin, B. A. *A Treasury of American Folklore.* New York: Crown, 1969.
This enormous anthology includes stories of Mike Fink and other raftsmen, steamboats, and rivermen's songs.

Byars, Betsy. *Trouble River.* New York: Viking, 1969.
To escape a hostile Indian, young pioneer Dewey and his grandma travel down Trouble River on a raft.

Coatsworth, Elizabeth. *Bob Braden and the Good Ship Rover.* Champaign, Illinois: Garrard, 1968.
In this tall tale, Bob leaves his pa's potato patch to become a sailor.

Dorson, Richard. *America in Legend: Folklore from the Colonial Period to the Present.* New York: Pantheon, 1972.
In this comprehensive anthology, find the story of "Mike Fink the Keelboatman," born in Fort Pitt (Pittsburgh) around 1770. Fink was a rough and ready river man prior to the coming of the steamboats.

Ferber, Edna. *Showboat.* New York: Fawcett Crest, 1954.
Showboat is the story of Magnolia Ravenal and her marriage to river gambler Gaylord, and of their daughter Kim's success on Broadway, with the color and mood of the Mississippi when steamboats plied its muddy waters.

Forester, C. S. *The African Queen.* London: Michael Joseph, 1950.
Under the stress of wet heat, Charlie and Rosie steer the "African Queen" through Central African riverways, trying to hide from the German military.

George, Jean. *River Rats, Inc.* New York: Dutton, 1979.
To avoid the patrols, Joe and Crowbar float down the Colorado River at night through the Grand Canyon, depending upon the services of a feral boy.

Graham, Margaret. *Benjy's Boat Trip*. New York: Harper and Row, 1977.
A small dog takes a surprise boat trip and meets an angry ship's cat.

Grahame, Kenneth. *The Wind in the Willows*. London: Methuen, 1978.
When Mole feels the call of spring, and finds the river for the first time, the tale of Rat, Badger, and Toad unfolds in this classic story which was first published in 1908.

Kelly, Regina. *New Orleans: Queen of the River*. Chicago: Reilly and Lee, 1963.
This is a fictionalized history of New Orleans from the original settlement to Reconstruction Days after the Civil War.

Partridge, Jenny. *Hopfellow*. New York: Holt Rinehart and Winston, 1980.
Hopfellow the frog shows mouse children how to make boats from horse chestnut shells in this picture book.

Shapiro, Irwin. *Heroes in American Folklore*. New York: Julian Messner, 1967.
"Steamboat Bill and the Captain's Top Hat" is about the greatest river man of them all, who, in matching wits in a river race with Captain Carter, almost burns up the Mississippi. Four other tall tales are in the book.

Twain, Mark. *The Adventures of Huckleberry Finn*. New York: Penguin, 1986.
Of all the contenders for the title of Great American Novel, none has better claim than this idyll of a boy's voyage down the Mississippi with his friend Jim. It is at once an adventure, a classic of American humor, and a metaphor of the American predicament.

————. *The Adventures of Tom Sawyer*. New York: Penguin, 1976.
Tom Sawyer has passed, along with Huck Finn, into world legend, and the boy is synonymous with childish pranks, innocence

faced with the ugliness of life, and All-American small town living.

―――. *The Family Mark Twain*. New York: Harper and Brothers, 1935.
This large book contains the complete *Life on the Mississippi, Huck Finn, Tom Sawyer, Connecticut Yankee,* and excerpts from Twain's other stories.

Watson, Ian. *The Book of the River*. London: Panther Books, 1984.
This science fiction epic tells of "the river" that cuts right across the known world, dividing civilizations by its black current, which only certain women have the power to cross, and at their peril.

Rivers in Drama

Charlesworth, John, and Tony Brown. *Tom Sawyer, A Play*. London: Heinemann Educational Books, 1987.
A ninety-minute production of Mark Twain's classic with over twenty-two speaking roles and songs for soloists and chorus, this version highlights the fence painting and the graveyard scenes.

Gallina, Jill and Michael. *Steamboatin': A Musical Journey Down the Mississippi*. New Berlin, Wisconsin: Jensen Publications, 1985.
Eight musical numbers in this young people's drama draw on gospel, vaudeville, and blues to create an entertaining hour-long journey down Big Muddy.

Kendall, Jane. *Huckleberry Finn: A Comedy in Three Acts*. Chicago: The Dramatic Publishing Company, 1942.
Based on the Twain classic, this version of the classic tale will keep audiences in their seats for nearly three hours.

Hammerstein, Oscar, and Jerome Kern. *Show Boat*. London: Chappells, 1982.
Based on Edna Ferber's novel, this musical contains, among other classic tunes, the famous "Old Man River."

Mander, Charles. *The River*. London: Samuel French, 1980.
For generations, fishermen have trapped and netted salmon in the dangerous tidal waters that surge and flood across the Somer-

set flats, but advancing civilization has polluted the river, fish are dying, and there are only three fishermen left. The play encapsulates pollution vs. nature, and employment vs. environment.

Miller, Roger, and William Hauptman. *Big River*. Nashville: Tree Publishing, 1986.
Based on *Huck Finn,* this is an exciting vehicle for a large cast, with music based on spirituals, ballads, and contemporary folk-rock.

From Rivers to Seaways

Angel, Nicolas. *Capsize! A Story of Survival in the North Atlantic*. Trans. from original French by Alan Wakeman. New York: Norton, 1980.
The crew has to survive high seas, gale force winds, and cold in this true story of friendship.

Bond, Bob, and Steven Sleight. *Small Boat Sailing*. New York: Alfred Knopf, 1983.
This step-by-step illustrated course in sailing is arranged sequentially to acquaint novices with technique, clothing, equipment, and safety.

Chapelle, Howard Irving. *The History of American Sailing Ships*. New York: Bonanza, 1935.
This is a complete history, illustrated with line drawings, of the development of various types of sailing vessels and rigs from earliest colonial craft to cruising and racing yachts.

Landstrom, B. *Sailing Ships in Words and Pictures from Papyrus Boats to Full Riggers*. London: Allen and Unwin, 1969.
This history of ships is clearly illustrated in both color and pen and ink plans and sketches.

Sports Illustrated *Book of Small Boat Sailing*. Philadelphia: Lippincott, 1960.
After introducing the landlubber to the language of sailing, the editors of *Sports Illustrated* discuss sailing to windward, sailing to leeward, and racing.

Stammers, M. K. *Steamboats.* Aylesbury, England: Shire, 1986.

This small illustrated book traces the development of steamboats, from the first time steam was tried on British waters in the late 1700s to their gradual replacement by diesel in the 1920s, and shows where these boats may still be seen and ridden.

Periodicals: A Select List

American White Water. Box 51, Wallingford, Connecticut 06492.

Published six times annually, this magazine has been in circulation since 1967, and carries advance reviews of books relating to white water sports.

Canal and Riverboat Monthly. 15 Newstead Grove, Nottingham NG1 4G2, England.

With a circulation of over 15,000, this periodical, of special interest to enthusiasts about traditional long boats and canal preservation, has been in print since 1978.

River World. 1400 Stierlin Road, Mountain View, California 94043.

Published monthly from April to October, this magazine covers river sports, canoeing, kayaking, and rafting, with news of individuals, competitions, weekend events, and conservation.

Water Newsletter, Water Information Center, 6800 Jericho Turnpike, Syosset, New York 11791.

Since 1958 *Water Newsletter* has been issued twice a month, with news about waste disposal, conservation, pollution, and water supply.

Index

About the Author

ALAN HEATH earned his master's degrees from Vanderbilt University, Nashville, TN, and the University of Exeter, England. Since 1973 he has taught at the American School in London. During his recent sabbatical year, he earned a certificate in art history at the Royal Academy of Arts, London. In his art classes, Heath emphasizes a cross-disciplinary approach in order to link and reinforce learning. He now teaches sixth grade language arts and social studies within an integrated arts program. He has organized many all-school festivals using cultural, ethnic, literary, and historical themes. Heath has also worked in the international theatre, television, and film industries as a dialogue coach, singer, and actor, as in Mario Puzo's *The Fortunate Pilgrim* with Sophia Loren, Kurt Weill's *Three Penny Opera,* under Hans Werner Henze, and the BBC's *English Parish Churches* series. He has travelled extensively with the Academy of St. Martin in the Fields under Sir Neville Marriner with whom he also made numerous classical recordings. Heath has been active in the European Council of International Schools (ECIS) where he served as chair of its Media Services Committee and edited the *Link* magazine. He is book reviews editor of *The International Schools Journal.* Heath has regularly served on accreditation teams for The Middle States Association and the ECIS in schools across Europe. He is a member of the American Art Development Committee of the British Museum, London. His first book, *Off the Wall* (Teacher Ideas Press, 1986), relates artwork to the development of reading enjoyment. *Common Threads,* Heath's second Scarecrow Press publication, is a companion volume to *Windows on the World* (1995).